VAT and Property

Guidance on the application of VAT to UK property transactions and the property sector

Ann Humphrey LLM MBA
Solicitor and tax specialist
London

Published February 2015 by

Spiramus Press Ltd
102 Blandford Street
London W1U 8AG
United Kingdom

www.spiramus.com

© Spiramus Press Ltd

| Paperback | ISBN 978 1904905 60 8 |
| Ebook | ISBN 978 1904905 74 5 |

This publication is based on the law and HMRC practice as at 31 August 2014

All statutory references are to VATA unless otherwise stated.

The right Ann L Humphrey to be identified as the authors of this work has been asserted by them in accordance with the Copyright, Designs and Patents Act, 1988.

Printed and bound in Great Britain by
Grosvenor Group (Print Services) Ltd

Contents

Tables of authorities

Cases

CONTENTS

CONTENTS

Statutes

CONTENTS

Regulations

European Directives

Abbreviations

CGS	Capital Goods Scheme
EU	European Union
European Court	European Court of Justice
FA 2012, etc	Finance Act 2012, etc
HMRC	HM Revenue & Customs
ICTA 1988	Income and Corporation Taxes Act 1988
Sixth Directive	Directive 77/388 of 17 May 1977 on the harmonisation of the laws of the Member States relating to turnover taxes - common system of value added tax: uniform basis of assessment
TOGC	Transfer of a going concern
VATA	Value Added Tax Act 1994
VAT Directive	Directive 2006/112/EC of 28 November 2006 on the common system of value added tax
VAT Regulations	Value Added Tax Regulations 1995 SI 1995/2518

About the author

Ann Humphrey is an English solicitor who specialises in UK property taxation. She is a member of the VAT Practitioners' Group and the Stamp Taxes Practitioners' Group. Ann is the co-author (with Philip Freedman) of *Stamp Duty Land Tax – a Practical Guide for Lawyers* (Spiramus). Ann's firm, Ann L. Humphrey Solicitors, was ranked as one of the top firms in the category 'Highly Regarded - London - VAT' by Chambers Directory of the Legal Profession 2012.

1 Introduction

VAT, when it was introduced in the UK on 1 April 1973, was billed as a simple tax.[1] Unfortunately, VAT in the UK has, over the ensuing 40 years, proved to be anything but simple. The complexities of VAT are, perhaps, brought into sharpest relief where VAT comes up against UK property law. As a result, there are many traps which can catch even the most experienced professional.

This book aims to provide an understanding of VAT framework for many of the common property transactions as well as explaining how to deal with some of the problems that can arise. The object is to provide simple explanations, but, nevertheless, to include sufficient detail for the book to be useful to professional and layman alike. No consideration is given to the other taxes which may need to be taken into account when entering into or advising on a property transaction. This book provides general guidance in respect of the potential VAT issues only.

The basic principle of a VAT system is that all transactions are subject to tax unless a relief applies. The reliefs are: exemption; taxation at a reduced rate; and taxation at the zero-rate. Any of these can apply to property transactions. It is settled case law of the European Court[2] that the scope of a relief, in particular, exemption and zero-rating, is construed narrowly and an exception to a relief is to be construed broadly.

Exempt and zero-rated supplies have different consequences for the supplier. A supplier who makes exempt supplies will not, generally, be able to recover all the VAT charged on supplies made to him so this irrecoverable VAT becomes an extra cost of his business whereas a supplier making zero-rated supplies can, in general, recover the VAT charged to him in full. Irrecoverable input tax incurred by a VAT-registered business is often referred to as 'sticking tax.'

The UK legislation provides that zero-rating (referred to as 'exemption with credit' in the EU legislation to differentiate it from 'true' exemption) takes priority over exemption and all other rates.[3] The zero-rate is allowed in the UK as a 'transitional' measure and was negotiated on the UK's accession to the EU. It has been transitional since the introduction of VAT in 1973, but

---

[1] By the then Chancellor of the Exchequer, Anthony Barber MP

[2] See, for example, cases cited by the European Court in *HMRC v Axa UK plc* (Case C-175/09) [2010] STC 2825 at paragraph 24

[3] Section 30(1)

there is no sign that it will be withdrawn, even though the transitional period has ended.

The European Commission has, in the past, challenged the UK's ability to continue to zero-rate supplies of property, but the European Court has held[4] that the zero-rate could continue apply in the UK to non-commercial property transactions provided that there was a clearly defined social reason for its application and it was for the benefit of the 'final consumer[5]'. However, the European Court did not allow commercial property transactions, and construction work, to continue to benefit from the UK's zero-rate. This would have meant that commercial property transactions would, in the main, have become exempt while many of the inputs in relation to that supply were taxable, giving rise to sticking tax and raising costs. To alleviate this effect, the UK Government in 1989 (when the changes required by the judgment of the European Court were made to the UK VAT system) introduced an option to tax certain property transactions (as permitted by article 13C of the Sixth Directive[6]) so that the VAT incurred on those transactions would be recoverable, under certain circumstances.

The UK cannot extend the scope of zero-rating, but it is possible to apply to the European Commission for certain supplies of other goods or services listed in Annex III to the VAT Directive to be taxed at a reduced rate 'as part of a social policy'. The list in Annex III includes 'the provision, construction, renovation and alteration of housing' and the 'renovation and repairing of private dwellings, excluding materials which account for a significant part of the value of the service received'. The UK has introduced reduced rates for certain property transactions.

Articles 132 to 136 of the VAT Directive provide for a number of exemptions from VAT. Article 135.1(l) exempts 'the leasing or letting of immovable property', excluding:

(a) the provision of accommodation, as defined in the laws of the Member States, in the hotel sector or in sectors with a similar function, including

---

[4] In *EC Commission v United Kingdom* (Case C-416/85) [1988] STC 456 (ECJ)

[5] The final consumer is the 'person who acquires goods or services for personal use, as opposed to an economic activity, and thus bears the tax. ...The provision of goods or services at a stage higher in the production or distribution chain which is nevertheless sufficiently close to the consumer to be of advantage to him must also be considered to be for the benefit of the final consumer as so defined...' *EC Commission v Ireland* (Case C-108/11) (unreported) at paragraph 51

[6] Now article 137 of the VAT Directive

the provision of accommodation in holiday camps or on sites developed for use as camping sites;

(b) the letting of premises and sites for parking of vehicles;

(c) the letting of permanently installed equipment and machinery;

(d) the hire of safes.

1.1 Overview of the UK VAT rules for property transactions and the property sector

Property transactions are normally exempt, but there are various exceptions to this and also the 'option to tax' which allows owners to choose taxation in preference to exemption, and so to recover VAT they incur. Exemption applies unless:

(1) The transaction falls short of the exemption, or perhaps includes other services to which the property element is incidental. In this case, it will normally be standard rated.

(2) The transaction is covered by a statutory exception to exemption. The main exceptions cover some freehold new buildings, car parking, hotel and holiday accommodation and various recreational and similar activities. These are generally standard rated.

(3) The owner has opted to tax. In this case the transaction is normally standard rated.

(4) The transaction is outside the scope of VAT. This might be because it is between members of a VAT group, it is the transfer of a going concern or the payment is not consideration for a supply, for example, a payment of damages.

(5) The transaction is zero-rated. This is relevant to dwellings, and certain other residential or charity buildings, where a developer is selling the freehold or granting a long lease. Zero-rating can also apply to sales of grazing rights, and the sale in situ of a residential caravan or houseboat. Zero-rating overrides exemption.

Where VAT is chargeable on a property transaction it will increase the chargeable consideration for stamp duty land tax purposes.

Building work is generally standard rated, although some work on dwellings, and other residential or charity properties, is zero-rated or subject to the reduced rate of 5%. In some cases, businesses must account for VAT on building work that they carry out for themselves. Professional services are generally standard rated.

Businesses can recover the VAT they pay broadly to the extent that their activities are taxable. Most can recover VAT in full, but the finance, insurance, health and education sectors, and parts of the public sector, cannot. Landlords and developers can recover VAT where their sales or lettings are taxable, including zero-rated, but not generally otherwise.

Businesses with both taxable and exempt activities need to determine their VAT recovery under the partial exemption rules. Their initial VAT recovery may have to be adjusted in the light of later events, notably under the capital goods scheme which involves revisiting the position for a period of up to ten years. VAT related to non-business activities is normally irrecoverable, but there are special arrangements allowing VAT refunds to local authorities, museums and academies and for certain work to dwellings, charity buildings, churches and memorials.

The definitions used in this book are set out in section **1.2** below.

1.1.1   Zero-rated supplies

Group 5 Schedule 8 (*Construction of buildings etc*) provides for the following to be zero-rated:

(1) The first grant by a person constructing a building designed as a dwelling or dwellings of a major interest in it.

(2) The first grant by a person constructing a building intended for use for a relevant residential purpose of a major interest in it.

(3) The first grant by a person constructing a building intended for use for a relevant charitable purpose of a major interest in it.

(4) The first grant by a person converting a non-residential building or a non-residential part of a building into a dwelling or dwellings of a major interest in it.

(5) The first grant by a person converting a non-residential building or a non-residential part of a building into a building intended for use solely for a relevant residential purpose of a major interest in it.

(6) Certain works relating to the construction falling within (1) to (5) above.[7]

(7) Civil engineering works necessary for the development of a permanent park for residential caravans.[8]

---

[7] See **Chapter 0**
[8] See **Chapter 13**

(8) Certain services supplied to a 'relevant housing association'[9] in the course of conversion of a non-residential building or a non-residential part of a building into a dwelling or dwellings.[10]

(9) The supply of building materials by a contractor supplying services falling within (6) to (8) above.[11]

Item 1, Group 6, Schedule 8 (*Protected buildings*) zero-rates the first grant by a person substantially reconstructing a protected building of major interest in it.

Until 1 October 2012 Items 2 and 3 of Group 6 permitted the zero-rating of approved alterations to protected buildings and the supply of building materials incorporated into the building during the course of that work. There is transitional relief in certain circumstances for supplies made before 1 October 2015.[12]

1.1.2   Supplies taxable at the reduced rate
Groups 6 and 7, Schedule 7A

In the UK, a reduced rate applies to the following:
(1) the supply of certain services and building materials in the course of a qualifying conversion.[13]
(2) the supply of certain services and building materials in the course of a renovation or alteration of qualifying residential premises.[14]

1.1.3   Supplies taxable at the standard rate
Items 1(a) to 1(n), Group 1, Schedule 9

Property-related supplies that are taxable at the standard rate are supplies of:
- the freehold in a new or uncompleted commercial building or a new or uncompleted civil engineering work
- fishing and shooting rights
- hotel accommodation
- holiday accommodation
- seasonal caravan pitches[15] etc.

---

[9] For definition of '**relevant housing association**' see **1.2.29** below
[10] See **Chapter 1**
[11] See **Chapter 10**
[12] See **Chapter 1**
[13] See **Chapter 10**
[14] See **Chapter 10**
[15] Residential caravan pitches are treated differently – see **Chapter 13**

- camping
- parking
- rights to fell timber
- mooring for boats and aircraft storage etc.
- entertainment facilities
- sports facilities
- self-storage of goods (from 1 October 2012)
- hairdressers' chair rentals (from 1 October 2012)
- any right to call for an interest falling within any of the above categories

1.1.4   Exempt supplies
Item 1, Group 1, Schedule 9

Most other property transactions are exempted by Group 1 Schedule 9. In some cases these supplies are exempt subject to the option to tax.

1.1.5   The option to tax[16]
Part 1, Schedule 10

In some cases, an option to tax can be exercised to change a transaction that would otherwise be exempt into a standard rated one. The advantage of exercising the option is that any VAT incurred in relation to the transaction can be reclaimed, but VAT needs to be accounted for on the transaction.

Paragraphs 5 to 11 of Schedule 10 prevent the option to tax from having effect where the supply is of:
(1) a building is designed or adapted for use as a dwelling or solely for a relevant residential purpose;
(2) a building which is to be converted for use as a dwelling or for a relevant residential purpose, subject to provision of a certificate of intended use;
(3) a building intended for use solely for a relevant charitable purposes, other than as an office and subject to provision of a certificate of intended use;
(4) a pitch for a residential caravan;
(5) facilities for the mooring of a residential houseboat;
(6) any land if a certificate is given by a relevant housing association that the land is to be used as a dwelling or for a relevant residential purpose;
(7) land to be used for the construction of a dwelling by a DIY builder who is an individual and intends to use the dwelling.

---

[16] The option to tax is considered in detail in **Chapter 1**

1.2   Definitions

The definitions which follow are those used in the VAT legislation and also those used in this book. Where the definitions are statutory the source is given. The statutory definitions must be considered in the context of that part of the legislation in which they are used as the meaning can differ according to the context.

1.2.1   Approved alteration
Notes (6) to (8), Group 6, Schedule 8

This definition is relevant for the zero-rating of eligible good and services provided by Items 2 and 3, Group 6, Schedule 8 until 1 October 2012.[17]

'Approved alteration' means:

(a) in the case of a 'protected building' which is an ecclesiastical building to which section 60 of the *Planning (Listed Buildings and Conservation Areas) Act 1990* applies, any works of alteration; and

(b) in the case of a protected building which is a scheduled monument within the meaning of the *Historic Monuments Act (Northern Ireland) 1971* and in respect of which a protection order, within the meaning of that Act, is in force, works of alteration for which consent has been given under section 10 of that Act; and

(c) in any other case, works of alteration which may not, or but for the existence of a Crown interest or Duchy interest could not, be carried out unless authorised under, or under any provision of:

    (i) Part I of the *Planning (Listed Buildings and Conservation Areas) Act 1990*,

    (ii) Part I of the *Planning (Listed Buildings and Conservation Areas) (Scotland) Act 1997*,

    (iii) Part V of the *Planning (Northern Ireland) Order 1991*,

    (iv) Part I of the *Ancient Monuments and Archaeological Areas Act 1979*,

and for which, except in the case of a Crown interest or Duchy interest, consent has been obtained under any provision of that Part, but does not include any works of repair or maintenance, or any incidental alteration to the fabric of a building which results from the carrying out of repairs, or maintenance work.

An 'ecclesiastical building' for this purpose does not include a building used or available for use by a minister of religion wholly or mainly as a residence from which to perform the duties of his office. 'Crown interest'

---

[17] Subject to transitional rules for certain supplies made before 1 October 2015 – see **Chapter 1**

and Duchy interest' have the same meaning as in section 50 of the *Ancient Monuments and Archaeological Areas Act 1979*.

For 'protected building' see **1.2.25** below.

1.2.2 Building materials

'Building materials' are defined in Note (22) to Group 5 of Schedule 8 as goods of a description 'ordinarily' incorporated by builders in a building of the same description as the one in question or its site. Building materials when supplied in conjunction with building services taxable at the zero or reduced rate can benefit from the same relief (see **10.7.1** below for more details). The VAT charged on supplies of building materials to a DIY builder is refundable to him in certain circumstances (see **5.1** below for more details).

1.2.3 Capital goods scheme ('CGS')

Part XV, VAT Regulations

The capital goods scheme adjusts VAT input tax deductions on certain 'capital items' (including property assets) over a fixed period (the capital goods scheme adjustment period). The adjustments are intended to reflect any change in use of the item between taxable and exempt activities so if there is no change there is no adjustment.

The capital goods scheme has little impact on businesses making only taxable supplies. Such businesses do, however, need to keep appropriate records in relation to capital items in case exempt supplies are made within the capital goods scheme adjustment period.

Input tax adjustments are made over a maximum of five intervals (for leases of less than ten years falling within the capital goods scheme) and ten intervals (other land and property falling within the capital goods scheme). Intervals are normally, but not always, a year in length.

The capital goods scheme is considered in more detail in **11.4**.

1.2.4 Capital items

Regulation 113, VAT Regulations

'Capital items' for the purposes of the capital goods scheme are specified items on which VAT-bearing capital expenditure is incurred to a value of not less than a specified amount. Some of the specified items are property-related and these items are:

(1) land;
(2) a building or part of a building;
(3) a civil engineering work or part of a civil engineering work.

The specified amount of VAT-bearing capital expenditure in the case of these items is £250,000. 'Capital expenditure' is not defined for VAT purposes although there is extensive case law on its meaning for direct tax purposes[18].

The expenditure taken into account is the acquisition expenditure in the case of land and, in the case of a building or civil engineering work, is the expenditure relating to its acquisition, construction, refurbishment, fitting out, alteration or extension (including the construction of an annexe).

1.2.5   Commercial building
For the purposes of this book, a commercial building is a building which is neither designed as a dwelling or number of dwellings, nor is it intended for use solely for a relevant residential purpose or a relevant charitable purpose.

1.2.6   Completed (in relation to a building or civil engineering work)
Note (2), Group 1, Schedule 9

Note (2) to Group 1 of Schedule 9 deals when a building or civil engineering work is completed. This is important in deciding whether a building or civil engineering work is 'new' or 'uncompleted' for the purposes of Item 1(a) Group 1, Schedule 9 which imposes a charge to VAT on the grant of the fee simple in a new or uncompleted building or civil engineering work by removing that supply from exemption. The Note also applies deciding when a building is completed for the purposes of Part 1 of Schedule 10 which deals with the option to tax.[19]

A building is completed on the earlier of:
*   when an architect issues a certificate of practical completion in relation to it; or
*   when it is first fully occupied.

A civil engineering work is completed on the earlier of the following events:
*   when an engineer issues a certificate of completion in relation to it; or
*   when it is first fully used.

---

[18] For example, *Strick v Regent Oil Co. Ltd* (1965) 43 TC 1 (HL) and *CIR v British Aero Engines* (1938) 22 TC 29 (CA)
[19] Paragraph 33, Schedule 10

1.2.7   Dwelling

Note (2) Group 5, Schedule 8

The zero-rating provided for in Items 1 to 3 of Group 5 of Schedule 8 applies to the first grant of a major interest in a building 'designed as a dwelling or number of dwellings' (and certain supplies in the course of construction of such a building). There is no definition of 'dwelling'. However, Note (2) provides that a building is 'designed as a dwelling or number of dwellings' where all of the following conditions are met:

(a)   the dwelling consists of self-contained living accommodation;

(b)   there is no provision for direct internal access from the dwelling to any other dwelling or part of a dwelling;

(c)   the separate use, or disposal of the dwelling is not prohibited by the terms of any covenant, statutory planning consent or similar provision; and

(d)   statutory planning consent has been granted in respect of that dwelling and its construction or conversion has been carried out in accordance with that consent.

These restrictions on the meaning of 'designed as a dwelling' contained in Note (2), Group 5, Schedule 8 (and discussed in more detail at **4.3.2** below) do not apply when considering what is a 'non-residential building'[20] for the purposes of the zero-rating in Item 1(b), Group 5, Schedule 8. However, Note (2) does apply when deciding whether the building which results from the conversion of a non-residential building is 'designed as a dwelling or a number of dwellings'.

Note (2), Group 5, Schedule 8 also applies for the purposes of paragraph 5, Schedule 10 which disapplies the option to tax in relation to a building or part of a building 'designed as a dwelling or number of dwellings'[21].

1.2.8   Election to waive exemption

An alternative term for the 'Option to tax' (see **1.2.21** below).

---

[20] For '**non-residential building**' see **1.2.20** below
[21] See **9.12** below

1.2.9 Exempt supplies

Section 31(1) and Schedule 9

Exempt supplies are supplies that are exempt from VAT. VAT is not charged on these supplies, but no VAT can be claimed on any expenditure that relates to them.[22]

1.2.10 Freehold interest or 'freehold'

The freehold interest (also referred to as the fee simple or the fee simple absolute in possession) is the most complete interest in land that can be held in England and Wales, where all land is technically held subject to the Crown. In practice it means the outright ownership of land or property for an unlimited period. With effect from 27 September 2004 freehold also includes commonhold under the *Commonhold and Leasehold Reform Act 1992*.

1.2.11 Grant

A grant is a sale of a freehold or other interest, or a lease or letting of land. For the purposes of zero-rating under Group 5 of Schedule 8 a grant includes an assignment or a surrender.[23]

For the purposes of Group 1 Schedule 9 'grant' also includes the supply made by the person to whom an interest is surrendered when there is a reverse surrender (i.e. where the person to whom the interest is surrendered is paid by the person by whom the interest is being surrendered to accept the surrender).[24]

For the purposes of Part 1 of Schedule 10 (the option to tax) Note (1), Group 5, Schedule 8 and Notes (1) and (1A), Schedule 9 are applied by paragraph 33 of Schedule 10 in construing the meaning of 'grant.'

An assignment is the transfer of a lease or other 'lesser' interest in or right over land. A surrender is the giving up of an interest in or right over land to the grantor.

The grant of any interest frequently gives rise to a number of further supplies at later times. For example, a supply is made each time that a payment of rent is received. In such cases, the liability of each subsequent supply is determined at the time when that supply is made rather than by reference to the time of the original grant.

---

[22] For the consequences of making exempt supplies **see Chapter 1** below
[23] Note (1), Group 5, Schedule 8
[24] Notes (1) and (1A), Group 1, Schedule 9

1.2.12 Inputs

'Inputs', sometimes referred to, particularly in proceedings before the European Court,[25] as 'cost components,' are the goods or services supplied to a taxable person which are used or to be used for the purposes of his business.

1.2.13 Input tax
Section 24(1)

'Input tax' is VAT on the supply to a taxable person of any goods or services, on the acquisition by him of goods from another Member State and on the importation of goods from outside the EU. The goods or services in question must be used or to be used for the purposes of a business. In other words, input tax is the VAT charged on a business's inputs.

1.2.14 Institutional purpose
Note 7, Group 6, Schedule 7A

This definition forms part of the definition of a special residential conversion which applies for the purposes of the reduced rate for 'qualifying conversions'.[26] The reduced rate reliefs are covered in **Chapter 0**.

An 'institutional purpose' is use as:

(a) a home or other institution providing residential accommodation for children;

(b) a home or other institution providing residential accommodation with personal care for persons in need of personal care by reason of old age, disablement, past or present dependence on alcohol or drugs or past or present mental disorder;

(c) a hospice;

(d) a monastery, nunnery or similar establishment; or

(e) an institution which is the sole or main residence of at least 90 per cent of its residents, except use as a hospital, prison or similar institution or a hotel, inn or similar establishment.

1.2.15 Long lease

In this book, the term 'long lease' is used to describe a lease granted for a term in excess of 21 years in England and Wales or in excess of 20 years in Scotland. This forms part of the definition of 'major interest' which is

---

[25] See, for example, *BLP Group plc v CCE* (Case C–4/94) [1995] STC 424 and *Midland Bank plc v CCE* (Case C–98/98) [2000] STC 501

[26] See **1.2.26** below

relevant for zero-rating under Groups 5 and 6 of Schedule 8 (see **1.2.16** below).

The term of a lease under a time-share arrangement is determined by the period of occupation, not the number of years for which the arrangement is expressed to run.[27]

1.2.16   Major interest
Section 96(1)

In England, Wales and Northern Ireland, a freehold interest or a 'long lease' (see **1.2.14** above). This definition is relevant for zero-rating under Groups 5 and 6 of Schedule 8.

1.2.17   Mixed use
'Mixed use' is used in this book to describe a building part of which eligible for zero-rating under Item 1, Group 5, Schedule 8 and part not.

1.2.18   Multiple occupancy dwelling
Note 4(2), Group 6, Schedule 7A

This definition is relevant in deciding whether there is a qualifying conversion for the purposes of Schedule 7A (*reduced rate for certain supplies*).[28]

A multiple occupancy dwelling is, broadly, hostel-type accommodation, and is defined in Note 4(2), Group 6, Schedule 7A as:

(a) a dwelling that 'is designed for' occupation by persons not forming a single household and that is not to any extent used for a 'relevant residential purpose';[29]

(b) in relation to which the following four conditions are satisfied:

   (1) it consists of self-contained living accommodation;
   (2) there is no provision for direct internal access from it to any other dwelling or part of a dwelling;
   (3) separate use is not prohibited by the terms of any covenant or planning permission; and
   (4) separate disposal is not prohibited by the terms of any covenant or planning permission.

---

[27] *Cottage Holiday Associates Ltd v CCE* [1983] STC 278, where one week's occupation per annum for 80 years was held to be a lease for a term certain of 80 weeks.

[28] See **1.2.26** below

[29] See **1.2.29** for the meaning of 'use for a relevant residential purpose'

A dwelling is 'designed for' occupation of a particular kind if it is so designed as a result of having been originally constructed for occupation of that kind and not having been subsequently adapted for occupation of any other kind, or as a result of adaptation.[30]

Note 2(4) to Group 7 of Schedule 7A applies the definition of multiple occupancy dwelling in Note 4(2) to Group 6 of Schedule 7A to Group 7 also. Group 7 applies the reduced rate of VAT to certain residential renovations and alterations.[31]

1.2.19 New (in relation to a building or civil engineering work)
Note (4), Group 1, Schedule 9

This definition is important as the supply of a freehold in a new commercial building or in a new civil engineering work is standard rated, rather than exempt. A building or civil engineering work is new if it was completed less than three years before the grant. For 'completed' see **1.2.5** above.

Special rules (in Notes (5) and (6), Group 1, Schedule 9) apply where the building or civil engineering work was completed before 1 April 1989.

1.2.20 Non-residential building
Notes (7) and (7A), Group 5, Schedule 8

There are two definition of non-residential building for the purposes of the zero-rating provided for in Group 5. In neither case do references to a non-residential building or a non-residential part of a building include a reference to a garage occupied together with a dwelling.[32]

Note (7), Group 5, Schedule 8
The definition of 'non-residential' in Note (7) is relevant for the zero-rating[33] of the first grant of a major interest in a building converted from a non-residential building or from a non-residential part of a building, into a building designed as a dwelling or number of dwellings or intended for use solely for a 'relevant residential purpose'.[34]

A building or part of a building is 'non-residential' if:
(a) it is neither designed, nor adapted, for use as a dwelling or number of dwellings, or for a relevant residential purpose; or

---

[30] Note 2(4) Group 6, Schedule 7A
[31] See **Chapter 10**
[32] Note (8), Group 5, Schedule 8
[33] In Item 1(b), Group 5, Schedule 8
[34] See **1.2.29**

(b) it is designed, or adapted, for such use but it was constructed more than ten years before the grant of the major interest and no part of it has, in the period of ten years immediately preceding the grant, been used as a dwelling or for a relevant residential purpose.

Note (7A), Group 5, Schedule 8

The definition of 'non-residential building' in Note (7A) is relevant for the zero-rating[35] of the supply of qualifying services and building materials to a 'relevant housing association'[36] in the course of conversion of a non-residential building or a non-residential part of a building into a building or part of a building designed as a dwelling or number of dwellings or intended for use solely for a relevant residential purpose and also for the DIY builders' refund scheme[37].

Note (7A) provides that a building or part of a building is 'non-residential' if:

(a) it is neither designed, nor adapted, for use as a dwelling or number of dwellings, or for a relevant residential purpose; or

(b) it is designed, or adapted, for such use but it was constructed more than ten years before the commencement of the works of conversion, and no part of it has, in the period of ten years immediately preceding the commencement of those works, been used as a dwelling or for a relevant residential purpose, *and no part of it is being so used.*

The italics highlight the difference between the two definitions.

In *Salter (Paul) v Revenue & Customs Comrs*[38] an individual purchased a building that had been used as a commercially-run residential home for children suffering from a mental disability or drug addiction and claimed repayment of VAT on buildings works to convert the building into a family home. HMRC refused the claim on the basis that, while under section 35 the conversion of a non-residential building into a building designed as a dwelling could result in VAT refunds, in this case the previous use of the building meant that it had not been a 'non-residential building' within Note (7A), Group 5, Schedule 8. The tribunal considered that it was clear that the use of the building for the vast majority of the relevant ten year period

---

[35] In Item 3, Group 5, Schedule 8

[36] For definition of **'relevant housing association'** see **1.2.29** above

[37] See **5.2** below

[38] (TC03556) [2014] UKFTT 427

before the conversion was use for a 'relevant residential purpose' within Note (4)(b), Group 5. The appeal was dismissed.

1.2.21 Option to tax

The option to tax which is exercisable by the person making a specified supply can convert certain exempt supplies of interests in or rights over land into supplies taxable at the standard rate. The option to tax is considered in detail in **Chapter 1**.

1.2.22 Outputs

Outputs are the taxable supplies made by a business which is or should be VAT-registered. Zero-rated supplies are included.

1.2.23 Output tax

Section 24(2)

Output tax is the VAT chargeable on the supply by a taxable person of any goods or services, and on the acquisition by him of goods from another Member State. In other words, output tax is the VAT on a business's outputs.

Taxable property transactions are charged at either a reduced rate of 5 per cent or the standard rate. No output tax is charged on zero-rated supplies as the rate of tax is 0 per cent.

1.2.24 Partial exemption

Part XIV, VAT Regulations

A registered business which makes both taxable and exempt supplies cannot charge VAT on the exempt supplies and equally cannot normally reclaim the VAT incurred on the purchases used to make those supplies. Where input tax cannot be claimed because it relates to an exempt supply, it is known as exempt input tax and the registered business is known as partially exempt. Exempt supplies are not unusual in a property context and they are those supplies which fall within Item 1, Group 1, Schedule 9.[39] There is a list of these supplies in the introduction to **Chapter 1**.

A partially exempt business will normally have to use an approved partial exemption method to work out how much of its input tax can be reclaimed. This would usually be the standard method unless it feels that this would not give a fair or reasonable result, in which case it can apply to HMRC for a special method. All methods should provide for direct attribution and apportionment of the input tax incurred. Direct attribution involves

---

[39] See **3.1**

identifying VAT on goods and services which are used exclusively to make taxable supplies or exempt supplies; the former is deductible, the latter is not. Apportionment is required for the remaining input tax (e.g. on overheads) which cannot be directly attributed.

Partial exemption in a property context is considered in **Chapter 1**.

1.2.25 Protected building
Note (1), Group 6, Schedule 8

This definition is used in Group 6 of Schedule 8 which zero-rates substantial reconstructions of protected buildings and, before 1 October 2012,[40] supplies of qualifying services and 'building materials' in the course of an 'approved alteration'[41] to a protected building.

'Protected building' means a building which is:
(1) designed to remain as or become a dwelling or number of dwellings (as defined in Note (2), Group 6)[42]; or
(2) intended for use solely for a 'relevant residential purpose' or a 'relevant charitable purpose' after the reconstruction or alteration,

and which, in either case, is:
(a) a listed building, within the meaning of:
   (i)   the Planning (*Listed Buildings and Conservation Areas) Act 1990*; or
   (ii) the *Planning (Listed Buildings and Conservation Areas) (Scotland) Act 1997*; or
   (iii) the *Planning (Northern Ireland) Order 1991*; or
(b) a scheduled monument, within the meaning of:
   (i)   the *Ancient Monuments and Archaeological Areas Act 1979*; or
   (ii) the *Historic Monuments and Archaeological Objects (Northern Ireland) Order 1995*.

1.2.26 Qualifying conversion
Notes 2, 3, 5, 7, 9 and 10, Item 1, Group 6, Schedule 7A

Certain supplies in the course of a 'qualifying conversion' are taxable at the reduced rate. There are three types of qualifying conversions:

(1) A 'changed number of dwellings conversion' (Note 3, Group 6, Schedule 7A)

---

[40] There are transitional rules extending to 30 September 2015 – see **Chapter 8**
[41] See **1.2.1** above
[42] See **4.1** below

This is a change in the number of dwellings in a building or part of a building. The change can be an increase or a decrease but after the conversion there must be at least one 'single household dwelling'[43]

(2) A 'house in multiple occupation conversion' (Note 5, Group 6, Schedule 7A)

This is a conversion from a building or part of a building that does not contain any 'multiple occupancy dwellings[44]' into a multiple occupancy dwelling or dwellings. After the conversion the premises must contain only a multiple occupancy dwelling or dwellings and the intended use after the conversion must not, to any extent, be use for a 'relevant residential purpose'[45].

(3) A 'special residential conversion' (Note 7, Group 6, Schedule 7A)

This is a conversion of a building or buildings or part or parts of a building or a combination of buildings or parts of buildings which were not being used for a 'relevant residential purpose'[46] into premises intended for use solely for such a purpose. Where the intended relevant residential purpose use after conversion is an 'institutional purpose'[47] the premises being converted must be intended to form the entirety of an institution used for that purpose after conversion.

In all three cases, any necessary planning consents and building control approvals must have been obtained. A qualifying conversion can include garage works.

Conversions qualifying for the reduced rate are dealt with in **Chapter 0**.

1.2.27   Qualifying residential premises
Note 2(1), Group 7, Schedule 7A

This definition is relevant for Items 1 to 3, Group 7, Schedule 7A which apply the reduced rate to certain supplies of goods and services in the course of residential renovations and alterations. 'Qualifying residential premises' means:

(1) a 'single household dwelling'[48];

(2) a 'multiple occupancy dwelling'[49]; and

---

[43] For 'single household dwelling' see **1.2.32**

[44] See **1.2.18**

[45] See **1.2.29**

[46] See **1.2.29**

[47] See **1.2.14**

[48] See **1.2.32**

(3) a building or part of a building which, when it was last lived in, was used for a 'relevant residential purpose'[50].

Where a building formed part of a 'relevant residential unit[51]' when it was last lived in, it is treated as having been used for a relevant residential purpose and therefore falls within (3) above (Note 2(2), Group 7, Schedule 7A).

The reduced rate for residential renovations and alterations provided for in Group 7 Schedule 7A is considered in detail at **10.6** below.

1.2.28   Relevant charitable purpose
Note (6), Group 5, Schedule 8

Certain supplies of or in relation to buildings intended to be used solely for a relevant charitable purpose fall within Group 5, Schedule 8 and are zero-rated.

'Use for a relevant charitable purpose' means use by a charity, in either or both of the following ways:

(1) otherwise than in the course or furtherance of a business;
(2) as a village hall or similarly in providing social or recreational activities for a local community.

1.2.29   Relevant housing association
Note (21), Group 5, Schedule 8 and paragraph 10(3), Schedule 10

A 'relevant housing association' is defined as:
• a private registered provider of social housing
• a registered social landlord within the meaning of Part 1 of the Housing Act 1996 (Welsh registered social landlords)
• a registered social landlord within the meaning of the *Housing (Scotland) Act 2010* which is either a society registered under the *Co-operative and Community Benefit Societies and Credit Unions Act 1965*, or a company within the meaning of the *Companies Act 2006*
• a registered housing association within the meaning of Part 2 of the *Housing (Northern Ireland) Order 1992* (Northern Irish registered housing associations)

---

[49] See **1.2.18**
[50] See **1.2.29**
[51] See **1.2.31**

1.2.30 Relevant residential purpose
Note 6, Group 6, Schedule 7A and Note (4), Group 5, Schedule 8

There are two definitions of relevant residential purpose, one in Note 6, Group 6, Schedule 7A and the other in Note (4), Group 5, Schedule 8. They are in identical terms.

Group 6, Schedule 7A applies the reduced rate to certain supplies in the course of a 'qualifying conversion' (see definition in **1.2.26** above). One of the types of qualifying conversion is a special residential conversion. Note 6, Group 6, Schedule 7A sets out the definition of relevant residential purpose which applies in determining whether there is a special residential conversion.

Certain supplies of or in relation to buildings intended to be used solely for a relevant residential purpose fall within Group 5, Schedule 8 and are zero-rated. Note (4), Group 5, Schedule 8 applies for this purpose.

'Use for a relevant residential purpose' means use as:
(a) a home or other institution providing residential accommodation for children;
(b) a home or other institution providing residential accommodation with personal care for persons in need of personal care by reason of old age, disablement, past or present dependence on alcohol or drugs or past or present mental disorder;
(c) a hospice;
(d) residential accommodation for students or school pupils;
(e) residential accommodation for members of any of the armed forces;
(f) a monastery, nunnery or similar establishment; or
(g) an institution which is the sole or main residence of at least 90 per cent of its residents, except use as a hospital, prison or similar institution or a hotel, inn or similar establishment.

except use as a hospital, prison or similar institution or an hotel, inn or similar establishment.

1.2.31 Relevant residential unit
Note 2(3) Group 7, Schedule 7A

This definition forms part of the test of 'qualifying residential premises'[52] in applying the reduced rate relief to certain supplies in the course of residential renovations and alterations.

---

[52] See **1.2.27**

A building is part of a 'relevant residential unit' when it is one of a number of buildings on the same site and the buildings are used together for a 'relevant residential purpose'[53].

1.2.32   Reverse surrender
Note (1A)), Item 1, Group 1, Schedule 9

A reverse surrender is where the person to whom the interest is surrendered is paid by the person by whom the interest is being surrendered to accept the surrender.

1.2.33   Single household dwelling
Note 4, Group 6, Schedule 7A

This definition applies to determine whether there is a 'changed number of dwellings conversion' to which the reduced rate in Group 6, Schedule 7A applies (see 'Qualifying conversion' at **1.2.26** above).

A 'single household dwelling' means a dwelling designed (either originally or as a result of adaptation) for occupation by a single household, that is not to any extent used for a relevant residential purpose, and, in relation to which the following four conditions are satisfied:
(1)   it consists of self contained living accommodation;
(2)   there is no provision for direct internal access from it to any other dwelling or part of a dwelling;
(3)   the separate use of it is not prohibited by the terms of any covenant, statutory planning consent or similar provision; and
(4)   the separate disposal of it is not prohibited by any such terms.

1.2.34   Supplies outside the scope of VAT
A supply may be outside the scope of VAT for a variety of reasons. It may be made outside the UK or it may be a supply that is disregarded for VAT purposes such as a transfer of a business as a going concern.[54]

No VAT is chargeable on such supplies, but related input tax may, depending on the circumstances, be recoverable.

1.2.35   Taxable person
Section 3

A taxable person is a person who is or is required to be registered for VAT.

---

[53] See **1.2.29**
[54] Discussed in a property context in **Chapter 1**

1.2.36   Taxable supplies
Section 4

Taxable supplies are supplies of goods or services in the UK, other than exempt supplies, made by a taxable person.

1.2.37   Transfer of a business as a going concern ('TOGC')
Article 5, Value Added Tax (Special Provision) Order 1995[55]

When a VAT registered business sells assets, each asset is subject to VAT at the applicable rate. However, if a business, or a part of a business is sold as a TOGC then the supply of the assets is disregarded, subject to certain conditions and this can have advantages where the sale would otherwise be exempt. The TOGC rules as they apply to property transactions are considered in detail in **Chapter 1**.

---

[55] SI 1995/1268

2 The General VAT Rules as they apply to Property-Related Supplies

This chapter deals with the general VAT rules as they apply to property-related supplies. The VAT liability of the most common property supplies is discussed in **Chapter 1** below.

UK VAT is chargeable where there has been a taxable supply in the UK by a 'taxable person[1] in the course or furtherance of a business. Supplies of interests in real property and of property-related services[2], such as building work, take place where the underlying land is situated. This means that, in certain circumstances, the reverse charge[3] may apply to UK land-related services.[4] However, the reverse charge cannot apply to services of any of the descriptions specified in Schedule 9.[5] This covers most property letting, since even if the landlord opts to tax under Schedule 10 the supply is still of a 'description' in Schedule 9.

2.1 Goods or services?

Section 5 sets out the rules for deciding whether a supply is a supply of goods or of services. Subject to Schedule 4 and any Treasury Orders made under section 4, anything which is not a supply of goods but is done for a consideration is a supply of services.

Paragraph 4, Schedule 4 provides that 'the grant, assignment or surrender of a major interest[6] in land is a supply of goods'. This means that any supply of a lesser interest (such as a lease for ten years) or of a major interest that does not amount in law to a grant, assignment or surrender (such as a declaration of trust) will be a supply of services for VAT purposes.

---

[1] For the meaning of '**taxable person**' see **1.2.35**

[2] Article 45 VAT Directive enacted in UK law as paragraph 1(2) Schedule 4A. See, for example, *RCI Europe v HMRC* (Case C-37/08) [2009] STC 2407 in which the European held that the place of supply of timeshare rights was the place where the property over which the timeshare rights had effect was situated

[3] The 'reverse charge' is a deemed supply by a taxable person to himself in the course of his business – see section 8

[4] Section 8 (considered in *Muster Inns Ltd* [2014] UKFTT 563 (TC) which concerned a supply of refurbishment works by a company based in Guernsey to a UK pub-owner)

[5] Section 8(4A)

[6] For '**major interest**' see **1.2.16**

The classification of a supply as a supply of goods or a supply of services can be important. In particular, the rules identifying the time of supply[7] differ according to whether there is a supply of goods or a supply of services. Also there are provisions in paragraph 4, Schedule 4 deeming a supply to be made, even where there is no consideration, where goods which are business assets cease to form part of those assets. An example would be where goods are given away. Where such goods are sold under a power exercisable by a third party in satisfaction of a debt owed by a taxable person there is a deemed supply under paragraph 7, Schedule 4. There is also a deemed supply of goods which are business assets on deregistration.[8]

The rules for recovery of input tax incurred before a person was or was required to be registered[9] differ depending on whether the supply in respect of which the VAT was charged was a supply of goods or a supply of services. VAT incurred before registration on supplies of services cannot be claimed unless the services were supplied six months or less before the date the person was registered or required to be registered[10]. In relation to goods the period is four years provided that the goods have not been supplied or 'consumed' before the date the person was registered or required to be registered.[11] This can give rise to problems in relation to pre-registration fit-outs.[12]

2.2 Time of supply

VAT is due by reference to the time of supply, or tax point. This may not be the same as the time payment is received. Regulation 13(5) VAT Regulations provides that a VAT invoice must be issued within 30 days of the time when the supply is treated as taking place under section 6 (or such longer period as HMRC may allow, either specially or generally).

---

[7] See **2.2** below

[8] Paragraph 8, Schedule 4 – there will be no charge if no input tax has been claimed on the supply of those goods or any of the conditions in paragraph 8(1) are fulfilled

[9] In regulation 111 VAT Regulations

[10] Regulation 111(2)(c) VAT Regulations

[11] Regulation 111(2)(a) and (b) VAT Regulations

[12] See, for example, *Ann Khoshaba T/A Cinnamon Café* [2013] UKFTT 481(TC)

2.2.1 The general rules

Section 6

The basic tax point for a supply of goods is when the goods are removed or made available,[13] and for a supply of services is when the services are performed.[14]

Where the supply is of goods that is an interest in property, the basic tax point is completion as that is the time when the interest is 'made available', even if the purchaser is allowed into occupation at an earlier date. This was confirmed by the Court of Session in *Cumbernauld Development Corporation v CCE.*[15]

A basic tax point is overridden in the following circumstances:[16]

(1) If payment is received and/or a tax invoice is issued *before* the basic tax point, then, to the extent of the amount paid or invoiced, this creates what HMRC refer to as an 'actual tax point'.

(2) If (1) does not apply and the supplier issues a tax invoice within 14 days *after* the basic tax point, this creates an actual tax point unless the supplier has notified HMRC in writing that it does not wish to use this rule. HMRC can also agree an extension to the 14 day time limit.

Where a tax point occurs, the supplier becomes liable to account for any VAT on the supply to which it relates whether he has received payment or not.

If the purchaser of an interest in land pays a deposit to the seller or his agent, this becomes the seller's money and creates an actual tax point to the extent of the deposit. There is then a further tax point when the balance is paid, normally on completion. This does not apply if a deposit is paid to a stakeholder. For an example of the problems these tax point rules can cause for purchases at auction see the discussion of *Higher Education Statistics Agency v CCE*[17] at section **9.16** below.

2.2.2 Special tax point rules for interests in land giving rise to periodic payments

The basic tax point rules do not apply where there the interest in land gives rise to consideration which is payable periodically or from time to time.

---

[13] Section 6(2)
[14] Section 6(3)
[15] [2002] STC 226 (CS)
[16] Section 6(4) and 6(5)
[17] [2000] STC 332 (QBD)

Under regulation 85 VAT Regulations (which applies to leases treated as supplies of goods) and regulation 90 (which applies in other cases) there is a separate tax point at the earlier of and each time that there is a receipt of payment by the supplier or a tax invoice is issued.

The taking of a rent deposit will be a receipt of payment if and when it becomes the landlord's money, but not while it is held in an escrow or similar account. Similarly, the receipt of a contribution to a sinking fund etc, could create a tax point if the fund belongs to the landlord, but not if it belongs to the tenants, or to the parties jointly when there will be a tax point on the earlier of when the landlord draws amounts down from the fund or issues a tax invoice.

Interest on rent paid late is outside the scope of VAT as it is treated as damages for breach of the terms of the agreement.

Some landlords delay issuing a tax invoice until the rent has been paid and issue a rent demand to secure payment. This avoids having to account for VAT on unpaid rent. There can also be a cash-flow advantage to a landlord in having particular VAT return periods – if rents are due in on the quarter-days in March, June etc, it will be preferable to have return periods ending in February, May etc.

There is a facility under both regulation 85 and regulation 90 for the issue of a single tax invoice for up to a year in advance, without creating a tax point – tax points occur when rents fall due or, if earlier, are paid. The form of this invoice differs from a standard tax invoice as it must contain the following additional information:

(1) the dates on which an parts of the consideration are to become due for payment;

(2) the amount payable (excluding VAT) on such date; and

(3) the rate of VAT in force at the time of issue of the VAT invoice and the amount of VAT chargeable in accordance with that rate on each of the payments.

Anti-avoidance rules

There are compulsory annual tax point rules in regulation 94B VAT Regulations. These are an anti-avoidance measure and are intended to prevent the deferral of tax points for more than a 12 month period. The rules apply where there has been no supply under the normal tax point rules and to the extent that the services have been 'provided':

(1) rent is subject to VAT other than as a result of the exercise of an option to tax – such as where there is a supply of parking or sports facilities[18];

(2) the recipient cannot recover that input VAT in full; and

(3) the supplier and recipient are 'connected'[19] or one party is an 'undertaking' in relation to which the other is a 'group undertaking' for the purposes of section 1161 *Companies Act 2006*.

Where the anti-avoidance rules apply, the supplier must recognise a tax point for any difference between the supplies under the lease or licence disregarding any supplies in respect of which VAT have fallen due under the normal rules for the 12 month period determined in accordance with regulation 94B(5) and any subsequent 12 month period. This rule can be displaced by the issue of a tax invoice or receipt of payment within six months of the end of the period.[20]

2.2.3   Time of supply for 'building work' (including alteration, demolition, repair and maintenance and civil engineering work)

For building work, the position depends on whether the contract provides for a single payment (with or without retentions) or stage payments:

- Where there is a single payment, the general rule described in **0** above applies to determine the time of supply. This means that there is a basic tax point on completion of the work, overridden by an actual tax point to the extent of any earlier payment or tax invoice, or by the issue of a tax invoice within 14 days after completion.

- Where the contract provides for retentions, regulation 89 VAT Regulations provides that there is a tax point for these only when, and to the extent that, they are actually received by the supplier or a tax invoice is issued in respect them.

- Where a contract for building work provides for payment to be made 'periodically or from time to time', regulation 93 provides for a tax point in relation to each payment, at the earlier of when it is received by the supplier or a tax invoice is issued for it. In practice, many contractors issue a request for payment, followed by an authenticated receipt, rather than tax invoices, so that VAT is only due when payments are received.

---

[18] See **3.2.14** for further examples

[19] Within the meaning of section 839 *ICTA 1988* as modified by regulation 94B(4)(b) VAT Regulations

[20] Regulation 94B(6) VAT Regulations

Completion of the building work does not create a tax point unless the anti-avoidance rule in regulation 93 of the VAT Regulations applies. These cover cases where the contractor, or someone financing the contractor, intends or expects that the property will be occupied by one or other of them, or by someone 'connected[21]' with either of them, other than 'wholly or mainly' for 'eligible purposes.' 'Eligible purposes' means the making of taxable supplies or certain public sector use. The anti-avoidance rule is covered in detail in **10.9.4** below.

2.2.4 Time of supply for professional services

Where professional services are provided for a single payment, the general rules described in **2.2** above apply, so that there is a basic tax point when the services are completed, overridden by an actual tax point to the extent of any earlier payment or tax invoice, or by the issue of a tax invoice within 14 days after the basic tax point.

If there are periodic payments, tax points will be determined either by regulation 93 or by regulation 90. Regulation 93, as discussed in **2.2.3** above covers any services supplied in the course of 'building work' and this extends to the services of architects, surveyors, consultants and others acting in a supervisory capacity in relation to such work.

Regulation 90 (discussed in **2.2.2** above) applies in any other case where there are periodic payments, and provides that:
(1) There is no tax point on completion, but there will be a tax point on receipt of each payment or, if earlier, the issue of a tax invoice.
(2) There is a facility for a tax invoice to be issued up to a year in advance without creating a tax point.

For services involving connected persons, regulation 94B can create an annual tax point if VAT on the services is not wholly recoverable by the client, (as described in **2.2.2** above).

2.2.5 Time of supply - unascertainable consideration
Regulation 84 VAT Regulations

In some cases, the full sale price may not be known at the tax point, for example, there could be a supply of freehold land for a fixed sum together with an overage payment calculated by reference to building density in planning permission. Regulation 84 VAT Regulations provides:

---

[21] Within the meaning of section 839 *ICTA 1988* as modified by regulation 94B(4)(b) VAT Regulations

(1) If property is compulsorily purchased, and the amount of compensation is not known at the time, tax points only arise as and when payment is received.

(2) If the full price of a freehold sale is not known at completion, the normal rules apply to the extent it is known. A further tax point will be created by the receipt of any additional payment, or the issue of a tax invoice for it.

There is an anti-avoidance rule in regulation 84(3) which provide that in the case of the sale of a freehold there is a tax point for the full sale price at completion even if the sale price is not actually known. Regulation 84(3) applies if the following conditions are met:

(1) the sale is compulsorily standard rated under Item 1(a) Group 1 Schedule 9;[22]

(2) the seller, someone financing or agreeing to finance the seller's development or acquisition, or someone connected with any such person, intends or expects to occupy the property within ten years of the completion of the building or civil engineering work; and

(3) that person intends or expects that occupation not to be 'wholly or substantially wholly, for eligible purposes'. 'Substantially wholly' means at least 80%, whilst 'eligible purposes' essentially means the making of taxable supplies or certain public sector use.

2.3 The value of the supply (the amount on which VAT is chargeable)

Section 19

The value of a supply which is made for a consideration in money is the amount which, with the addition of the VAT chargeable, is equal to the consideration[23]. If a sale contract does not oblige a purchaser to pay VAT in addition to the consideration, the amount payable under the contract will be regarded as inclusive of any VAT, meaning that the seller will have to account to HMRC for the VAT out of the contract price. In *Hostgilt v Megahart Ltd*[24], a decision of the High Court, where the contract price was stated to be exclusive of VAT but the contract lacked an express obligation

---

[22] Item 1(a) covers the 'grant' of the 'fee simple' in a 'new' or 'uncompleted' 'commercial building' or civil engineering work – for definitions see **1.2** above

[23] Section 19(2)

[24] [1999] STC 141 cited by Lord Walker in *National Transport Authority v Mauritius Secondary Industry Ltd* [2010] UKPC 31

on the purchaser to pay the VAT, it was held that the purchaser was liable for the VAT.

In *CLP Holding Co Limited v Singh and Kaur*[25] the Court of Appeal considered whether the purchasers of an opted freehold property were contractually liable to pay VAT on the purchase price[26]. A VAT-registered seller sold a freehold commercial property for £130,000. Although the seller had opted to tax the property a number of years earlier, the issue of VAT was not addressed by the parties until HMRC assessed the seller for VAT on the sale. In March 2008, after HMRC had made an assessment, the seller wrote to the purchasers requesting an amount equal to VAT on the contractual purchase price. The buyers refused to pay arguing that the price was VAT-inclusive.

The sale contract incorporated the Standard Conditions of Sale (4th edition), even though the sale was of commercial property. The incorporated standard conditions stated that:
(1) Any obligation to pay money included an obligation to pay any related VAT.
(2) All sums payable under the contract were exclusive of VAT.
(3) Any liability to perform an outstanding obligation under the contract survived completion.

However, the special conditions in the sale contract, which took priority over any conflicting Standard Conditions, defined the purchase price as the sum of £130,000.

The Court of Appeal held that the sale contract, unlike the contract in *Hostgilt*, did not oblige the buyers to pay the VAT amount. The contractual price was inclusive of VAT and the seller therefore had to account to HMRC for VAT out of the £130,000 it received.

The Court's reasoning was that it is necessary to consider what a reasonable person, with 'all the background knowledge' at their disposal, would have understood the contracting parties to have meant. In this case, the purchase monies were agreed and paid a considerable time before completion. The seller, through its solicitors, had confirmed that it had received 'all of the sale monies of £130,000 on this matter', with no mention of VAT. In response to a standard requisition seeking confirmation of the exact amount payable on completion, there was no mention of the VAT. As a result, the

---

[25] [2014] EWCA Civ 1103
[26] For the **option to tax** see **Chapter 1**

buyers were not aware and had no reason to suspect that the price would be subject to VAT.

The judgment in *CLP Holding Co Ltd* serves as a useful reminder to consider VAT at an early stage in property sale negotiations, and to ensure that VAT wording in sale contracts is clear and unambiguous.

2.4   Supplies spanning change of VAT rate or change in liability of a supply

Sections 88 and 89 VATA, and regulation 95 VAT Regulations

The provisions of section 88 apply where there is a change in the rate of VAT or a change in the liability of a supply (because of a change of the description in the legislation) and a basic tax point falls on one side of the change and a tax point arising from receipt of payment or the issue of an invoice falls on the other. Any such change affects supplies made on or after the effective date of the change.

Section 88 allows suppliers can choose to apply the rate or the liability in force at the basic tax point. For continuous supplies (for example, where there are stage payments for building work or rents payable under a lease) the supplier can choose to split the charges (for example, on the basis of building work actually done before or after the change, or the number of days in the rental period falling before and after the change).

Section 89 (adjustment of contracts on changes in VAT) provides that where, after the making of a contract for the supply of goods or services and before those goods or services are supplied, there is a change in the VAT charged, then, unless the contract provides otherwise, the consideration for the supply is increased or decreased by an amount equal to the change. These provisions apply in relation to a tenancy or lease as they apply in relation to a contract.

This means that where the option to tax is exercised after exchange of contracts (or after agreement for lease) and the terms of that contract (or the agreement for lease) do not either specifically exclude section 89 or state that the agreed consideration is inclusive of any VAT charge arising from the exercise of the option to tax the consideration will be increased by statute to include VAT.

3 The VAT Liability of the Most Common Property-Related Supplies

This chapter begins by setting out the VAT liability of most of the common property transactions to give a feel for the subject before moving on to examine leases in detail. The chapter concludes by considering some more specialised issues, such as joint ownership and commonhold. Reference should be made to **1.2** above for defined terms.

The default position for property transactions is that the supply will be exempt[1]. There are a number of exceptions to this, as there are items that are compulsorily standard rated, or the supplier may be able to opt to tax the transaction[2], changing the liability from exempt to standard rated. In addition, there are property-related supplies that benefit from zero-rate or reduced rate relief. The zero-rate and reduced rate reliefs are deal with in detail in other chapters, as is the option to tax.

3.1 Exempt or taxable at the standard rate?

Item 1, Group 1, Schedule 9

Article 135.1(j) of the VAT Directive exempts 'the supply of a building or parts thereof, and of the land on which it stands, other than the supply of building land as referred to in point (b) of Article12(1).'

Article 135.1(k) of the VAT Directive exempts 'the supply of land which has not been built on other than the supply of building land as referred to in point (b) of Article12(1).'

'Building land' for the purposes of article 12(1)(b) means 'any unimproved or improved land as defined as such by Member States'.

Article 135.1(l) of the VAT Directive exempts 'the leasing or letting of immovable property', excluding:
(a) the provision of accommodation, as defined in the laws of the Member States, in the hotel sector or in sectors with a similar function, including the provision of accommodation in holiday camps or on sites developed for use as camping sites;
(b) the letting of premises and sites for parking of vehicles;
(c) the letting of permanently installed equipment and machinery;
(d) the hire of safes.

---

[1] Group 1, Schedule 9
[2] The option to tax is dealt with in detail in **Chapter 1**

Item 1, Group 1, Schedule 9 provides that exemption applies to the 'grant of any interest in or right over land or of any licence to occupy land' other than the types of supplies listed at (a) to (n) of that Item (which are dealt with at **3.2.14** below). Zero-rating takes precedence over exemption[3] so all zero-rated grants fall outside Item 1 of Group 1.

Any other use of land (that does not flow from the grant of an interest in or right over land or a licence to occupy land), such as the right to share business premises or the right to sell ice creams from vans on the sea front, or hamburger from vans at sporting events, will also fall outside Item 1 of Group 1 and be taxable at the standard rate.

3.1.1 Building land

In *Norbury Developments Ltd v CCE*[4] the tribunal found that building land should be taxable under EU law rather than exempt (as it was and remains in UK law) unless the exemption was authorised by article 28(3)(b) Sixth Directive (which allowed countries to continue to exempt certain supplies, including building land, for a transitional period and which is now article 371 of the VAT Directive). The tribunal referred the case to the European Court which held that the UK was entitled to exempt the supply under article 28(3)(b).

3.1.2 Interest in or right over land

An interest in land for this purpose can be a legal interest or a beneficial interest. A beneficial interest may be held and transferred separately from the legal interest. Rights over land include rights of entry, easements, wayleaves, and profits à prendre.

Some rights over land, such as the right to fell and remove timber and shooting and fishing rights, are taxable at the standard rate under the exceptions to exemption in UK law[5]. In addition, the right granted to harvest and remove crops may in some cases be treated as a zero-rated supply of food or animal feed stuff.

3.1.3 Licence to occupy

A 'licence to occupy' is a written or oral agreement which falls within the European concept of 'leasing or letting of immovable property' but falls short of being a lease under UK land law. For a licence to occupy to exist, the agreement has to have all characteristics of a leasing or letting of

---

[3] By reason of section 30(1)

[4] (Case C-136/97), [1999] STC 511

[5] See **3.2.14** below

immovable property. Exclusivity of occupation is not an essential characteristic of a licence[6].

A definition of a 'licence to occupy' was also offered by the House of Lords in *CCE v Sinclair Collis Ltd*[7]:

> 'a licence to go into possession, not necessarily exclusive possession, or to go on to the land and take some degree of control of it. If neither of these features is present, the licence cannot, in my opinion, properly be described as a licence to occupy.'

3.1.4   The exclusions from exemption in general[8]

The exclusions from exemption at paragraphs (c) to (ma) of Item 1, Group 1, Schedule 9 are 'carve-outs' from the more general wording in Item 1. In some cases. there can be what may seem like overlap so it is important to consider the wording of the exclusions carefully and identify exactly what is being supplied. This is illustrated by the case of *Abbotsley Golf & Squash Club Ltd.*[9]

In *Abbotsley* a company which owned two golf courses granted a golf club a non-exclusive licence to occupy its courses, receiving a licence fee of £280,000. G did not account for output tax on this fee, treating it as being consideration for a licence to occupy land and exempt.

HMRC issued an assessment on the basis that the payment was taxable, considering that it was excluded from exemption by Item 1(m), Group 1, Schedule 9, as being 'the grant of facilities for playing any sport'. The tribunal allowed the company's appeal, holding that the fact that the licence was not exclusive did not prevent it from constituting a 'licence to occupy land' within Item 1. Applying dicta of Lord Templeman in *Street v Mountford*[10], exclusivity of occupation was an essential condition of a tenancy but was not an essential condition of a licence. The tribunal chairman observed that 'what distinguishes a tenancy from a licence is that the former grants a legal right to exclusive possession of the land for a

---

[6] See discussion at **3.1.4** below and also *Altman Blane & Co (VTD 12381)* where payments for use of a room were held to be payments for a licence to occupy land and therefore exempt even though the licence did not grant exclusive occupation.

[7] [2001] STC 989 (HL) per Lord Scott at paragraph 74

[8] Considered in more detail at **3.2.14** below

[9] [1997] VATDR 355

[10] [1985] 1 AC 809 (HL)

particular period'. The chairman declined to follow *Mount Edgcumbe Hospice Ltd[11]*, (which HMRC had cited as an authority).

The tribunal in *Abbotsley* also held that Item 1(m) did not apply to take the supply out of exemption, since the company had granted the club 'a licence to occupy land, not facilities for playing any sport or participating in any physical recreation'. The club had occupied the land for the purpose of granting such facilities to its members, but what the company had granted to the club was a licence to occupy land. The tribunal chairman observed that 'the licence envisaged that the club would occupy the property for use as a golf course and club, but that object of the licence is not the grant of the facilities which would be created after the grant. It would be a distortion of language to say that [the company] was granting facilities for playing sport or participating in physical recreation to the club.'

3.2 Treatment of the most common supplies of land and buildings

3.2.1 Supply of bare land
Item 1, Group 1, Schedule 9

A supply of bare land is exempt, subject to the option to tax.[12]

3.2.2 Supply of a civil engineering work
Item 1, Group 1, Schedule 9

A supply of the freehold in a new or uncompleted civil engineering work is taxable at the standard rate. Any other supply of a civil engineering work is exempt subject to the option to tax. The definition of 'new' is set out at **1.2.19** above. The definition of when a civil engineering work is 'completed' is at **1.2.6**.

Special rules (in Notes (5) and (6), Group 1, Schedule 9) apply where the civil engineering work was completed before 1 April 1989.

3.2.3 Supply of an uncompleted dwelling
Item 1, Group 5, Schedule 8

Where an uncompleted dwelling is supplied that supply is zero-rated provided that it is the first grant of a major interest by a 'person constructing' the building. Others supplies are exempt and the option to tax has no effect.

---

[11] (VTD 14807)

[12] The **option to tax** is considered in detail in **Chapter 1**

See **Chapter 0** for a more detailed analysis.

3.2.4 Supply of an uncompleted building intended for use solely for a relevant residential or relevant charitable purpose

Item 1, Group 5, Schedule 8

Where an uncompleted building intended for use solely for a relevant residential or a relevant charitable purpose, is supplied and the relevant certificate is given as required by Note (12) to Group 5, the supply is zero-rated provided that it is the first grant of a major interest by a 'person constructing' the building. Others supplies of the building are exempt (apart from those 'lesser interests' falling within items (b) to (n), Group 1, Schedule 9[15]) and an option to tax has no effect.

See **Chapter 1** for a more detailed analysis.

3.2.5 Supply of a completed dwelling

Item 1, Group 5, Schedule 8

Where a completed dwelling is supplied, that supply is zero-rated provided that it is the first grant of a major interest by a 'person constructing' the building. Others supplies of the building are exempt (apart from those 'lesser interests' falling within items (b) to (n), Group 1, Schedule 9) and an option to tax has no effect.

See **Chapter 0** for a more detailed analysis.

3.2.6 Supply of a completed building intended for use solely for a relevant residential or relevant charitable purpose

Item 1, Group 5, Schedule 8

Where a completed building intended for use solely for a relevant residential or a relevant charitable purpose, is supplied is supplied and the relevant certificate is given as required by Note (12) to Group 5, that supply is zero-rated provided that it is the first grant of a major interest by a 'person constructing' the building. Others supplies of the building re exempt (apart from those 'lesser interests' falling within items (b) to (n), Group 1, Schedule 9) and the option to tax has no effect provided that the appropriate certificate is provided.

See **Chapter 1** for a more detailed analysis.

---

[15] These supplies are always taxable at the standard rate - see **3.2.14** below

3.2.7 Supply of an uncompleted conversion of a non-residential building or part of such a building into a dwelling or dwellings

Item 1, Group 5 Schedule 8

Where an uncompleted conversion of a 'non-residential'[21] building or part of such a building into a dwelling or dwellings is supplied that supply is zero-rated provided that it is the first grant of a major interest by a 'person converting' the building. Other supplies of the building are exempt (apart from those 'lesser interests' falling within items (b) to (n), Group 1, Schedule 9[22]) and an option to tax has no effect provided that the appropriate certificate is provided.[23]

See **Chapter 0** for a more detailed analysis.

3.2.8 Supply of a completed conversion of a non-residential building or part of such a building into a dwelling or dwellings

Item 1, Group 5 Schedule 8

Where a completed conversion of a 'non-residential building' or part of such a building into a dwelling or dwellings is supplied that supply is zero-rated provided that it is the first grant of a major interest by a 'person converting' the building. Others supplies of the building are exempt (apart from those 'lesser interests' falling within items (b) to (n), Group 1, Schedule 9) and the option to tax has no effect provided that the appropriate certificate is provided.

See section **4.4** for a more detailed analysis.

3.2.9 Supply of an uncompleted conversion of a non-residential building or part of such a building into a building intended for use solely for a relevant residential purpose

Item 1(b), Group 5, Schedule 8

Where an uncompleted conversion of a 'non-residential building' or part of such a building into a building intended for use solely for a relevant residential purpose is supplied that supply is zero-rated provided that it is the first grant of a major interest by a 'person converting' the building. Other supplies of the building are exempt (apart from those 'lesser interests' falling within items (b) to (n), Group 1, Schedule 9) and the option to tax has no effect provided that the appropriate certificate is provided.

---

[21] For '**non-residential building**' see **1.2.20** above

[22] These supplies are always taxable at the standard rate - see **3.2.14** below

[23] The **option to tax** is considered in detail in **Chapter 1**

3.2.10 Supply of a completed conversion of a non-residential building or part of such a building into a building intended for use solely for a relevant residential purpose

Item 1(b), Group 5, Schedule 8

The first grant of a major interest in a 'non-residential building' or part of such a building into a building intended for use solely for a relevant residential purpose is zero-rated provided that the supply is by a person 'converting' it. Other supplies of the building are exempt (apart from those 'lesser interests' falling within items (b) to (n), Group 1, Schedule 9) and the option to tax has no effect provided that the appropriate certificate is provided.

See **Chapter 1** for more detailed analysis.

3.2.11 Supply of a new or uncompleted commercial building

Item 1(a), Group 1, Schedule 9

The supply of the freehold in a new or uncompleted commercial building is standard rated. The leasing or letting is exempt subject to the option to tax.

See **Chapter 1** for a more detailed analysis of supplies of commercial property and the option to tax. The definition of 'new' is as set out at **1.2.19** above and of 'commercial building' is in **1.2.5** above. The definition of when a building is 'completed' is at **1.2.6**.

There are anti-avoidance rules in section 96(10B)(*a*) and (b) which provide that:

(1) Where the grant of the freehold in a commercial building is standard rated because the building is less than three years old any subsequent supply arising from that grant will also be standard rated. This is designed to block avoidance schemes that deliberately made the price uncertain in order to take advantage of the provisions of regulation 84(2) VAT Regulations[33] allowing VAT to be declared when the payment is received rather than at the date of sale.

(2) Where the grant of the freehold in land is exempt any further supply arising from that grant will also be exempt. This is designed to block avoidance schemes involving the sale of vacant land and the subsequent construction of a commercial building.

---

[33] See **2.2.5** above

Special rules (in Notes (5) and (6), Group 1, Schedule 9) apply where the building was completed before 1 April 1989.

3.2.12 Supply of a commercial building which is neither new nor uncompleted
Item 1, Group 1, Schedule 9

The supply of a commercial building which is neither new nor uncompleted is exempt, subject to the option to tax. See **Chapter 1** for a more detailed analysis of supplies of commercial property and the option to tax. The definition of 'new' is as set out at **1.2.19** above and of 'commercial building' is in **1.2.5** above. The definition of 'new' is as set out at **1.2.19** above and of 'commercial building' is in **1.2.5** above. The definition of when a building is 'completed' is at **1.2.6**.

3.2.13 Supply of a mixed use building or a mixture of buildings

Where there is a supply of mixed use buildings (for example, shops with residential accommodation above them) it will be necessary to apportion the consideration between the various exempt, zero-rated or standard rated elements. For example, if a new housing development is sold which includes bare land, dwellings, shops and a village hall, the supplies will be: zero-rated for the first sale of the village hall (as a relevant charitable use building), zero-rated for the dwellings, standard rated for the new shops and exempt (subject to the option to tax) for the bare land. Apportionment of the consideration for each of these properties will be necessary.

3.2.14 Supply of interests in and rights over land
Paragraphs (a) to (n), Item 1, Group 1, Schedule 9

Supplies of most rights over land are exempt subject to the option to tax. However, certain supplies of rights over land are always subject to VAT at the standard rate. These supplies are specifically excepted from exemption under Item 1 (paragraphs (a) to (n)), Group 1, Schedule 9 and are supplies of:

* the fee simple in certain new or uncompleted buildings and civil engineering works
* fishing and shooting rights
* hotel accommodation
* holiday accommodation
* seasonal caravan pitches
* camping
* parking
* rights to fell timber

- boat mooring and aircraft storage
- self-storage of goods (from 1 October 2012)
- entertainment facilities
- sports facilities
- hairdressers' chair rentals (from 1 October 2012)
- certain rights to call for or be granted an interest or right that would be taxable at the standard rate

Each of these is dealt with in turn below, apart from the first which is dealt with at **3.2.11** (buildings) and **3.2.2** (civil engineering works) above.

A 'developmental tenancy, developmental lease or developmental licence' is not covered as this relates to interests subject to the developer's self-supply charge, which was abolished with effect from 1 March 1997, although it is still included Item 1 (paragraph (b)), Group 1, Schedule 9.

In the case of parking, camping and caravanning, boat mooring and aircraft storage, self storage of goods, entertainment, sports and hairdressers' chair rental, the standard rate applies where there is a grant of 'facilities' for any of those things. In the case of hotel and holiday accommodation, and tent and caravan pitches the standard rate applies where there is a grant of the 'provision' of any of those things. This may be intended to distinguish between a supply of use and a supply of the thing itself, for example, the supply of camping in a tent for a week and the supply of a camp site.

Options
The supply of an option to purchase property or a right over property will follow the VAT liability of the underlying supply. Thus, if the right is to acquire bare land (that is not subject to the option to tax) the supply of a 'call option' (a right to buy the land) will be exempt. If the call option is over land with a new commercial buildings on it, the supply is standard rated. Options to buy rights that are standard rated are also standard rated.

Put options are not interests in or over land. It has been held[34] that an agreement to give the first refusal or a right of pre-emption confers no immediate right upon the prospective purchaser. It imposes a negative obligation on the possible vendor requiring him to refrain from selling the land to any other person without giving the holder of the right of first refusal the opportunity of purchasing in preference to any other buyer. It is not an offer and in itself imposes no obligation on the owner of the land to

---

[34] Per Street J in *Mackay v Wilson* (1947) 47 SR (NSW) 315 at 325, approved by Goff and Stephenson LJJ in *Pritchard v Briggs* [1980] 1 All ER 294 at 305, 331 (CA)

sell the same. He may do so or not as he wishes. But if he does decide to sell, then the holder of the right of first refusal has the right to receive the first offer which he also may accept or not as he wishes. The right is merely contractual and no equitable interest in the land is created by the agreement.

Fishing and shooting rights
Paragraph (c), Item 1, Group 1, Schedule 9

The grant[35] of any interest, right or licence consisting of a right to take game or fish is standard rated unless, at the time of the grant, the grantor grants to the grantee the fee simple of the land over which the right to take game or fish is exercisable.

Where a grant of an interest in, right over or licence to occupy land (which is exempt subject to the option to tax by reason of falling within Item 1, Group 1, Schedule 9) includes a valuable right to take game or fish, an apportionment must be made to determine the supply falling outside exemption.[36]

Hotel accommodation
Paragraph (d), Item 1, Group 1, Schedule 9

The provision in an hotel, inn, boarding house or 'similar establishment' of sleeping accommodation or of accommodation in rooms which are provided 'in conjunction with' sleeping accommodation or for the purpose of a supply of catering is standard rated. The sale of the hotel itself will be exempt subject to the option to tax.

'Similar establishment' includes premises in which there is provided furnished sleeping accommodation, whether with or without the provision of board or facilities for the preparation of food, which are used by or held out as being suitable for use by visitors or travellers[37].

HMRC (in VAT Notice 709/3[38]) have expressed the view that the supply of a serviced flat is caught by this provision where the supply is 'other than for permanent residential use'. In the author's view, this goes further than is provided for by the legislation.

---

[35] Note (1), Item 1, Group 1, Schedule 9 extends the meaning of 'grant' to include an assignment or surrender and the supply made by the person to whom an interest is surrendered when there is a reverse surrender
[36] Note (8), Group 1, Schedule 9
[37] Note (9), Group 1, Schedule 9
[38] 'Hotels and holiday accommodation' (June 2013) at paragraph 2.1

There is a long stay discount in respect of stays of more than 28 days in paragraph 9 of Schedule 6. Tax is charged on a reduced value from the 29th day.

Holiday accommodation[39]
Paragraph (e), Item 1, Group 1, Schedule 9

The grant[40] of any interest in, right over or licence to occupy holiday accommodation is standard rated. 'Holiday accommodation' includes any accommodation in a building, hut (including a beach hut or chalet), caravan, houseboat or tent which is advertised or held out as holiday accommodation or as suitable for holiday or leisure use, but excludes any accommodation falling within Item 1(d) (hotel accommodation – see above).[41]

Note (11), Group 1, Schedule 9 provides that Item 1(e) includes:
(a) any 'grant'[42] excluded from zero-rating under Item 1, Group 5, Schedule 8 by Note (13) to that Group;
(b) any supply made pursuant to a tenancy, lease or licence under which the grantee is or has been permitted to erect and occupy holiday accommodation.

Note (13), Group 5, Schedule 8 excludes from zero-rating the supplies of interests in dwellings where:
(1) the interest granted is such that the grantee is not entitled to reside in the building or part, throughout the year; or
(2) residence there throughout the year, or the use of the building or part as the grantee's principal private residence, is prevented by the terms of a covenant, statutory planning consent or similar permission.

This type of dwelling is taxed as holiday accommodation.

Note (12), Item 1, Group 1, Schedule 9, provides that Item 1(e) does not include a 'grant' in respect of a building or part which is not a new building of the freehold or the grant of a tenancy, lease or licence to the extent that the grant is made for a consideration in the form of a premium. This is

---

[39] See also discussion at **4.3.6**

[40] Note (1), Item 1, Group 1, Schedule 9 extends the meaning of 'grant' to include an assignment or surrender and the supply made by the person to whom an interest is surrendered when there is a reverse surrender

[41] Note (13), Group 1, Schedule 9

[42] For the meaning of '**grant**' see **1.2.11** above

necessary to retain exemption for supplies of the building itself whilst taxing accommodation in the building at the standard rate.

Timeshares

The supply of timeshare holiday accommodation is the supply of an interest in, or right over, land and is exempt to the extent that the supply is made for a consideration in the form of a premium[44] otherwise it is taxable at the standard rate. The option to tax cannot apply where the timeshare relates to a dwelling.

Seasonal caravan pitches etc.

Paragraph (f), Item 1, Group 1, Schedule 9

The provision of 'seasonal pitches'[45] for caravans, and the 'grant' of facilities at caravan parks to persons for whom such pitches are provided are standard rated (see **Chapter 13** for more detail).

Camping

Paragraph (g), Item 1, Group 1, Schedule 9

The provision of pitches for tents or of camping facilities is standard rated.

Parking

Paragraph (h), Item 1, Group 1, Schedule 9

The 'grant' of facilities for parking a vehicle is standard rated (even if used for other purposes such as storage[48]).

The standard rate applies to the supply of parking 'facilities' for a 'vehicle' so the charge to tax at the standard rate is not limited to car-paring facilities. The normal meaning of 'vehicle' applies as it is not defined in *VATA*. The Oxford English Dictionary definition of 'vehicle' is:

> 'A means of conveyance provided with wheels or runners and used for the carriage of persons or goods; a carriage, cart, wagon, sledge, or similar contrivance.'

Standard rating applies to many other situations and includes the supply of taxi-rank spaces and the letting of bare land for car parking and the supply of a purpose-built car park.

Exemption applies when vehicles are 'parked' where the purpose is not parking or garaging, such as the supply of facilities to a motor dealer, motor

---

[44] Note (12), Group 1, Schedule 9
[45] Notes (14) and (14A), Item 1, Group 1, Schedule 9 define a 'seasonal pitch'.
[48] *CCE v Trinity Factoring Services Ltd* [1994] STC 504 (CS)

auctioneer, or vehicle distributor for their vehicles, their stock or goods for carriage. There are other examples in VAT Notice 742[49] at paragraph 4.3.

Where a garage is supplied with a new dwelling, zero-rating will also extend to the garage.[50] The letting of a garage together with an exempt dwelling is exempt. The letting of a garage separate from the letting of a dwelling, however, is standard rated.

In a Danish case[51], two blocks of twelve garages were constructed in conjunction with a building development comprising 37 linked houses. Some of the garages were let to residents of the development and some were let to non-residents. The case was referred to the European Court for a ruling on whether the letting of the garages was exempt from VAT under article 13B(b) of the Sixth Directive, as the 'letting of immovable property', or was excluded from that exemption by article 13B(b)(2), as the 'letting of premises and sites for the parking of vehicles'. The European Court held that where the letting of parking places was 'closely linked to lettings of immovable property' which were themselves exempt from VAT under article 13B(b), such lettings could not be excluded from exemption.

This should be contrasted with the decision in *Civilscent Ltd*[52] where a company, that leased out 97 residential apartments and 22 car parking spaces, did not account for VAT on the income from leasing the car parking spaces. HMRC issued an assessment charging tax on this income, and the representative member of the company's VAT group appealed, contending that the leases of the apartments and the car parking spaces should be treated as an a 'single economic transaction'. The First-tier Tribunal rejected this contention and dismissed the appeal, holding that the leasing of the car parking spaces was a separate standard-rated supply.

Whilst the supply of a freehold interest in a new garage/parking facility or partly completed garage, car park or other parking facility is standard rated as the supply of a civil engineering work, the supply of the freehold in any other car park is exempt subject to the option to tax as it is the supply of the car park itself not of 'facilities for parking a vehicle'. The nature of the supply needs to be considered to determine the VAT liability. For example, fees charged to exhibitors/sellers at a car boot sale will be exempt (subject to

---

[49] 'Land and property' (June 2012)
[50] Note (3), Group 5, Schedule 8
[51] *Skatteministeriet v Henriksen (Case C-173/88)* [1990] STC 768
[52] *Civilscent Ltd v Revenue & Customs* [2009] UKFTT 102 (TC)

the option to tax), despite the fact that cars are parked land on which is usually used as a car park. The fee charged to the potential buyers visiting the car boot sale for them to park their cars will be standard rated.

The fee charged by a local authority for on- or off-street parking is also taxable at the standard rate.[53]

Felling timber
Paragraph (j), Item 1, Group 1, Schedule 9

The 'grant'[54] of any right to 'fell and remove' standing timber is standard rated. The sale of the land on which the timber stands is exempt, subject to the option to tax. Other profits à prendre (other than the right to take game or fish) are not caught.

Boat mooring and aircraft storage etc.
Paragraph (k), Item 1, Group 1, Schedule 9

The grant of facilities for housing, or storage of, an aircraft or for mooring, or storage of, a ship, boat or other vessel is standard rated. 'Mooring' includes anchoring or berthing.[56] Mooring fees for 'residential houseboats'[57] are exempt and the option to tax has no effect.

Self storage
Paragraph (ka), Item 1, Group 1, Schedule 9[58]

Before 1 October 2012, HMRC took the view that a charge for storing goods was liable to VAT, unless it involved the provision of a clearly defined space, that is, there was a licence to occupy land. In which case, the supply was exempt, subject to the option to tax.

From 1 October 2012 'the grant of facilities for the self storage of goods' is specifically excluded from exemption and is brought into line with supplies of other types of storage (such as those provided by traditional removal companies, where the customer is not provided with a discrete area and the supplier is able to move the customer's goods around within its premises). A charge to VAT can no longer be avoided by the allocation of a discrete area to a customer.

---

[53] *Isle of Wight Council (and related appeals)* [2014] UKUT 446 (TCC)

[54] For the meaning of 'grant' see **1.2.11** above

[56] Note (15), Item 1,Group 1, Schedule 9

[57] Defined in Group 9, Schedule 8

[58] Added to *VATA* by *FA 2012*

'Facilities for the self storage of goods' are defined in Note (15A) of Group 1, as the use of a 'relevant structure' for the storage of goods (other than live animals) by the grantee. Use by another person with the permission of the grantee is also caught[59]. 'Relevant structure' means[60] the whole or part of:

(1) a container or other structure that is fully enclosed; and

(2) a unit or building.

Where the 'relevant structure' is a capital item or is part of a capital item for the purposes of the capital goods scheme and is still subject to adjustments under the scheme by the person making the supply; then if the person making the supply and any person using the facility for storage are connected,[61] the new rules do not apply.[62] The supply of facilities to a charity where they are used solely for non-business purposes is also excluded as is ancillary use of part of a building for storage of goods.

The VAT liability of supplies of self-storage is, to a certain extent, determined by the use of the space, although, as a matter of law, it will be necessary establish whether the grant was of 'facilities for the self storage of goods' or of something else. HMRC guidance (in VAT Information Sheet 10/13)[63] is that the grantor should obtain written confirmation from the grantee of how the space will be used, if this is not already defined in the terms of an agreement. HMRC consider[64] that suppliers consider requiring grantees to notify any proposed change of use of space where this may result in different VAT treatment.

Entertainment facilities
Paragraph (l), Item 1, Group 1, Schedule 9

The 'grant' of any right to occupy a box, seat or other accommodation at a sports ground, theatre, concert hall or other place of entertainment is standard rated.

---

[59] Note (15B), Group 1, Schedule 9

[60] Note (15D), Group 1, Schedule 9

[61] Within the meaning of section 1122 *Corporation Tax Act 2010*

[62] Notes (15C) and 15(E), Group 1, Schedule 9

[63] 'Provision of storage facilities' (8 August 2013) at paragraph 2.8

[64] Ibid.

Sports facilities
Paragraph (m), Item 1, Group 1, Schedule 9

The grant of 'facilities' for playing any sport or participating in any physical recreation is standard rated unless[65] the grant of the facilities is for:

(1) a continuous period of use exceeding 24 hours; or

(2) a series of ten or more periods, whether or not exceeding 24 hours in total, where:

    (a) each period is in respect of the same activity carried on at the same place;

    (b) the interval between each period is not less than one day and not more than 14 days;

    (c) consideration is payable by reference to the whole series and is evidenced by written agreement;

    (d) the 'grantee'[66] has exclusive use of the facilities; and

    (e) the grantee is a school, a club, an association or an organisation representing affiliated clubs or constituent associations.

Hairdressers' chair rentals
Paragraph (ma), Item 1, Group 1, Schedule 9

From 1 October 2012, any charge for chair rental at a hairdresser's salon is standard rated. Paragraph (ma), Item 1, Group 1, Schedule 9[67] provides that from that date the grant of facilities to a person who uses them wholly or mainly to supply hairdressing services is standard rated.

For many years salon owners allowed self-employed stylists to 'rent' a chair, with a wash basin, and the surrounding area, arguing that it was a licence to occupy land, and therefore exempt. If the argument was successful, this allowed the salon owner not to register for VAT. However, in view of the decisions of the Courts in cases such as *Denyer*[68] the change was probably unnecessary.

Paragraph (ma) does not apply to a grant of facilities which provides for the exclusive use, by the person to whom the grant is made, of a whole building, a whole floor, a separate room or a clearly defined area, unless the person making the grant or a person connected with that person provides

---

[65] See Note (16), Item 1, Group 1, Schedule 9

[66] 'Grantee' is not defined but must be presumed to be the person to whom the 'grant' is made

[67] Introduced by *FA 2012*

[68] *HMRC v Denyer* [2008] STC 633 (Chancery Division)

or makes available (directly or indirectly) services related to hairdressing for use by the person to whom the grant is made[69].

'Services related to hairdressing' means the services of a hairdresser's assistant or cashier, the booking of appointments, the laundering of towels, the cleaning of the facilities subject to the grant, the making of refreshments and other similar services typically used in connection with hairdressing, but does not include the provision of utilities or the cleaning of shared areas in a building, and it does not matter if the services related to hairdressing are shared with other persons[70].

Right to call for certain interests or rights
Paragraph (n), Item 1, Group 1, Schedule 9

The 'grant'[71] of any right, including an equitable right, a right under an option or right of pre-emption, or in relation to land in Scotland, a personal right to call for or be granted an interest or right which would fall within any of paragraphs (a) or (c) to (ma) of Item 1, Group 1, Schedule 9 is also VATable at the standard rate.

3.3   Supplies of and under leases

The application of the VAT rules for place of supply, time of supply, and invoicing to leases are dealt with in **Chapter 2** above. The granting of a lease usually gives rise to a number of further supplies at later times. For example, a supply is made each time that lease is surrendered or assigned. In such cases, the liability of each subsequent supply is determined at the time when that supply is made rather than by reference to the time of the original grant[72].

3.3.1   VAT liability of service charges

HMRC's current practice[73] is that a service charge assumes the same VAT liability as the premium or rent payable under a lease provided that the service charge relates to the external fabric or the common parts of the building (as opposed to the demised areas of the property), and is paid for by all the occupants.

---

[69] Note (17), Group 1, Schedule 9
[70] Note (18), Group 1, Schedule 9
[71] For the meaning of 'grant' see **1.2.11** above
[72] Section 96 (10A)
[73] Set out in VAT Notice 742 'Land and property' (June 2012) at paragraph 11.2

If the landlord has opted to tax[74] the premises the service charge will, in relation to the lease-holders of non-residential premises, be treated as the consideration for a taxable supply, giving rise to an obligation on the landlord to account for VAT and issue a valid VAT invoice. In relation to residential lease-holders the service charge will remain exempt.

Taxable service charges would often be preferable where there are commercial tenants. If the rent and service charge are exempt, the landlord will be unable to recover VAT on related costs, and will recharge the costs gross of this irrecoverable VAT. This is disadvantageous if the tenant would otherwise have been able to recover the VAT. To deal with this, some landlords who do not want to opt to tax have established a separate management company which is engaged direct by the tenants, making taxable supplies to them.

Doubt was been cast on HMRC's practice in relation to service charges by the decision of the European Court in the Czech case of *RLRE Tellmer Property sro v Finanční ředitelství v Ústí nad Labem*[75]. In *Tellmer*, a company owned apartment blocks, and rented out the apartments in them to tenants. It made separate charges to its tenants for cleaning services. The Czech tax authority issued a ruling that the company was required to account for VAT on these charges. The company appealed, contending that for VAT purposes the letting out and cleaning of the apartments should be treated as a single supply which was exempt from VAT. The case was referred to the European Court which rejected the company's argument, holding 'the letting of immovable property and the cleaning service of the common parts of the latter must, in circumstances such as those at issue in the main proceedings, be regarded as independent, mutually divisible operations, so that the said service does not fall within that provision'. For HMRC's practice following this decision which was, in effect, to ignore it, see Revenue and Customs Brief 67/09.[76]

In *Field Fisher Waterhouse LLP v HMRC*[77], a firm of solicitors leased serviced office accommodation. Its landlords treated their supplies as exempt in accordance with HMRC's advice. The firm appealed, contending that the effect of the European Court's decision in *Tellmer*, was that the service

---

[74] The option to tax is considered in detail in **Chapter 1**

[75] (Case C--572/07) [2009] STC 2006

[76] VAT – Liability of property service charges following the European Court of Justice case of RLRE Tellmer (C-572/07) (27 October 2009)

[77] (Case C-392/11) [2013] STC 136

charges should be treated as taxable supplies (so that it should be allowed to reclaim input tax). The tribunal directed that the case should be referred to the European Court.

The European Court held that:

> 'the leasing of immovable property and the supplies of services linked to that leasing, such as those at issue in the main proceedings, may constitute a single supply from the point of view of value added tax. The fact that the lease gives the landlord the right to terminate it if the tenant fails to pay the service charges supports the view that there is a single supply, but does not necessarily constitute the decisive element for the purpose of assessing whether there is such a supply. On the other hand, the fact that services such as those at issue in the main proceedings could in principle be supplied by a third party does not allow the conclusion that they cannot, in the circumstances of the dispute in the main proceedings, constitute a single supply.'

It was for the national court to determine whether 'the transactions in question are so closely linked to each other that they must be regarded as constituting a single supply of the leasing of immovable property.'

3.3.2 Assignments of leases

Where a lease is assigned, the VAT liability of that supply will normally follow the liability of the supplies made under the lease.[78] Thus, if the letting of the property is exempt, the assignment of the lease under which the letting takes place will be exempt.

The VAT treatment of assignments was considered in *Abbey National plc v CCE (No.4)*,[79] a case concerning property that had been occupied by Abbey National plc (Abbey) as a tenant and other properties in which Abbey held a leasehold interest but had sub-let to third parties. Abbey sought to divest itself of its property interests and make use of an expert property manager, (Mapeley) for this purpose. The simplest route would have been for Abbey to assign all its leases to Mapeley and for Mapeley to lease these back to Abbey or the third-party sub-tenants. However, this was not possible in practice, mainly because the landlord would not allow such assignments. An arrangement was entered into, a 'virtual assignment' of the 'economic benefits and burdens' of the leases. After this was done, Abbey paid rent to

---

[78] Except where zero-rating applies to the first grant of a major interest – see Note (14), Group 5, Schedule 8

[79] [2006] STC 1961, ([2006] EWCA Civ 886

Mapeley (which paid the rent due to the landlord) and Mapeley collected rent from Abbey's sub-tenants.

This virtual assignment was treated by Abbey as if it were, in fact, the assignment of its leases and exempt. Abbey would not want VAT to be charged, as it was unable to reclaim all of the VAT (because much of its business consisted of making exempt supplies of finance). HMRC did not agree that the 'virtual assignment' was a supply that came within the exemption[80] on the basis that it was not the 'leasing or letting of immovable property'[81]. In HMRC's view the supply was standard rated as a supply of property management services. HMRC's position was that as Abbey could not legally transfer its interest to Mapeley, Mapeley could not be granting it a right of occupation (as it had no power to make such a grant). The tribunal had agreed with this view.

The tribunal had accepted Abbey's second contention, holding that the effect of what is now paragraph 40(1) Schedule 10[82] was that following the agreement, the exempt supplies to the sub-tenants were to be treated as having been made by Mapeley, and that the payments by the sub-tenants did not represent consideration for the standard rated supplies which Mapeley made to Abbey. The Court of Appeal unanimously upheld the tribunal decision. Jonathan Parker LJ held that 'a right of occupation is an essential and fundamental element of a transaction of leasing or letting for the purposes of Article 13B(b)' of the Sixth Directive. Since Mapeley had 'acquired no right of occupation of the properties', its supply to Abbey was not a supply of 'leasing or letting' and was not exempt from VAT.

3.3.3   Reverse premiums and surrenders
Introduction
Reverse premiums or inducements are often paid as a way of maintaining the rental value of a property. If a key tenant is identified, this tenant may not wish to pay the full market rate for the rent, but the landlord would be keen to attract the tenant. Even though the landlord may offer this tenant a discount, it would want the full rent paid so that it could demonstrate to other tenants of the complex or tower block the market rent payable. The way to resolve this problem is to reach an agreement with the key tenant that they will pay a full market rental, but will receive a reverse premium to compensate them for the excess they are paying, a sort of future rent

---

[80] In Group 1, Schedule 9
[81] See article 135(1)(l) VAT Directive
[82] See **3.6** below

discount. So, if the market rate was £10 per square foot per month for a ten year lease of 20,000 square foot, but the key tenant only was to pay £8 a square foot, the key tenant may agree to pay £10 a square foot if it then received a reverse premium of £4.8 million [(£10-£8) X 20,000 X 10 X12)], although this amount would undoubtedly be altered due to the effect of present value discounting.

Reverse premium on grant of lease

In *Mirror Group plc v CCE*[83] the European Court held that where a prospective tenant is paid by the prospective landlord to take a lease then the payment is for a standard rated supply by the tenant to the landlord. The European Court said that 'a person who does not initially have any interest in the immovable property and who enters into an agreement for lease of that immovable property with a landlord and/or accepts the grant of a lease of the property in return for a sum of money paid by the landlord' did not make an exempt supply within article 13B(b) of the Sixth Directive.

Reverse premium on assignment of lease

In *Cantor Fitzgerald International*[84] the European Court held that where an outgoing tenant pays an incoming tenant to take an assignment of his lease then the payment is for a standard rated supply by the incoming tenant to the outgoing tenant. The European Court said that article 13B(b) of the Sixth Directive did 'not exempt a supply of services which is made by a person who does not have any interest in the immovable property and which consists in the acceptance, for consideration, of an assignment of a lease of that property from the lessee'.

In *British Eventing Ltd*[85], the appellant, who was the tenant, paid a reverse premium of £340,000 (plus VAT) to assign an onerous lease. The assignee paid a nominal consideration of £10 on the assignment of the lease. Judge Mosedale held that the lease had a 'negative value', and the appellant had 'paid £340,000 to be rid of it'. On this basis the assignment 'was not a supply for VAT purposes' and it was 'impossible for the input tax on the reverse premium to be attributable to it'. The tribunal held, after considering the decisions of the European Court in *Midland Bank*[86] (costs incurred after a transaction may not normally be attributed to that

---

[83] See Joined Cases of (Case C-409/98) *CCE v Mirror Group plc* [2001] STC 1453 and (Case C-108/99) *CCE v Cantor Fitzgerald International* [2001] STC 1453
[84] Ibid
[85] British Eventing Ltd v Revenue & Customs [2010] UKFTT 382 (TC)
[86] *Midland Bank plc v CCE* (Case C-98/98) [2000] STC 501

transaction) and *Fini*[87] (such an attribution may be made in particular circumstances), that the occupation of the premises in question pre-dated the appellant's letting activity, and the costs on which the reverse premium was based did not relate to the letting charges. Thus the input tax on the reverse premium fell into the residual category, and was recoverable in accordance with the appellant's partial exemption method[88].

Payment by a landlord for surrender of a lease
Note 1, Group 1, Schedule 9

The European Court held in *Lubbock Fine & Co v CCE*[89] that a surrender is exempt from VAT subject to the option to tax[90].

Payment to a landlord to accept a surrender of a lease
Notes 1 and 1A, Group 1, Schedule 9

This is normally an exempt supply, subject to the option to tax[91], made by the person accepting the surrender. It is referred to in Notes (1) and (1A) to Group 1 of Schedule 9 as a 'reverse surrender' and is defined as where 'the person to whom the interest is surrendered is paid by the person by whom the interest is being surrendered to accept the surrender'.

Statement of Practice agreed by HMRC with the Law Society on variations to leases[92]

Property law can result in the surrender and re-grant of a lease where there are certain variations in a lease, such as an extension of the term. Normally this would mean that any consideration received would be treated according to the rules outlined above. The Law Society agreement with HMRC has determined that these rules will not apply in certain circumstances.

The full text of the Statement of Practice is set out below:

---

[87] *I/S Fini H v Skatteministeriet* (Case C-32/03) [2005] STC 903
[88] For partial exemption see **Chapter 1**
[89] (Case C-63/92) [1994] STC 101
[90] In the UK there is the possibility of zero-rating if it is the first grant of a major interest and the other conditions are fulfilled
[91] The option to tax is considered in detail in **Chapter 1**
[92] Reproduced from HMRC Manuals at VATLP27000

'VATLP27000 - Statement of Practice

Copy of the Statement of Practice agreed with the Law Society on variations to leases

This Statement of Practice deals with a situation where there is a potential conflict between land law and VAT legislation. Under land law, the variation of a lease can sometimes require a deemed surrender of the old lease and the grant of a new lease. HMRC recognises that in certain circumstances, which are explained in this Statement of Practice, the economic reality of the situation is that the original interest granted to the tenant continues and the variation of the original lease does not in itself result in any supply of the surrender of the old lease or the grant of a new one.

This Statement of Practice does not apply to situations where a surrender and re-grant actually occur rather than being deemed to occur by operation of the law. Furthermore, as made clear in this Statement of Practice, a consideration may attach to a supply or supplies that result from obligations under the new lease. These supplies are quite separate and the consideration, whether monetary or otherwise, cannot put value on the surrender of the original lease and the grant of the new one.

Where there is no monetary consideration paid by the lessor to the lessee
Where there is no monetary consideration passing from lessor to lessee as a result of or in connection with the variation, then HMRC policy is that there is no surrender of the old lease for non-monetary consideration when:
- the new lease is for the same building (or the same part thereof) but the new lease is for an extended term;
- the new lease is for a larger part of the same building than the old lease but the term is for the same or an extended term; or
- the new lease is for the same land and for an extended term.

Where the surrender and re-grant involves ground leases or building leases i.e. leases granted on condition that the lessee will undertake development, very often the negotiations between the parties will result in the demolition of an old building and the construction of a new one or partial demolition and reconstruction or enlargement. HMRC may find that the terms of the new lease will be more favourable to both the lessee and lessor but do not consider this in itself indicates that the old lease was surrendered in consideration of the grant of the new one.

However, if the lessee receives a direct benefit in return for undertaking the construction works (e.g. a rent-free period, or reduced rent for a period) HMRC are likely to see a consideration passing from the lessee to the lessor in return for the benefit. In cases where there is doubt you should agree the position with HMRC.

Where there is monetary consideration

Where monetary consideration passes from lessor to lessee, HMRC would normally regard the monetary consideration as the sole consideration for the surrender. Where monetary consideration passes to the lessor from the lessee, HMRC would normally see this as consideration for the grant of the new lease which would be exempt subject to the lessor's election to waive exemption (option to tax).

However, the circumstances may indicate that the payment is consideration for the lessor's supply of the acceptance of the surrender of an onerous lease from the lessee, (sometimes known as a reverse surrender). From 1 March 1995 we say these payments are for an exempt supply, with the option to tax. When the payment received by the lessor is seen as consideration for the grant of a new lease, there would be no surrender by the lessee.'

3.3.4   Rent-free periods

The grant by a landlord of a rent-free period is not a supply for VAT purposes except where the rent-free period is given in exchange for something which the tenant agrees to do, for example, carry out works for the benefit of the landlord.

3.3.5   Payments under rent guarantees

Property developers and other sellers of commercial property may guarantee that they will pay the open market rent of the property to a purchaser if a tenant or tenants cannot be found. These guarantee payments are not normally consideration for a supply by the purchaser to the seller.

The payments are not regarded as reductions in the value of the original lease or freehold sale unless the documentation shows the parties agree that they are to be taken as such. There is often a difference between the value of a transaction and the price paid. HMRC, however, will usually accept that the netting-off of rental guarantee payments against the purchase value does not alter the purchase value unless the document states that it does.

The payments under such rental guarantee agreements are therefore usually not consideration for VAT purposes and fall outside the scope of the tax. In some cases purchasers may formally let the empty property back to the seller. This is a supply for VAT purposes.

3.3.6   Payments under leases which are outside the scope of VAT

The following are not consideration for a supply when paid under or in consequence of the termination of a lease:
- dilapidations payments;
- payments in respect of mesne profits; and

- statutory compensation under the terms of the *Landlord and Tenant Act 1954* or the *Agricultural Tenancies Act 1995*.

3.4 Commonhold

A new form of land ownership, commonhold, was introduced by the *Commonhold and Leasehold Reform Act 2002* in addition to the existing forms of ownership, freehold and leasehold. With effect from 27 September 2004 'freehold' also includes commonhold.

A commonhold association is responsible for the upkeep of the common parts; on the acquisition of a commonhold unit the acquirer will also acquire an interest in the commonhold association and common parts. In reality this is little different from previous forms of ownership. For example, the owners or leaseholders of residential flats may have been able to form a company to hold the common parts. Instead of the commonhold association there may have been a corporate body owning the common parts. Alternatively, where the flats were all let on lease, the freeholder would own the common parts and be responsible for its upkeep and make a charge to the leaseholders for their maintenance.

The VAT liability for a supply of commonhold is the same as it is for freehold property. The transfer of the interest in the commonhold association and the common parts is usually for no consideration.

Commonhold can come into existence either by being created following the construction of a building or by conversion of freeholds or leasehold into commonhold. The supply of the units of a commonhold property takes its normal VAT liability.

Where a leasehold interest is converted into a commonhold the existing leases is terminated. If the same person owns the commonhold unit as previously held under the lease there is no supply for VAT purposes. Where, however, there is a change in ownership or a change in area covered there is a supply of the surrender in the property and the acquisition of the interest in the unit and commonhold association. The surrender will usually be exempt, unless there is a new commercial property or commercial property is subject to the option to tax. Similarly, the acquisition is exempt unless there is a new commercial property or commercial property is subject to the option to tax where the supply is standard rated, or there is a supply of new residential property, which is zero-rated.

3.5 Joint ownership

Where more than one person owns land or a building they will be treated for VAT purposes as a single person. Any option to tax must be made jointly.

Where they are required to register for VAT, joint owners will be registered by HMRC as a partnership even though they are not partners in law[93]. This is not a statutory requirement, but it is the only way that HMRC can deal with the situation and has the disadvantage that they will be treated, for VAT purposes, as being jointly and severally liable for VAT as partners are. Those in this situation are advised to write to HMRC pointing out that they are not partners and should not have joint and several liability for VAT purposes. Their liability will usually be determined in accordance with their joint ownership agreement.

3.6 Beneficial interests

Paragraph 40(1), Schedule 10

A supply is treated as made by the person to whom 'the benefit of the consideration' for the grant of an interest, right over, or licence to occupy land accrues. This person may not be the same as the legal owner actually making the grant. This is because of paragraph 40, Schedule 10 which is in the following terms:

'(1) This paragraph applies if the benefit of the consideration for the grant of an interest in, right over or licence to occupy land accrues to a person ("the beneficiary") other than the person making the grant.

(2) The beneficiary is to be treated for the purposes of this Act as the person making the grant.

(3) So far as any input tax of the person actually making the grant is attributable to the grant, it is to be treated for the purposes of this Act as input tax of the beneficiary.'

This is sometimes the case where property is held on trust. In such circumstances, the legal owner (the trustee) is not treated as making the supply; the supply is made by the beneficial owner (the beneficiary). It is the beneficiary who is required to register for VAT and account for any VAT that is due.

In *Abbey National plc v CCE (No.4)* (see **3.3.23.3.2** above) a virtual assignment was treated by Abbey as if it were, in fact, the assignment of its

---

[93] Paragraph 7.2 Notice 742 'Opting to tax land and buildings' (June 2013)

leases and exempt. The tribunal rejected this but accepted Abbey's second contention, that the exempt supplies to the sub-tenants were to be treated as having been made by Mapeley, and that the payments by the sub-tenants did not represent consideration for the standard rated supplies which Mapeley made to Abbey. The Court of Appeal unanimously upheld the tribunal decision.

The question of what is meant by 'directly receiving the benefit of the consideration' in this context was also considered by the First-tier Tribunal in *Hills*[95]. In that case, a commercial property was the principal asset of a Self-invested Personal Pension Plan (a SIPP). The property was sold by the trustees of the SIPP to the appellants, and was subject to the option to tax (although this was a further matter of dispute). The appellants contended that since the option had been exercised by the trustee, rather than the beneficiary of the SIPP, it had no effect as a result of paragraph 40, Schedule 10. The tribunal held, however, that what the beneficiary was entitled to under the terms of the SIPP (and UK legislation) was the tax-free sum and annuity which could be obtained from the sale of the property, rather than the proceeds of the sale itself. Thus the beneficiary was not the person 'directly receiving the benefit of the consideration'; consequently paragraph 40, Schedule 10 did not apply and the option did have effect.

The HMRC manual at VATLP04250 says:

'Paragraph 40 does not normally apply where there are a large number of beneficiaries, such as in a pension fund. This is because the beneficiaries will not be entitled to the benefit of the consideration (for example, rent), but to a different sort of asset, such as a pension or proceeds from a financial investment. In addition, paragraph 40 only applies where the benefit of the consideration accrues to the beneficiaries collectively or as a class. It would not, for example, apply where the consideration accrues to some beneficiaries, but not others.'

---

[95] *Darren Hills and Lynn Hills* [2014] UKFTT 646 (TC)

4 VAT Reliefs for Supplies of Dwellings

Group 5, Schedule 8

This chapter examines the VAT reliefs in relation to supplies of dwellings. Similar reliefs are available for supplies of buildings which are to be used for a 'relevant residential purpose' or for a 'relevant charitable purposes' and these are discussed in **Chapter 1**. There are related reliefs which apply to building work and certain other work on these qualifying buildings and those reliefs (which are in Groups 6 and 7, Schedule 7A) are considered in **Chapter 0**.

In outline the reliefs considered in this chapter are:

Description of supply:	VAT Liability
(1) The first sale of the freehold in a newly constructed dwelling by a person constructing it	Zero-rated[1]
(2) The first sale of the freehold in a dwelling which has been converted from a non-residential building by a person converting it[2]	Zero-rated
(3) The first sale of the freehold in a dwelling converted from a non-residential part of a building by a person converting it	Zero-rated
(4) The first 'grant'[4] of a 'long lease' in a newly constructed dwelling by a person constructing it	Zero-rated
(5) The first 'grant' of a 'long lease'[7] in a dwelling converted from a non-residential building by a person converting it	Zero-rated

4.1 Meaning of 'dwelling'

As can be seen from the table above, VAT reliefs in relation to sales of dwellings are given in respect of the first 'grant' by a 'person constructing' a building designed as a dwelling or a number of dwellings (Item 1(a)(i), Group 5, Schedule 8) or by a person converting a 'non-residential building' or a non-residential part of a building into a building designed as a

---

[1] Item 1, Group 5, Schedule 8
[2] See **1.2.20** for definition of a '**non- residential building**'
[4] For the meaning of '**grant**' see **1.2.11** above
[7] See **1.2.15** for definition of '**long lease**'

dwelling or a number of dwellings (Item 1(b), Group 5, Schedule 8) of a major interest in, or in any part of, the building, dwelling or its site[12].

A 'dwelling' is not defined for VAT purposes and so the word bears its ordinary meaning. The Oxford English Dictionary meaning is 'a place of residence, a dwelling-place, a habitation, a house' and some of the relevant case law on the question is considered at **4.2** below. In Revenue & Customs Brief 47/11[13] HMRC have confirmed that 'extra care accommodation' can, in their view, be a building 'designed as a dwelling' for the purposes of zero-rate relief. 'Extra care accommodation' is 'self contained flats, houses, bungalows or maisonettes that are sold or let with the option for the occupant to purchase varying degrees of care to suit his or her needs as and when they arise. It does not apply to accommodation where the occupant needs care or supervision of a type typically provided by an institution.'

The distinction between Item 1(a)(i), (person constructing a dwelling) and Item 1(b) (person converting a non-residential building into a dwelling) is important because of the effect of Note (2) and Note (7) Group 5 Schedule 8.

Note (2) provides that a building is 'designed as a dwelling or a number of dwellings' where in relation to each dwelling four conditions[14] are satisfied:
(1) the dwelling consists of self-contained living accommodation;
(2) there is no provision for direct internal access from the dwelling to any other dwelling or part of a dwelling;
(3) the separate use, or disposal of the dwelling is not prohibited by the terms of any covenant, statutory planning consent or similar provision; and
(4) statutory planning consent has been granted in respect of that dwelling and its construction or conversion has been carried out in accordance with that consent.

Note (2) prevents what is in effect an extension to an existing dwelling qualifying as a new dwelling and benefiting from zero-rating.

Note (7) which applies only for the purposes of Item 1(b) (person converting a non-residential building into a dwelling) provides that a building or part of a building is 'non-residential' if:
(1) it is neither designed nor adapted 'for use as[15]' a dwelling or number of dwellings or for a 'relevant residential purpose[16]'or

---

[12] Item 1, Group 5, Schedule 8
[13] 'VAT – zero-rate – 'extra care accommodation'' (30 December 2011)
[14] These conditions are considered in detail at **4.3**

(2)   it is designed or adapted for such use but it was constructed more than ten years before the 'grant' of the major interest; and no part of it has, in the period of ten years immediately preceding the grant been used as a dwelling or for a relevant residential purpose.

Note (2) does not apply to the definition of non-residential in Note (7) as that Note does not use the phrase 'designed as a dwelling or a number of dwellings.' Note (7) defines non-residential as a building that is not designed or adapted 'for use as' a dwelling therefore a building which is not designed as a dwelling for Item 1(a)(i) (because of the conditions in Note (2)) may nevertheless be regarded as not non-residential within Note (7).[17] The consequence of this is that the conversion of such a property into a dwelling will not fall within Item 1(b), Group 5, Schedule 8.

Example

A new pub is constructed which has living accommodation for the landlord above the public rooms which are on the ground floor. The washrooms and kitchen were built on the ground floor rather than in the living accommodation above. The kitchen was used to serve pub customers of the pub and the washrooms were also available for use by them.

As the living accommodation is not self-contained it could not be zero-rated under Item 1(a), Group 5, Schedule 8 as Note (2) prevents it. That the living accommodation be self-contained accommodation is a pre-requisite for a property to be regarded as being dwelling.

If the pub is later converted into a single dwelling, a subsequent sale would not be zero-rated, as it was a dwelling before conversion (for the purposes of Note (7)) as the upstairs accommodation was being used as a dwelling and so part of the building was being used as dwelling making the pub not 'non-residential', even though it did not have self-contained accommodation.

It should be noted that where a building designed or adapted for use as a dwelling has not been used a dwelling for ten years it is treated as non-residential property for the purposes of the conversion relief in Item(1)(b).

4.2   Case law on meaning of 'dwelling'

In some of the early cases the tribunal did read Note (2) into Note (7). In these cases it was held that where the accommodation (such as the

---

[15] Not 'designed as' a dwelling so Note (2) does not apply

[16] For the meaning of **relevant residential purpose** see **1.2.29**

[17] Note (2) *does* apply in relation to the building resulting from the conversion which must be a building 'designed as a dwelling or number of dwellings' or, not relevant here, a building intended for sue solely for a relevant residential purpose

publican's accommodation above the pub in the example above) was not self-contained it would not be a dwelling and, therefore, was non-residential for Item 1(1)(b) purposes[18]. In these earlier cases, the restrictions on the definition in 'dwelling' in Note (2) were imported into the meaning of 'dwelling' in Note (7).

Later decisions moved against this view. In *Look Ahead Housing Association*[19] the zero-rating of a conversion of bed-sitting rooms into self-contained flats was considered. It was held that to be a dwelling all the bed-sits had to have the major facilities of life, sleeping, washing and cooking facilities, and there was, therefore, a conversion from non-residential to a dwelling. Although the tribunal agreed that Note (2) should not be applied to Note (7), it applied a test of self-containment (found in Note (2)) in deciding that the bed-sits were non-residential for the purposes of Note (7). The decision in *Look Ahead Housing Association* was distinguished in *Calam Vale Ltd*[20] where it was held that Note (7) did not import the various restrictions on the meaning of 'dwelling' from Note (2). It was held that that private accommodation in a pub was a dwelling because it was where a family lived. Conversion relief was therefore not available.

In the later case of *Amicus Group Ltd*[21] which concerned the conversion of bedsits into self-contained flats the *Look Ahead* decision was specifically disapproved and dicta of the House of Lords in *Uratemp Ventures Ltd v Collins*[22] (a Housing Act case) were applied. In *Uratemp* Lord Irvine said that a 'dwelling' should be interpreted as 'a place where one lives, regarding and treating it as a home'. It was no less a person's home because he did not cook there, and therefore bed-sits could be dwellings. It did not matter that there was no cooking facilities other than a power point.

Uratemp followed a number of other Rent Act cases in which it was held that a 'dwelling' included all the major activities of life, including sleeping, cooking and eating so that at an unfurnished room without cooking facilities or a water supply was not a dwelling[23]. In *St Catherine's College v Dorling*[24] it was held that a house which contained a number of 'units of

---

[18] For example, see *Temple House Developments Ltd* (VTD 15583)
[19] (VTD 16816)
[20] (VTD 16869)
[21] (VTD 17693)
[22] [2002] 1 AC 301, [2001] UKHL 43
[23] For example, *Wright v Howell* (1947) 150 EG 403 (CA)
[24] [1979] 3 All ER 250 (CA)

habitation' for students, with shared kitchens, was not let as a separate dwelling.

In *Agudas Israel Housing Association Limited*[25] a housing association provided different types of residential accommodation depending upon the needs of its tenants. Over a two year period an additional floor was added to a care home which the housing association owned. This provided eight additional flats for permanent occupation by persons with Alzheimer's and other similar diseases, although the intention of the housing association was to provide accommodation to persons who could live an independent life. The flats had limited cooking facilities (a fridge, kettle and microwave) although each 'dwelling' had separate and direct access from the street. Although cooking facilities were limited, some residents did prepare meals in their own homes, but others ate in the care home dining room and others ate out or had meals brought in. The question was whether supplies of services in the course of construction of the flats could be zero-rated under Item 2(a), Group 5, Schedule 8[26]. This would only be the case if the flats were designed as dwellings within the meaning of Note (2).

The tribunal in *Agudas* held that:

> 'premises with their own front door, en-suite bathing facilities and the ability to cook with a microwave cooker and kettle are self-contained living accommodation. The factor of the limited nature of the cooking facilities is outweighed by the factor of the direct access to the Square from the resident's own front door to which he or she has his or her own key'.

It should be noted, however, that usually, where a property is denied relief by Note (7), the building is likely to have benefitted from relief when it was originally constructed.

4.3   Zero-rating for new dwellings – the details of the relief
Item 1(a)(i), Group 5, Schedule 8

The zero-rate relief for newly constructed dwellings is available for two types of supply. First, relief is available in respect of most of the costs of construction. This relief is considered in **Chapter 0**. Secondly, there is a zero-rate relief which applies to the sale of newly constructed dwellings. This second relief is considered in detail below.

---

[25] (VTD 18798)

[26] See **Chapter 0** for services falling within Item 2(a), Group 5, Schedule 8

Most lettings of social housing are on short leases and these are exempt from VAT so no VAT can be reclaimed on the costs incurred. Most costs, however, are zero-rated (construction costs) or exempt (land costs – the option to tax does not apply to land to be used for housing)[27] and this is intended to avoid the burden of VAT being borne by tenants.

The relief under Item 1(a)(i), Group 5, Schedule 8 is only available where the supply is the first grant by a person constructing a building designed as a dwelling or number of dwellings of a major interest in, or in any part of, the building or its site.

Since the zero-rate for dwellings is based on the design of the building and for relevant residential purpose buildings is based on use, HMRC accept that a building may qualify for zero-rating under both of these provision. In such cases, a taxpayer is free to rely on either provision to achieve zero-rating for their building. As there is no claw-back of relief for dwellings, a claim under this head would seem to be preferable in these circumstances.[28]

4.3.1   First grant of a major interest by a person constructing a building

It does not matter if the first grant takes place many years after construction, as long as it is the *first* grant by a person who has been involved in the construction of the building[29]. If a building is sold during construction and completed by the buyer both parties can be 'a person constructing' a building.

With effect from July 2014 HMRC accept[30] that a person who acquires a building as a result of a transfer of a going concern[31] inherits 'person constructing' status for the purposes of the zero-rating of new qualifying buildings (dwellings and relevant residential or relevant charitable purpose) provided that:

(1) a zero rated grant has not already been made of the completed building or relevant part by a previous owner (for this purpose, HMRC consider that the grant that gives rise to the TOGC should be disregarded);

(2) the person acquiring the building as a TOGC would suffer an unfair VAT disadvantage if its first major interest grants were treated as

---

[27] The **option to tax** is considered in detail in **Chapter 1**

[28] See VAT Information Sheet 02/14 'Buildings that are used for a relevant residential purpose' (30 January 2014)

[29] *Link Housing Association* [1992] STC 178 (CS)

[30] See Revenue & Customs Brief 27/14 'Changes relating to the transfer of a business as a going concern (TOGC)' (27 July 2014) at section 3

[31] See **Chapter 1**

exempt. For example, a developer restructures its business. This entails the transfer (as a TOGC) of its entire property portfolio of newly constructed residential/charitable buildings to an associated company, which will make first major interest grants. If these were treated as exempt, the transferee might become liable to repay input tax recovered by the original owner on development costs under the capital goods scheme or partial exemption 'claw-back' provisions and would incur input tax restrictions on selling fees that would not be suffered by businesses in similar circumstances – HMRC would consider this to be an unfair disadvantage;

(3) that person would not obtain an unfair VAT advantage by being in a position to make zero-rated supplies (for example, by recovering input tax on a refurbishment of an existing building).

Stapenhill Developments Ltd[32] concerned the sale of a large development site on which the seller had undertaken some civil engineering work, and had commenced but abandoned the construction of three dwellings. The tribunal held that it was not 'a person constructing a building', and that for this to apply 'a building must be seen to be under construction on the land'. Similar decisions were reached in *Permacross Ltd*[33] and *Cameron New Homes Ltd*.[34]

Where legal and beneficial ownership are split it is the beneficial owner who is treated as making the grant[35] so it is the beneficial owner that needs to be involved in the construction.

To qualify for zero-rating a building must be constructed. Notes 16 and 18[36], Group 5, Schedule 8 are relevant here. Taken together these Notes set out the following rules for deciding whether a building has been constructed so as to fall within Item 1(a), Group 5, Schedule 8:

(1) The construction of a building does not include[37]:
  (*a*) the conversion, reconstruction or alteration of an 'existing building'; or

---

[32] [1984] VATTR 1 (VTD 1593)

[33] (VTD 13251)

[34] (VTD 17309)

[35] See **3.5**

[36] Note (17) modifies Note (16) but only in relation to annexes intended for use solely for a relevant charitable purpose – see **6.3.3**

[37] Note (16), Group 5, Schedule 8

(*b*) any enlargement of, or extension to, an existing building except to the extent the enlargement or extension creates an additional dwelling or dwellings; or

(*c*) the construction of an annexe to an 'existing building'[38].

(2) A building only ceases to be an 'existing building' when[39]:

(*a*) demolished completely to ground level; or

(*b*) the part remaining above ground level consists of no more than a single facade or where a corner site, a double facade, the retention of which is a condition or requirement of statutory planning consent or similar permission.

In *Central Sussex College*[40] a college campus was redeveloped in three phases. Outline planning permission for the phased replacement of the existing buildings to form a complete new campus was granted by Mid Sussex District Council on 9 February 2006. Detailed planning permission for Phase 1 (a new English Performing Arts Centre including auditorium, rehearsal and dance studios, music department, classrooms and ancillary accommodation) was also granted on 9 February 2006. The Phase 1 buildings were designed so that they could be used with the existing original buildings (pending completion of the entire project). They were aligned to the existing buildings for this reason. Reserved matters permission was granted in relation to Phases 2 and 3 on 24 October 2006. Phase 2 was described in the reserved matters permission as an 'extension [to the scope of the works within the planning permission for Phase 1] of the previously approved English and Performing Arts block, to provide a new Art and Media Department at lower ground floor, central kitchens on the ground floor and two storeys of classrooms above for business and humanities'. Phase 3 was described in the permission as a building comprising 'at ground floor the new principal college entrance hall, central canteen and reception area with admin, adult education and health and leisure classrooms. The first and second floor will provide new classrooms for maths and science with a new learning resources department centrally located above the entrance hall'. It was also stated in the permission that 'these two phases will enable the main section of the existing college to be removed …'.

---

[38] Subject to Note (17)

[39] Note (18), Group 5, Schedule 8

[40] [2014] UKFTT 1058 (TC)

The tribunal held that, as each phase was a stand-alone project which had to be considered separately, zero-rating did not apply by reason of Note (16) as, on that basis, the work (even though it was part of a 'master plan') was an enlargement of or extension to an existing building.

It is essential that the whole building is demolished before any rebuilding work is commenced if zero-rating is to be achieved. In *Alec A Bugg*[41] a building was demolished, and rebuilt, in stages. First the external walls were demolished and new walls built, and then the internal walls were removed and rebuilt. The building was also enlarged at the same time. There was nothing left of the old building when the works finished. It was held (for the purposes of the DIY-builder's scheme where Notes (16) and (18), Group 5, Schedule 8 are applied by section 35(4)) that this was not the construction of a building.[42]

A building that is reconstructed retaining a single or double facade of the old building will be regarded as a new building only if the retention of the facade is required by planning permission or similar permission, such as listed building consent[43]. It may be prudent to obtain HMRC written agreement to 'new building' status before the commencement of works, particularly where any other features of the old building are retained. Copies of the statutory planning consent showing the required retention should be provided (and retained).

Major interest

Zero-rating only applies to the *first* 'grant' of a major interest. Any subsequent grant will be exempt. Major interest is defined in section 96(1) as a freehold interest or a lease granted for a term in excess of 21 years in England and Wales or in excess of 20 years in Scotland. The term of a lease under a time-share arrangement is determined by the period of occupation, not the number of years for which the arrangement is expressed to run.[45]

Note (14), Group 5, Schedule 8 provides that where the major interest is a tenancy or lease then:

---

[41] (VTD 15123)

[42] Compare the result in *E D Bruce* [1991]VATTR 280

[43] Note (18)(b), Group 5, Schedule 8

[45] *Cottage Holiday Associates Ltd v CCE* [1983] STC 278, where one week's occupation per annum for 80 years was held to be a lease for a term certain of 80 weeks.

(a) if a premium is payable, the grant falls within Item 1 of Group 5 (and is therefore zero-rated) only to the extent that it is made for consideration in the form of the premium; and

(b) if a premium is not payable, the grant falls within Item 1 of Group 5 (and is therefore zero-rated) only to the extent that it is made for consideration in the form of the first payment of rent due under the tenancy or lease.

This is to ensure that only the first supply under the lease is zero-rated to release any input tax charged in relation to construction. Later supplies will be exempt and the option to tax will not apply.[46]

Zero-rating can still apply if there has been an earlier grant of an interest which was not a major interest but this earlier grant will have been exempt and there may be input tax recovery issues.[47]

4.3.2   Designed as a dwelling

Note (2), Group 5, Schedule 8 provides that a building is 'designed as a dwelling or number of dwellings' only if all of the following conditions are met in relation to each dwelling:

(1) it must consist of self-contained living accommodation;

(2) it must be without provision for 'direct internal access' to another dwelling or part of a dwelling;

(3) separate use or disposal is not prohibited by the terms of any covenant or planning permission;

(4) any necessary planning consents have been granted and adhered to.

Each of these conditions will be discussed in turn.

Where part of a building that is constructed is designed as a dwelling or number of dwellings or is intended for use solely for a relevant residential purpose or relevant charitable purpose (and part is not) an apportionment is necessary.[48]

In addition it should be borne in mind that Note (13), Group 5, Schedule 8 prevents the grant of a major interest in a building designed as a dwelling or number of dwellings being zero-rated in the following two cases:

---

[46] The **option to tax** is considered in detail in **Chapter 1**

[47] See **Chapter 1**

[48] Note (10), Group 5. Schedule 8

(1) where the interest granted is such that the grantee (the person acquiring the right to reside in the property) is not allowed to reside there throughout the year; and

(2) where the planning permission prevents residence throughout the year.

In *Jennings*[49] the tribunal decided that Note 13, Group 5, Schedule 8 only applies to cases which fall within Item 1 of Group. It does not apply to cases falling within Item 2 (i.e. where the supply is of the services of constructing a new dwelling). Also it should not be treated as applying to cases within section 35.[50]

Dwelling - Condition one: self-contained living accommodation

To be self-contained living accommodation, the property will need all the normal facilities, that is living and sleeping accommodation, and cooking and washing facilities. This does not necessarily mean that it is required to have a separate bedroom, bathroom or kitchen.[51]

In *Oldrings Development Kingsclere Ltd*[52] it was held that a building without all the usual facilities of a dwelling was a dwelling. In this case, a self-contained building was built near the main house. The new building contained one large main room which was usually used as a studio and was also occasionally slept in by the children of the family that occupied the main house. There was a further small room in the building with a WC and washbasin plus provision for a shower or bath (which had not been installed). The studio was held to be designed as a dwelling as defined in Note (2), Group 5, Schedule 8 despite not having all the usual facilities.

Dwelling - Condition two: no 'direct internal access' to another dwelling

Zero-rate relief is denied where there is any 'direct' internal access from the dwelling to any other dwelling or part of a dwelling. This is to prevent the relief being available for granny flats or accommodation for teenage (or older) children that still live at home but require a degree of independence. The use of the word 'direct' allows access from one dwelling to another by a corridor to be discounted.

---

[49] *Jennings v Revenue and Customs Commrs* [2010] UKFTT 49 (TC)
[50] The DIY builder's refund scheme – see **5.1** below
[51] See *Agudas Israel Housing Association* (VTD 18798)
[52] (VTD 17769)

Dwelling - Condition three: separate use or disposal not prohibited
The prohibition needs to be expressed in a covenant, planning consent or
similar provision. A mere requirement for landlord's consent should not
cause a problem. The test is applied at the time (or each time) of supply.

The question arose whether both separate use and separate disposal need to
be allowed or whether if *either* separate use *or* separate disposal is allowed
the building can qualify as a dwelling. In other words, is the word 'or'
conjunctive or disjunctive? It was held in *Hopewell-Smith*[53] that as separate
disposal was not prohibited by the planning permission the building was
not prevented from being a dwelling, even though separate use was
prohibited. It was, however, held in the later case of *Wiseman*[54] that both
separate use and separate disposal needed to be permitted.

In some cases it has been argued that a condition of planning permission
limiting occupation to persons working at a specific location did not
prohibit the separate use of the building. In *Roy Shields*[55] the Upper Tribunal
was not convinced and decided that such a provision fell within the
prohibition in Note (2)(c).[56]

In *Stevens*[57] a married couple constructed a farmhouse in the Exmoor
National Park. Somerset County Council granted planning permission
subject to a proviso that the farmhouse 'shall not be transferred, let or in
any way disposed of separately' from the land. The couple reclaimed tax
under the DIY builder's scheme. HMRC rejected the claim on the basis that
effect of the planning permission was that zero-rating was precluded by
Note (2)(c), Group 5, Schedule 8 as the farmhouse was not 'designed as
dwelling' by reason of the restriction in the planning permission.

The tribunal allowed the couple's appeal. Judge Cornwell-Kelly held that
the effect of section 4A of the *Town and Country Planning Act 1990* was that
the relevant planning authority was the Exmoor National Park Committee,
rather than Somerset County Council. It followed that the restriction which

---

[53] (VTD 16725)

[54] (VTD 17374)

[55] [2014] UKUT 0453 (TCC) in which the Upper Tribunal held that *Phillips* [2011]
UKFTT 372 and *Bull* [2013] UKFTT 92 which came to the contrary view on a
similar provision were wrongly decided

[56] See also decisions in *Wendells* [2010] UKFTT 476 (TC), *Burton* [2013] UKFT 104 (TC)
and *Brims Construction* [2013] UKFTT 35 (TC)

[57] [2011] UKFTT 835 (TC)

the County Council had sought to impose had no legal effect, and the farmhouse qualified as a 'building designed as a dwelling'.

Dwelling - Condition four: planning permission
To obtain zero-rating relief any necessary planning permission must have been sought at the appropriate time and complied with. Permission therefore needs to be obtained before the commencement of construction and not sought retrospectively.

It has been held that zero-rating was not available where a couple had built a dwelling in the grounds of their existing house as the planning consent stated that the new building had to be ancillary to the main building and was not consent for a separate unit of accommodation. The appellants later got the planning permission amended but it was held not to be sufficient to support zero-rating.[58]

4.3.3 Shared ownership: staircasing
Housing associations (and other bodies) frequently become involved in shared ownership schemes. The housing association will sell a part interest in the property and rent the remaining interest to the occupier.

Occupiers have the ability to increase the share that they own until they own the property outright. This is called 'staircasing' as the occupier climbs the staircase to full ownership. As each step to full ownership is climbed, the rental element is reduced accordingly.

The initial payment for the first tranche of equity in the property is zero-rated (provided that the housing association was the person constructing the building and all the other conditions are fulfilled). This enables the housing association to reclaim the costs incurred on construction (or make an adjustment under the capital goods scheme[59] if it had previously been let out) and to reclaim the VAT incurred on the selling costs. Subsequent rental payments and sales of further equity are all input taxed. The amount of input tax that can be reclaimed is limited.

4.3.4 Supply of an incomplete residential development
Civil engineering work on a site destined for dwellings becomes an incomplete residential development when the residential units rise above foundation level. At this stage the properties are regarded as dwellings and the sale can be zero-rated if all the other conditions are fulfilled.

---

[58] *Mr A E and Mrs J M Harris* (VTD 18822)
[59] See **Chapter 1**

Stapenhill Developments Ltd[60] concerned the sale of a large development site on which the seller had undertaken some civil engineering work, and had commenced but abandoned the construction of three dwellings. The tribunal held that it was not 'a person constructing a building', and that for this to apply 'a building must be seen to be under construction on the land'. Similar decisions were reached in *Permacross Ltd*[61] and *Cameron New Homes Ltd*.[62]

4.3.5   Garages
Note (3), Group 5, Schedule 8
Garages built at the same time as a dwelling and intended to be occupied with the dwelling can also be zero-rated. It is insufficient for the planning permission to have been obtained at the same time as the dwellings and for the garages to be built at a later date.

4.3.6   Holiday homes and holiday accommodation[63]
Holiday homes that are designed as dwellings are still dwellings and the first grant of a major interest in them can be zero-rated if all the other conditions are fulfilled. However Note (13), Group 5, Schedule 8 prevents the grant of a major interest in a building designed as a dwelling or number of dwellings being zero-rated in the following two cases:

(1) where the interest granted is such that the grantee (the person acquiring the right to reside in the property) is not allowed to reside there throughout the year; or

(2) where the planning permission prevents residence throughout the year

Note (11)(a), Group 1, Schedule 9 makes a grant standard rated under Item 1(e) where the grant is excluded from zero-rating by Note (13), Group 5, Schedule 8. However, this is subject to Note (12), Group 1, Schedule 9 which provides that Item 1(e) does not include a grant in respect of a building or part which is not a new building of the fee simple, or a tenancy, lease or licence to the extent that the grant is made for a consideration in the form of a premium. So, although holiday accommodation rental is always standard rated, the receipt of a capital sum, whether as lease premium or from the sale of the freehold, is exempt unless the building is new, in which case it is standard rated.

---

[60] [1984] VATTR 1 (VTD 1593)
[61] (VTD 13251)
[62] (VTD 17309)
[63] See also the section on holiday accommodation at **3.2.14**

In *Livingstone Homes UK Ltd*[64] sale contracts for new houses provided that they should be 'used as holiday dwelling houses only and for no other purpose'. The sales were zero-rated by the supplier. HMRC argued that Note (11)(a), Group 1, Schedule 9 applied with the result that the supply was taxable at the standard rate, saying that the restriction on use meant the properties were therefore excluded from zero-rating by Note (13), Group 5, Schedule 8. The tribunal disagreed on the grounds that use as holiday accommodation and use as a principal residence were not mutually exclusive, and held that the sales were zero-rated. This decision was specifically disapproved by the tribunal in *Loch Tay Highland Lodges Ltd* which was of the view that the earlier tribunal had 'ignored the word 'only' and the phrase 'for no other purpose''.

In *Loch Tay Highland Lodges Ltd*[65] the planning consent required that the properties, which were newly constructed lodges in a holiday development, should be used 'solely for holiday accommodation and shall not be occupied as the sole or main residence of any occupant', and the sale contracts said that the properties should be 'used and occupied solely as a holiday dwelling house and for no other purpose'. Note (11)(a), Item 1, Group 1, Schedule 9 applied because the planning consent clearly prohibited use as a principal private residence and that meant that the supply was excluded from zero-rating by Note (13), Group 5, Schedule 8. The tribunal also held that the sale contract precluded occupation throughout the year (a further obstacle to zero-rating) and that *Livingstone Homes* had been wrongly decided.

In *Herling Ltd*[66], a developer's sales of major interests in newly constructed houses were taxable at the standard rate because of a planning condition that the houses 'shall be used for holiday accommodation only and for no other purpose'.

In *Jennings*[67] the tribunal decided that Note 13, Group 5, Schedule 8 (which denies zero-rating relief for the construction of a new dwelling if residence throughout the year is not permitted) only applies to cases which fall within Item 1 of Group 5 (where a new dwelling is supplied by the person who has constructed it). It did not apply to cases falling within Item 2 (i.e. where the

---

[64] (VTD 16649)
[65] (VTD 18785)
[66] [2009] UKFTT 257 (TC)
[67] [2010] UKFTT 49 (TC)

supply is of the services of constructing a new dwelling). Also it should not be treated as applying to cases within section 35.[68]

4.3.7   Mixed development and live-work units

Where part of a building qualifies for zero-rating and part does not (e.g. a sale of shops with housing above them) then there is a need to apportion the price paid to establish the value of the zero-rated supply.

An increasingly common example of mixed use is live-work units. A live-work unit is a property that combines a dwelling and commercial or industrial working space. This mixed use is often a condition of planning permission. Zero-rating is only available for the dwelling element and there may be a need to apportion.

4.3.8   Communal facilities

Where communal facilities are provided in blocks of flats (for instance, a laundry, refuse facilities, gyms, pools etc.) then the sale of the building can be zero-rated where it is the intention that only the occupiers and their guests will use the communal facilities.[69] The sale of an individual flat can be zero-rated even though there it carries with it the right to use the communal facility.

4.4   VAT reliefs for conversions into dwellings

There are three reliefs available for conversions of buildings into dwellings:
(1) the zero-rate relief under Item 1(b), Group 5, Schedule 8 which applies to the first grant by a person converting a 'non-residential' building or non-residential part of a building into a building designed as a dwelling or number of dwellings of a major interest in that building;
(2) the zero-rate relief under Item 3, Group 5, Schedule 8 which applies to conversion works supplied to a 'relevant housing association';[70] and
(3) the reduced rate relief under Schedule 7A which applies to certain works.

Only the first relief is considered here. The second is dealt with in **Chapter 1** and the third in **Chapter 0**.

Zero-rate relief applies to the first grant by a person converting a 'non-residential' building or non-residential part of a building into a building designed as a dwelling or number of dwellings of a major interest in that

---

[68] The DIY builder's refund scheme – see **5.1** below

[69] See HMRC Business Brief 11/03 (25 July 2003)

[70] For definition of '**relevant housing association**' see **1.2.29** above

building. Reference should be made to the discussion of the first grant of a major interest by a person constructing a building at **4.3.1** above.

Note (7), Group 5, Schedule 8 provides that for the purposes of Item 1(b), and for the purposes of any other of the Notes having effect for the purposes of Item 1(b), a building or part of a building is 'non-residential' only if:

(1) it is neither designed, nor adapted, for use as a dwelling or number of dwellings, or for a 'relevant residential purpose'[71]; or

(2) it is designed, or adapted, for such use but it was constructed more than 10 years before the grant of the major interest; and no part of it has, in the period of 10 years immediately preceding the grant, been used as a dwelling or for a relevant residential purpose.

The restrictions on the meaning of 'designed as a dwelling' contained in Note (2), Group 5, Schedule 8 and discussed at **4.3.2** above do not apply when considering what is a non-residential building. However, Note (2) does apply when deciding whether the building which results from the conversion is 'designed as a dwelling or a number of dwellings'.

Note (9) further provides that the conversion, other than to a building designed for a relevant residential purpose, of a non-residential part of a building which already contains a residential part is not included within Item 1(b)[72] unless the result of that conversion is to create an additional dwelling or dwellings.

In *Jacobs*[73] a building was converted into a large private house, with three flats for staff. It had originally been a built as a house in the early 1900s. It was used as a boarding school from 1950 to 1995. The tribunal held that this was a conversion to a dwelling from a non-residential property as no child sees a school as his home or main residence. HMRC appealed against this decision and the High Court found against them, but for different reasons. It held that the conversion was one that created additional dwellings and was within Note (9) and its decision was confirmed by the Court of Appeal.

In *Alexandra Countryside Investments Ltd*[74] a company had converted a public house into two semi-detached houses by way of a vertical conversion. It reclaimed input tax on the work. HMRC rejected the claim on the basis that

---

[71] See **0** below for meaning of '**relevant residential purpose**'

[72] Or Item 3 – see **Chapter 1**

[73] [2005] STC 1518 [2005] EWCA Civ 930

[74] [2013] UKFTT 34 8 (TC)

part of the public house had been used as a flat for a manager, so that the work failed to qualify for zero-rating under Item 1(b), Group 5, Schedule 8 as parts of that flat had been incorporated in both new houses The First-tier Tribunal allowed the company's appeal, applying the Court of Appeal's decision in *CCE v Jacobs*[75], and declining to follow the VAT tribunal decision in *Calam Vale*[76].

Judge Kempster held that 'the fact that an additional dwelling has been created means that Note 9 does not prevent the conversion coming within Item 1(b). He also held that there was no justification for distinguishing between claims for recovery of input tax under section 35[77] (such as in *Jacobs*) and claims for input tax recovery under section 30 (such as in *Calam Vale*).

Note (10), Group 5, Schedule 8 deals with the case where only part of a building resulting from a conversion is designed as a dwelling or number of dwellings. In such a case a grant or other supply relating only to the part so designed (or its site) shall be treated as relating to a building so designed. A grant or other supply relating only to the part not so designed (or its site) shall not be so treated; and in relation to any other grant or other supply relating to, or to any part of, the building (or its site), an apportionment shall be made to determine the extent to which it is to be so treated.

---

[75] [2005] STC 1518
[76] (VTD 16869)
[77] By DIY builders – see **5.2** below

5   VAT Refund Schemes

There are three schemes which provide for the refund of VAT incurred in relation to certain building work and these are:

(1) The DIY builders scheme;
(2) The listed places of worship grant scheme; for VAT paid on eligible repairs and maintenance; and
(3) The memorials grant scheme ;which is a scheme for UK charities which refunds a proportion of the VAT incurred in the construction, renovation and maintenance (including professional fees) of statues, monuments and similar structures[1].

Only the first scheme is dealt with in this book. Details of the second scheme can be found on the scheme's website[2] and information on the Memorials Grant Scheme is provided by Topmark (MGS).[3] Both schemes are administered by the Department for Culture, Media and Sport.

5.1   DIY builders scheme – introduction
Section 35

VAT is not chargeable on land to be used for the construction of a dwelling by a DIY builder who is an individual and intends to use that dwelling himself. If the seller has opted to tax the land, the option is disapplied. Where the land is to be used for the construction of a building for use solely for a relevant residential or relevant charitable purpose an option to tax may be disapplied if the appropriate certificate is given, meaning that the supply is exempt from VAT. In addition, a special refund scheme exists to allow persons constructing a dwelling or converting a non-residential building into a dwelling or constructing a building for use solely for a relevant residential or relevant charitable purpose (a 'DIY builder') to reclaim the VAT incurred on certain goods used in that work.

The object of the refund scheme is to put the DIY builder in a broadly similar VAT position as a person who buys the finished building from a developer who has done the work as part of his business[5]. However, the refund is limited to VAT charged on goods – no relief is available for VAT

---

[1] Some of the work may benefit from zero-rating or be taxable at the reduced rate – see **Chapter 10**

[2] www.lpwscheme.org.uk

[3] www.memorialgrant.org.uk

[5] *CCE v Lady Blom-Cooper* [2003] STC 669 (CA), [2003] EWCA Civ 493

charged on services, although VAT on certain conversion services may be eligible for the reduced rate of VAT[6]. The refund can include repayment of an amount equal to VAT chargeable in accordance with the law of another Member State.[7]

The refund scheme is not limited to individuals but the DIY builder must be acting in a non-business capacity.[8]

5.2   Details of the DIY builder's refund scheme

A DIY builder is entitled to a refund where:

(1) The works are:
    (a) the construction of a building 'designed as a dwelling or a number of dwellings'[9]; or
    (b) the construction of a building for use solely for a 'relevant residential purpose'[10] or a 'relevant charitable purpose'[11]; or
    (c) a 'residential conversion'[12] being the conversion of a 'non-residential' building[13] or a 'non-residential' part of a building into a building:
        (i.) designed as a dwelling or number of dwellings; or
        (ii.) intended to be used solely for a relevant residential purpose; or
        (iii.)that would be a dwelling or a building to be used for a relevant residential purpose if different parts of the building were treated as separate buildings.[14]
(2) The works are carried out lawfully. This test is applied at the time the works are carried out.[15]

---

[6] See **10.5** below

[7] Section 35(3)(b)

[8] Section 35(1)(b) – see *Shinewater Association Football Club* (VTD 12938) and *Mr R and Mrs L Watson* [2004] VATDR 408

[9] See **4.3.2** above for when a building is '**designed as a dwelling**'

[10] See **0** above for what is meant by a '**relevant residential purpose**'

[11] See **1.2.28** above for what is meant by a '**relevant charitable purpose**'

[12] Section 35(1D)

[13] See **1.2.20** for the definition of a '**non-residential building**'

[14] Section 35(1D)

[15] *Bond & Baxter* (2010) TC00539, *Michael James Francis* and *Asim Patel* [2014] UKUT 0361 (TCC) but the position is different where planning permission is made retrospective to the start of the work as permitted by the planning legislation rather than granted from a current date but with retrospective effect – see *M Francis* [2012] UKFTT 359 (TC) distinguishing *Watson* [2010] UKFTT 526 (TC)

(1) VAT is chargeable[16] on the supply to him[17] of any goods used by him for the purposes of the works.

(2) A claim is made on the prescribed form and in the manner required by HMRC.

(3) The supplies in question are made to the DIY builder[18]

The usual rules as to when a building is 'designed as a dwelling', and what is a 'relevant residential' or 'relevant charitable purpose' apply. The Notes to Group 5, Schedule 8 apply for the purpose of construing the DIY builders scheme with the following modifications:

- the meaning of 'non-residential' is that given by Note (7)A, not Note (7), references to Item 3 in that Note are to be read as references to section 35[19] and paragraph (b)(iii) is be disregarded;[20] and

- Note (13) (which denies relief if residence throughout the year is not permitted) does not apply.[21] However, the requirement in Note (2)(c) that separate use or disposal of the building is not prohibited by the terms of any covenant or planning permission does apply.[22]

In *Catchpole*[23] an individual lived with his partner who had two children from a previous relationship. He decided to build a house comprising two separate buildings, one metre apart and linked by timber decking. Each of the buildings comprised two bedrooms, and the larger building also contained a bathroom, living-room and kitchen. The bedrooms in the smaller building were occupied by his partner's children. The individual claimed a refund of tax under section 35. HMRC rejected the claim but the tribunal allowed the individual's appeal. Judge Nowlan held that the fact that the dwelling contained two separate buildings did not prevent it from qualifying for relief under section 35.

---

[16] Where VAT is wrongly charged it is not recoverable under section 35 – confirmed in *R J Vincett* (VTD 10932)

[17] Including VAT charged on the acquisition from another Member State or importation from outside the EU

[18] *Mr and Mrs Barnes* (VTD 19407)

[19] Section 35(4)

[20] Section 35(4A)

[21] *Mrs I S Jennings* [2010] UKFTT 49 (TC)

[22] *D and Mrs E Sherratt* [2011] UKFTT 320 (TC)

[23] [2012] UKFTT 309 (TC)

In *Jennings*[24] the tribunal decided that Note 13, Group 5, Schedule 8 (which denies zero-rating relief for the construction of a new dwelling if residence throughout the year is not permitted) only applies to cases which fall within Item 1 of Group 5 (where a new dwelling is supplied by the person who has constructed it). It did not apply to cases falling within Item 2 (i.e. where the supply is of the services of constructing a new dwelling). Also it should not be treated as applying to cases within section 35.

The tribunal observed that if a DIY builder agrees with a contractor for the construction of the entire building, that supply is zero-rated by Group 5, Items 2 and 4, both of which are unaffected by Note 13. Where a DIY builder pays a contractor for building services which are zero rated within Item 2, but buys from someone else materials which are supplied to him and which are to be incorporated into the dwelling, then the supply of those materials is not zero rated by Group 5 but any VAY may be eligible for refund.

Following *Jennings*, HMRC accepted that the DIY builders refund scheme applies to the construction of new holiday homes and to the conversion of non-residential buildings into holiday homes. HMRC had previously not applied the scheme to holiday homes 'since their supply by a developer attracted VAT at the standard rate'. However, they have now stated[25] that the relevant legislation does allow the same recovery of VAT on building materials for holiday homes that have been constructed for a non-business purpose.

In *Tinker*[26] the appellant demolished part of a house and built a new part before demolishing and replacing the remainder. Since there was at all times an existing building the tribunal held that the works were not the construction of a building and there was therefore no right to a refund.

As a result of the decision of the Court of Appeal in *Jacobs*[27] on the construction of Note (9), Group 5, Schedule 8 in its application under section 35 HMRC accept[28] that, for the purposes of the DIY builders' refund scheme, the conversion of a building that contains both a residential part and a non-residential part comes within the scope of the scheme so long as

---

[24] [2010] UKFTT 49 (TC)
[25] In Revenue & Customs Brief 29/10 'VAT: DIY Housebuilders and Converters VAT Refund Scheme – treatment of holiday homes' (15 June 2010)
[26] (VTD 18044)
[27] [2005] All ER 326
[28] See Business Brief 22/05 (1 December 2005)

the conversion results in an additional dwelling being created. It is no longer necessary for the additional dwelling to be created exclusively from the non-residential part. However, VAT recovery is restricted to the tax attributable the conversion of the non-residential part.

It has been held that the requirement for the creation of an additional dwelling does not require the prior existence of a dwelling in the building to be converted. In *Clark*[29], the converted building comprised a residential part (a garage) and a non-residential part (a stable and tack room). Despite the existence of the residential part, the result of the conversion was to create an additional dwelling. Applying *Jacobs*[30], 'one counts the number of dwellings in the building before conversion and again after conversion'. The fact that the increase was from zero to one was no less apt than any other increase. An apportionment was required to exclude from the claim VAT attributable to the conversion of the garage area. Details of the method of apportionment are set out in *J Clark (No. 2)*.[31]

CCE v Blom Cooper[32] concerned the conversion of a public house into a single dwelling. The pub consisted of a non-residential area on the ground floor (the bar) and a residential area on the first floor (the living accommodation). Lady Blom Cooper argued that the conversion of the commercial part of the building to residential qualified for VAT relief, i.e. that HMRC should refund the VAT incurred on the conversion work under the DIY builder's scheme. HMRC refused the claim on the basis that the new dwelling was not being converted entirely from the non-residential part of the pub. Lady Blom-Cooper lodged an appeal. The Court of Appeal held that the dwelling resulting from the conversion used both the residential and non-residential parts of the pub and the works did not qualify for VAT relief under the DIY builders' scheme.

5.3   Amounts qualifying for refund

Any VAT charged on supplies of goods which are 'building materials[33]' to a DIY builder is eligible for refund provided that those building materials are incorporated in the building or its site in the course of works to which section 35 applies.[34] Where qualifying goods are bought by a DIY builder

---

[29] [2010] UKFTT 258 (TC)

[30] [2005] STC 1518, [2005] EWCA Civ 930 (CA)

[31] [2010] UKFTT 458 (TC)

[32] [2003] STC 669, [2003] EWCA Civ 493

[33] For what is meant by '**building materials**' see **10.7** below

[34] Section 35(1B)

and given to a specialist contractor to use or install, the VAT incurred can be reclaimed.

HMRC will not refund VAT to a DIY builder if, or to the extent that, that VAT has been incorrectly charged.[35] The DIY builder's remedy in such a case (if any) is against the supplier in contract.[36] VAT is not recoverable where the goods are incorporated after the construction or conversion work has been completed. In *V W McElroy*[37] the tribunal considered when construction works end:

> 'It seemed to us that the process described as 'constructing a dwelling' begins with the laying out of the site and continues through the foundation work, the erection of the external walls, floors and roof, the fixed internal walls, the installation of services such as the electrical, plumbing and central heating systems, the fitting of windows, doors and other joinery and ends with such floor and wall finishes and decorations internal and external as are customary in the building trade for dwellings of this size and type, and would be carried out by a seller before a sale takes place. Without the work required to complete the dwelling to a habitable standard the building does not appear to us to be a dwelling. It follows that until that work is done the construction of the dwelling is not complete.'

It was subsequently decided that, for the purposes of the DIY builder's scheme, a building is complete when it is 'habitable, safe and hygienic.'[38]

5.4 The form of claims by DIY builders

Regulations 200 to 201A VAT Regulations

Claims must be made within three months of completion of the conversion or construction of the building on Form VAT431NB where the works are construction works and Form VAT431C where the works are conversion works. All goods purchased and the eligible services must be listed and quantities given. Where, however, a prefabricated kit is purchased, the details of the kit can be given with a copy of the manufacturer's specification. Although the listing should be given on the claim form, HMRC will accept a spreadsheet or listing in the same format as the form.

---

[35] See, for example, *Lady Henrietta Pearson* [2014] UKFTT 890 (TC)

[36] See *PS George* (VTD 20400); *D O'Reilly* (VTD 20945); *P & M Bates* (VTD 20948); and *M O'Donnell* [2010] UKFTT 236 (TC)

[37] (VTD 490)

[38] *Dr BN Purdue* (VTD 13430)

Claimants must also include[39]:

(1) A certificate of completion from the local authority, or if such a certificate is not available HMRC will accept[40]:
  (a) a habitation letter from the local authority (a temporary habitation certificate in Scotland);
  (b) a VOA: Notice of making a New Entry into the Valuation List in England and Wales); or
  (c) a letter from a bank or building society stating that 'This is to certify that the [name] Bank/Building Society released on [date] the last instalment of its loan secured on the building at [address] because it then regarded that building as complete';

(2) Original invoices for goods supplied to the claimant for which a claim is being made showing the VAT registration number of the supplier; or
  (a) if the goods were obtained from other Member States, invoices for the goods with the VAT converted into sterling;
  (b) if the goods were imported, the proof of importation and evidence of VAT paid.
  Since the person making the refund claim will not normally be a taxable person the invoices provided need not be VAT invoices.[41] In *IS Jennings*[42] the tribunal held that, for these purposes, an invoice was 'a statement identifying a supply of goods or services, the amount payable for them and the time when payment is to be made.'

(3) Planning permission documentation;

(4) A certificate signed by a quantity surveyor or architect stating that he goods shown in the claim were, or, in his judgement, were likely, to have been incorporated into the building or site.

The claim should be sent to:

Local Compliance
National DIY Team S0987
PO Box 3900
GLASGOW
G70 6AA

---

[39] Regulation 201(b) VAT regulations
[40] See VAT431B Claim form notes at 14 (page 7)
[41] Regulation 13 VAT Regulations only requires a VAT invoice to be issued where the supply is made to a taxable person
[42] [2011] UKFTT 298 (TC)

HMRC will acknowledge the claim within five working days of receipt, and if no enquiries are to be made, will usually deal with the claim within 30 working days.

An appeal lies to a tribunal against an HMRC decision as to the amount of any refund.[43]

---

[43] Section 83(1)(g)

6 Buildings used for a Relevant Residential or Relevant Charitable Purpose

Item 1(a)(ii) and Item 1(b,) Group 5, Schedule 8

6.1 Introduction

The first grant of a major interest in, or in any part of, a building or its site intended for use solely for a 'relevant residential purpose' or solely for a 'relevant charitable purpose' by the person constructing the building is zero-rated. In addition, most of the services of constructing such a building are zero-rated.[1]

Since the zero-rate for dwellings is based on the design of the building and for relevant residential purpose buildings is based on use, HMRC accept that a building may qualify for zero-rating under both of these provision. In such cases, a taxpayer is free to rely on either provision to achieve zero-rating for their building. As there is no claw-back of relief for dwellings a claim under this head would seem to be preferable in these circumstances[2].

In *Astral Construction Ltd*[3] a company constructed a nursing home on the site of a redundant church, incorporating most of the church as a reception area. HMRC issued a ruling that the work constituted the conversion of the church into a 'relevant residential purpose building' chargeable to VAT at the reduced rate. The company appealed, contending that the work qualified for zero-rating as new construction. The First-tier Tribunal accepted this contention and allowed the appeal, observing that 'viewed structurally and as a whole the church can only be described as being dwarfed by the new build'.

Where part of a building that is constructed is designed as a dwelling or number of dwellings or is intended for use solely for a relevant residential purpose or relevant charitable purpose (and part is not) the building is treated as two separate buildings and an apportionment is made where a supply relates to both parts.[4]

---

[1] See **Chapter 0** below

[2] See VAT Information Sheet 02/14 'Buildings that are used for a relevant residential purpose' (30 January 2014)

[3] [2013] UKFTT 374 (TC)

[4] Note (10)(a), Group 5, Schedule 8

The first grant by a person converting a 'non-residential building'[5] or a non-residential part of a building into a building intended for use solely for a relevant residential purpose is zero-rated. The services of conversion will be taxable at the standard rate unless they qualify for the reduced rate as supplies in the course of a 'special residential conversion'.[6]

'First grant', 'major interest', and 'person constructing a building' are considered in detail in section **4.3.1** above. The special zero-rate for the construction of an annexe intended for use solely for a relevant charitable purpose is considered at **6.3.3** below.

All other supplies of an interest in the building (other than those 'lesser interests' falling within items (b) to (n), Group 1, Schedule 9[7]) will be exempt and the option to tax will not normally have effect[8].

The construction of annexes and extensions are excluded from the relief unless, in the case of an annexe, it is to be used solely for a relevant charitable purpose (see **6.3** below).

Where the use of the property changes within ten years of completion of the building which has been zero-rated under these provisions there will be a claw-back of the relief (see **6.5** below).

The reduced rate of VAT considered in detail in 10.5 below can apply to certain supplies in the course of the conversion of a building into relevant residential use property.

6.1.1   The reliefs apply only to 'buildings'

In *Upper Don Walk Trust*[9] a charity arranged for the construction of a bridge across the River Don, for cyclists and pedestrians. HMRC issued a ruling that VAT was chargeable on the work. The charity appealed, contending that the bridge should be treated as a building and as qualifying for zero-rating. The tribunal rejected this contention and dismissed the appeal, holding that the bridge was not a 'building'.

---

[5] For **'non-residential building'** see **1.2.20** above
[6] See **10.5** below
[7] These supplies are always taxable at the standard rate - see **3.2.14** above
[8] The **option to tax** is considered in detail in **Chapter 1**
[9] (VTD 19476)

6.2　Use solely for a relevant residential purpose
Notes (4),(5) and 12, Group 5, Schedule 8

As a general guide, premises that are to be used for residential occupation for groups of people, such as student accommodation, hospices or monasteries are used for a relevant residential purpose.

Note (4), Group 5, Schedule 8 defines use for a relevant residential purpose as use as:

(a) a home or other institution providing residential accommodation for children;

(b) a home or other institution providing residential accommodation with personal care for persons in need of personal care by reason of old age, disablement, past or present dependence on alcohol or drugs or past or present mental disorder;

(c) a hospice;

(d) residential accommodation for students or school pupils;

(e) residential accommodation for members of any of the armed forces;

(f) a monastery, nunnery or similar establishment;

(g) an institution which is the sole or main residence for at least 90 per cent. of its residents.

Buildings that are not to be regarded as relevant residential use properties are hospitals, prisons or 'similar institutions' or hotels, inns or 'similar establishments'. 'Residential accommodation' suggests the provision of lodging, sleeping or overnight accommodation, but it does not suggest the need for a stay of any minimum period[10].

Revenue & Customs Brief 03/14[11] sets out HMRC's revised guidance on what the term 'student' means in Note (4)(d), Group 5, Schedule 8:

'The term 'student' in this context refers to a person undertaking a course of educational study or instruction. It covers any person who is receiving education or vocational training from a university (or a centrally funded higher education institution or a further education institution) or from any other supplier who is providing similar, or the same type of, education or vocational training to a similar, or the same, academic standard.'

This replaces the previous guidance (which was in HMRC's VAT Manual at VCONST15360).

---

[10] *Urdd Gobaith Cymru* [1997] VATDR 273 (VTD 14881)

[11] 'Construction works to buildings used 'for a relevant residential purpose'' (31 January 2014)

The supply must be to a person who intends to use the building or part of the building for such a purpose.[12] Note (12)(b) to Group 5 provides that a building shall not be regarded as intended for use for a relevant residential purpose unless before the supply is made the recipient of the supply has given the supplier a certificate '… in such form as may be specified in a notice published by the Commissioners stating that the grant … so relates'. The form of the certificate in relation to the zero-rating of supplies of a major interest in such a building is set out at paragraph 18.2 of VAT Notice 708[13] which has the force of law. For more on Certificates see **6.3.3** below.

In *TGH (Construction) Ltd*[14] the facts were that the appellant TGH which was a wholly-owned subsidiary of a charity had entered into a design and build contract with the charity in respect of the construction of new buildings on land belonging to the charity. Holme Terrace, which is a two-storey, self-contained building, was constructed on the site of some demolished cottages owned by the charity and comprised eighteen self-contained flats for occupation by elderly licensees, who are offered accommodation by the charity on the basis that they were persons who are in need within the terms of its charitable objects.

TGN claimed that Holme Terrace was used for a relevant residential purpose as it was used as one or other of the following:

- a home or other 'institution' providing residential accommodation with personal care for persons in need of personal care by reason of old age, disablement, past or present dependence on alcohol or drugs or past or present mental disorder; or
- an 'institution' which is the sole or main residence for at least 90 per cent. of its residents.

HMRC's case was that Holme Terrace was not an 'institution' and that it did not provide 'personal care'.

The First-tier Tribunal decided that Holme Terrace was 'an institution' for the following reasons[15]:

'The residents of Holme Terrace have a great deal of autonomy (as is their right) but that autonomy exists within a framework of rules and regulations which they must agree to adopt and abide by. They could be

---

[12] Note (12)(a), Group 5, Schedule 8
[13] 'Buildings and construction' (August 2014)
[14] [2014] UKFTT 1039 (TC)
[15] At paragraphs 30 and 31 of the decision

made to leave Holme Terrace if they do not adhere to the rules, as they have no occupational rights. When they take up residence it is at the invitation of the charity, having been assessed as in need according the charity's governing Scheme. As the residents of Holme Terrace are merely licensees, the charity may (and, indeed does at times) move them to a different flat within the building; they may not have overnight guests at their flats; they may not decorate or make alterations to their flats; they must inform staff if they are to be away overnight; they must submit to inspections and works provided by the charity. I consider that these are all features more consistent with a life lived in an *"institution"* than they are with a completely autonomous life lived in a bought or rented flat and over which the resident has legal rights and sole control.

I find that the degree of compulsion or control necessary (or indeed permitted) for the residents of Holme Terrace as a client group is minimal and that the flexible test of whether an *"institution"* exists under VATA does not require there to be any element of compulsion in their daily lives if compulsion is not a feature of their care needs. Mr Ridley's cross examination of Mr Pellatt proceeded on the basis that, unless residents were compelled to participate in card games in the communal lounge, they could not be said to be living in an institution. I reject this approach. Taking instead the approach of assessing the degree of organisation required in respect of the relevant client group, it seems to me that Holme Terrace has the relevant features of an *"institution"* for the purposes of VATA in view of the overall organisational framework for its residents which I have already referred to.'

The tribunal also decided in favour of the appellant on the question of whether the residents were provided with personal care[16]:

'I am satisfied that the services provided by the charity for free are designed to address the particular care needs of the incoming residents of Holme Terrace, so that there is a match between the two elements of the test in note 4(b), namely the provision of personal care to persons in need of that personal care by reason of their old age. Some of these services may at times involve feeding and washing a resident (for example when respite care is required) but others involve the provision of a supportive milieu designed to allow for maximum independence, for example the call button, site security and maintenance, and laundry

---

[16] At paragraph 35 of the decision

services. I note that the charity may only provide accommodation to persons in need and that the individual care needs of prospective residents at Holme Terrace are assessed by the care manager so that it is ensured they may be met. I reject HMRC's argument that it is necessary to import a rigid definition of *"personal care"* from other sources into VATA and find that the *"personal care"* provided at Holme Terrace is of a kind which is carefully calibrated for its particular residents and that it meets the flexible definition of the term which is found in VATA.'

6.2.1 'Similar institution' and 'similar establishment'

Various types of residential accommodation are excluded from the definition of use for a relevant residential purpose, including use as a hospital, prison or 'similar institution'[17] and use as a hotel, inn or 'similar establishment'.

There can be particular difficulty in differentiating between a hospice and a hospital. There is no definition of 'hospital' in the VAT legislation. It was held in *General Healthcare Group Ltd* [18] that a residence that provided care but not medical treatment or diagnosis was not a hospital. The average stay was approximately two years which exceeded the length of stay expected in a hospital.

Section 275(1) *National Health Service Act 2006* provides that:

'"hospital" means -
(a) any institution for the reception and treatment of persons suffering from illness,
(b) any maternity home, and
(c) any institution for the reception and treatment of persons during convalescence or persons requiring medical rehabilitation,
and includes clinics, dispensaries and out-patient departments maintained in connection with any such home or institution, and hospital accommodation shall be construed accordingly;'

'"illness" includes any disorder or disability of the mind and any injury or disability requiring medical or dental treatment or nursing.'

The essential characteristic of a hospital is that its purpose or function is the treatment of 'illness' as defined in section 275(1) *National Health Service Act*

---

[17] The meaning of 'institution' was considered by the First-tier Tribunal in *TGH (Construction) Ltd* [2014] UKFTT 1039 (TC)
[18] [2001] VATDR 328

2006 and treatment for this purpose includes nursing by professionally trained nurses.[19] This will be the basis for deciding if an 'institution' is 'similar' to a hospital. The same reasoning would apply in deciding whether an institution is similar to a prison.

The High Court in *CCE v Fenwood Developments Ltd* [20] confirmed that there is a distinction 'between a home or institution providing residential accommodation with personal care for those that needed it ... and an institution providing medical treatment and associated care, usually on a short-term basis.' In *Fenwood* a company constructed a home for persons suffering from mental illness. Many of the occupants were detained under the *Mental Health Act 1983*. HMRC ruled that the home was similar to a hospital and not eligible for the zero-rating relief. The company argued that the home was not similar to a hospital and therefore was eligible for the relief. The tribunal agreed with the company, applying the dissenting judgment of Denning LJ in *Minister of Health v General Committee of the Royal Midland Counties Home for Incurables at Leamington Spa*[21] that there was a distinction between care and treatment. The nursing home constructed by Fenwood provided care and not treatment so it was not a similar institution to a hospital. A similar conclusion was reached in *Hospital of St John and St Elizabeth*[22] where it was held that a centre to accommodate elderly mentally infirm persons was not a similar institution to a hospital as the occupants were provided with a secure environment but did not require medical intervention or treatment.

The tribunal in *Atlas Property London Ltd*[23] considered whether supplies of accommodation for the homeless made, in the main, to local authorities, were exempt supplies of interests in land and not standard rated hotel supplies or supplies of accommodation in a 'similar establishment.' The tribunal decided that the supplies were exempt and observed that the properties were not used by travellers; the question was therefore whether they were 'similar' to a hotel by reference to other characteristics. It noted that periods of long stay are highly unusual features of the use of accommodation in hotels and pointed to the 'home-like' nature of the accommodation. The tribunal added that Atlas Property provided very few

---

[19] Applying the reasoning in *White v Chief Adjudication Officer* (R(IS) 18/94 (CA))
[20] [2006] STC 644, [2005] EWHC 2954 (Ch D)
[21] [1954] 1 Ch 530 (CA) at pages 547-548
[22] (VTD 19141)
[23] [2014] UKFTT 674 (TC)

'hotel-like' services. In particular, no food, cleaning or reception desk services were provided. Finally, it noted that the accommodation could not even be likened to 'serviced flats', as it was not cleaned daily.

6.2.2 Multiple buildings

Note (5), Group 5, Schedule 8 provides that a number of buildings that are constructed at the same time that are intended to be used for a relevant residential purposes are to be treated as intended for use solely for a relevant residential purpose even if they would not qualify on their own. The buildings must be built at the same time and on the same site and must be intended to be used together as a unit solely for a relevant residential purpose.

This means that service buildings (such as a boiler house, separate dining room or laundry) that are separate from the relevant residential property also benefit from the relief. Where there is separate building with a particular use (such as a dining room), then that property should be used exclusively by the residents to qualify for relevant residential use. Where it is used by non-residents the property will not benefit from zero-rating. This rule is applied strictly. Even if persons using other residential accommodation use the dining hall (in this example), the dining hall will not be residential accommodation unless all the buildings were constructed together and intended to be used collectively as living accommodation.

A bedroom block built in the grounds of a care home is not in itself a relevant residential purpose building as it is not a 'home or institution', but part of a larger home or institution. To determine if the block is to be used for a relevant residential purpose it is necessary to consider the use to which it is put, whether it is used in conjunction with other nearby buildings forming part of the care home, whether there is common ownership, the licensing of the building and the way its use is advertised. If the bedroom block was constructed at the same time as the rest of the institution then it would be zero-rated by reason of Note (5), Group 5, Schedule 8.

6.2.3 Solely

'Solely for a relevant residential purpose' means, in relation to student accommodation, solely in term time based on an HMRC concession which could be relied on by the taxpayer.[24] This concession is being withdrawn

---

[24] *R (on application of Greenwich Property Ltd) v CCE* [2001] STC 618 distinguishing *University of Bath* (VTD 14235)

with effect from 1 April 2015.[25]

From 1 July 2010 HMRC have confirmed[26] that they will regard the test of use 'solely' for a relevant residential purpose as satisfied provided that the relevant residential purpose use is 95% or more.

6.3   Use solely for a relevant charitable purpose
Notes (6) and (12), Group 5, Schedule 8

Use for a relevant charitable purpose is defined in Note (6), Group 5, Schedule 8 as use by a charity 'otherwise in the course or furtherance of a business', and/or as a village hall 'or similarly' in providing social or recreational facilities for a local community.

The supply must be to a person who intends to use the building or part of the building for such a purpose.[27] Note (12)(b) to Group 5 provides that a building shall not be regarded as intended for use for a relevant charitable purposes unless before the supply is made the recipient has given the supplier a certificate '…..in such form as may be specified in a notice published by the Commissioners stating that the grant … so relates'. The form of the certificate in relation to the zero-rating of supplies of a major interest in such a building is set out at paragraph 18.2 of VAT Notice 708[28] which has the force of law. For more on Certificates see **6.3.3** below.

6.3.1   Otherwise than in the course or furtherance of a business
A charity that is regarded as being in business for some activities may still be eligible for zero-rating if the building that is constructed or acquired is used by the charity for a non-business purpose, for example, a charity may have a separate building for its non-business activities.

'Business' is to be construed widely and even the carrying on of non-profit making activities by charities can be business activities. The provision of education for a fee is seen by HMRC as being 'in business' even where provided by a charitable entity. A different result would obtain where the education is provided free.[29]

HMRC may also seek to treat charities as being in business even where the

---

[25]See Revenue & Customs Brief 14/14 'Withdrawal of concessions for student accommodation and dining halls (7 April 2014)

[26] Revenue & Customs Brief 32/10 (3 August 2010)

[27] Note (12)(a), Group 5, Schedule 8

[28] 'Buildings and construction' (August 2014)

[29] *Leighton Park School* (VTD 9392)

business activity is small. For example, in *Leighton Park School*[30] HMRC argued that a playgroup was in business despite its turnover being less than £4,000 and derived wholly from voluntary donations made by parents. The tribunal dismissed the appeal which related to the zero-rating of a new classroom block on the grounds that the building was not intended for use for a relevant charitable purpose.

In *CCE v St Paul's Community Project Ltd*[31] a charity that reserved spaces in its nursery for children referred to it by a local authority had constructed a new building which it claimed was intended for use for a relevant charitable purpose. HMRC rejected the charity's claim for zero-rating on the basis that the nursery was a business. The tribunal found that the charity's activities in operating the nursery were not predominantly concerned with the making of taxable supplies for consideration. The High Court, upholding the tribunal's decision, held that the intrinsic nature of the entity meant that it was not carrying on a business, identifying the distinguishing features as social concern for the welfare of disadvantaged children, lack of commerciality in setting fees and an overall intention simply to cover costs.

In *Longridge on the Thames*[32] the Upper Tribunal (Rose J) confirmed that a building could be used for a relevant charitable purpose, even though recipients of the services provided in the building paid for those services.

Longridge, a charity, provided a wide range of day and residential courses and activities (principally water-based). The building at the centre of the dispute was a training centre.

HMRC's main contention was that the First-tier Tribunal in finding in favour of Longridge[33] had erred in law by focusing on the price charged by Longridge, which in most cases did not cover its costs, to conclude that its activities were not profit making. However, the Upper Tribunal observed that there is a 'dividing line' between situations where the activities do amount to the furtherance of a business, even though they are not aimed at making a profit;[34] and situations where the activities are not conducted as a business, even though payment is made by the recipient.[35]

---

[30] *Newtownbutler Playgroup Ltd* (VTD 13741)

[31] [2005] STC 95; [2004] EWHC 2490 (Ch D)

[32] [2014] UKUT 0504 (TCC)

[33] [2013] UKFTT 158 (TC)

[34] *CCE v Morrison's Academy* [1978] STC 1

[35] *Commission v Finland* (C-246/08) unreported

The Upper Tribunal in *Longridge* added that the First-tier Tribunal had considered the scale of the payments, the way they were calculated and the finances of Longridge in a way that showed an understanding of the law. Looking at the 'totality of the observable features[36]' of the activities carried out by Longridge, the First-tier Tribunal had held that these activities were not economic and the Upper Tribunal could not interfere with this finding.

The Upper Tribunal rejected the notion that, following *Commission v Finland*, where consideration is paid for services that establishes a presumption that there is an economic activity.

The decision in *Longridge* casts doubt on the First-tier Tribunal's decision in *Capernwray Missionary Fellowship of Torchbearers*,[37] where the First-tier Tribunal decided that the construction of a community hall for a charity was not zero-rated. In particular, the tribunal, having considered the judgement of the European Court in *Commission v Finland*, found that the relevant charitable purpose test was not met because the charity's activity of putting on courses in the hall for remuneration was an economic activity, even though this was not carried out with a view to profit.

HMRC state in Notice 701/1/04[38] at paragraph 4.1, their view that the answers to the following questions are relevant as indicators of business activity for a charity:

- Is the activity a serious undertaking earnestly pursued?
- This considers whether the activity is carried on for business or daily work rather than pleasure or daily enjoyment.)
- Is the activity an occupation or function that is actively pursued with reasonable or recognisable continuity?
- (When considering this test one should consider how frequently the supplies will be made.)
- Does the activity have a certain measure of substance in terms of the quarterly or annual value of taxable supplies made?
- Is the activity conducted in a regular manner and on sound and recognised business principles?
- Is the activity predominately concerned with the making of taxable supplies for a consideration[39]?

---

[36] See *CCE v Yarburgh Children's Trust* [1999] STC 207

[37] [2014] UKFTT 626 (TC)

[38] 'Charities' (May 2004)

[39] This has in many instances been seen as the most important and arguably the most problematic indicator. In *The Institute of Chartered Accountants in England and Wales v CCE* [1999] STC 398 the House of Lords found that the test was 'what is the real

- Are the taxable supplies that are being made of a kind which, subject to differences of detail, are commonly made by those who seek to profit from them?

In *The Royal Academy of Music*[40] the tribunal held that the fact that the Academy's objectives were charitable and philanthropic was not conclusive of the question of whether it was carrying on a business.

6.3.2 Use as village hall 'or similarly' in providing social or recreational facilities for a local community

The legislation permits zero-rating of certain supplies of a building intended for use by a charity 'as a village hall or similarly in providing social or recreational facilities for a local community'. This means that even where the building used by a charity is a village hall to qualify for relief it must be used to provide social or recreational facilities for a local community

A building will be regarded by HMRC as a village hall used in providing social or recreational facilities for a local community when there is a high degree of local community involvement in the building's operation and activities and there is a wide variety of activities carried on in the building, the majority of which are for social and/or recreational purposes (including sport).[41]

Buildings that are regarded by HMRC as having a use similar to village halls in providing social or recreational facilities for a local community are:
- scout or guide huts
- sports pavilions
- church halls
- community centres
- community sports centres

Buildings that are not regarded by HMRC as having a use similar to village halls providing social or recreational facilities for a local community include:
- community swimming pools
- community theatres

---

nature of the activity?' i.e. is the real nature of the activity the making of taxable supplies for consideration or is it something else?

[40] [1994] VATTR 105 (VTD 11871)

[41] VAT Notice 708 'Buildings and construction' (August 2014) at paragraph 14.7.4

- membership clubs (although community associations charging a nominal membership may qualify)
- community amateur sports clubs

The decision in *Hanbury Charity*[44] concerned the question of whether a community hall was used by a charity as a village hall in providing social or recreational facilities for a local community. HMRC argued that the charity's objectives were educational rather than social or recreational; that the charity was not a village hall charity, and so the community hall did not qualify. HMRC also argued that as the original 19th century charitable trust was to promote education and not social and recreational purposes, the building could not be afforded the relief. The tribunal held that HMRC were ignoring the actual use – evidence had been presented of the various social and recreational activities that were undertaken in the hall for the benefit of a local community. The charity's appeal succeeded.

'For a local community'

There must be a high degree of local community involvement in the building's operations and activities. *Jubilee Hall Recreation Centre Limited v CCE; CCE v St Dunstan's Educational Foundation*[45] is the leading case on the definition of village hall and local community activity. In this case a charity ran a commercial gym for persons that came to the Covent Garden area to work. It was held by the Court of Appeal that for the premises to be regarded as similar to a village hall it had to be owned, organised and administered by the community that lived in that vicinity rather than persons whose only link was that they worked in the area.

A local community had to be the user of the hall (through a body of trustees or a management committee acting on its behalf) and the only economic activity in the building must be one in which they participated directly and which was an ordinary incident of the use by a local community for social, including recreational, purposes. The obvious examples were the bring-and-buy or jumble sale, the performance of a play by local players and similar activities. The village hall was the model of that case. The appeal failed as the Jubilee Hall was not used in a similar way to use of a village hall in providing social or recreational facilities for a local community.

HMRC have subsequently argued on the basis of the decision in *Jubilee Hall*

---

[44] (VTD 20126) - see also *The New Deer Community Association* [2014] UKFTT 1028 (TC)
[45] [1999] STC 381 (CA)

that the relief is only intended for small-scale charities that own organise and administer the village hall or other building. The tribunal in *Hanbury Charity*[46] held that this was not a sustainable interpretation of the legislation. The tribunal quoting the following passage from *The South Molton Swimming Pool Trustees* decision:[47]

> '...it is necessary to have in mind the purpose of the provision[48] and the statement of the Court of Justice.[49] In this appeal the supplies were made to the Trustees who were carrying on an economic activity, albeit non-profit making. Thus the Trustees do not come within the normal meaning of 'the final consumer'. Accordingly, it has to be considered whether the supplies to the Trustees were 'nevertheless sufficiently close to the consumer to be of advantage to him'[50].'

The issue in the *Hanbury Charity*[51] case was whether the charity was sufficiently close to the community for the hall to be of benefit to the community. It was held there was such a close connection – so zero-rating was allowed.

Broadly, for a village hall to be eligible for zero-rating, there needs to be social and recreational use by a local community; that is the community that lives in the area, not those that work or travel to the area. Use of the hall for other purposes can prevent the relief being available.

6.3.3   Annexes

The construction of an annexe to a building is zero-rated[53] when the following conditions are met:

---

[46] (VTD 20126)

[47] (VTD 16495)

[48] Note (6)(b), Group 5, Schedule 8 – use for a relevant charitable purpose

[49] In *European Commission v United Kingdom* (Case C-416/85) [1988] STC 456 where the European Court said that the term 'final consumer' could be applied only to a person who did not use exempted or zero-rated goods or services in the course of an economic activity and:

'The provision of goods or services at a stage higher in the production and distribution chain which is nevertheless sufficiently close to the consumer to be of advantage to him must also be considered to be for the benefit of the final consumer as so defined.'

[50] Quoting from *European Commission v United Kingdom* (Case C-416/85) [1988] STC 456

[51] (VTD 20126)

[53] Note (17) overriding Note (16)(c), Group 5, Schedule 8

(1) It is an annexe that is constructed, not an extension or enlargement to an existing building.

(2) The whole or part of the annexe is intended for use solely for a relevant charitable purpose.

(3) The annexe is capable of functioning independently of the existing building.

(4) The only access or, where there is more than one means of access, the main access, to the annexe is not via the existing building and the main entrance to the existing building is not via the annexe.

(5) The relevant certificate is issued (see **6.3.3**. below).

It was held in *Bryan Thomas Macnamara*[54] that the term 'annexe' connotes something that is adjoined but either not integrated with the existing building or of tenuous integration. In *Colchester Sixth Form College*[55] the tribunal found that:

'The correct approach, we think, is to consider the existing building as it was and then to consider the end result of the construction works and ask whether, viewed objectively and in the light of all the relevant information, the work done amounts to the enlargement of, or an extension to, the existing building, or to the construction of an annexe to it. This was the two-stage approach, recommended in relation to the earlier but comparable legislation, by McCullough J in *CCE v The London Diocesan Finance*[56] and endorsed by the Court of Appeal in *CCE v Marchday Holdings*[57].'

In *Knowsley Associates Limited*[58] it was held that a 'real and substantial measure of integration of new and old' means that the works are the extension of an existing building and the result is therefore not an annexe.

In *Allan Water Developments Ltd*[59] a company operated a nursing home for 81 residents (a 'relevant residential purpose' building). A new building was constructed which was to be used by those suffering from dementia and mental illness. The two buildings were linked by a corridor, which was used to transport meals from the nursing home to the new building, but was not used by residents or patients. HMRC believed that the new

[54] [1999] VATDR 171 (VTD 16039)
[55] (VTD 16252)
[56] [1993] STC 369 at 380
[57] [1997] STC 272
[58] (VTD 18180)
[59] (VTD 19131)

building was an 'annexe' to the nursing home and its construction was, therefore, excluded from zero-rating by Note 16. The tribunal disagreed and allowed the appeal holding that the construction of the new building qualified for zero-rating. The tribunal applied dicta of Sir Andrew Morritt V-C in *Cantrell and Another (trading as Foxearth Lodge Nursing Home) v CCE (No. 2)*:[60]

> 'an annexe is an adjunct or accessory to something else, such as a document. When used in relation to a building it is referring to a supplementary structure, be it a room, a wing or a separate building.'

In *Cantrell* a couple operated a nursing home comprising two separate units, one for medical patients and one for mentally infirm patients. They arranged for building work which involved extending the unit which housed the mentally infirm patients so that it joined onto the unit comprising the medical patients. However, there was no internal access. HMRC issued a ruling that VAT was chargeable on the work on the grounds that the new building was an annexe. Sir Andrew Morritt V-C found that on the evidence, the works 'did not constitute the construction of an annexe to any existing building', and qualified for zero-rating.

So it has been established that not all forms of attachment make a building an annexe. Clearly, it is important to consider what constitutes an annexe. Buildings that are extensions rather than annexes will be integral and so adjoined to a building that it becomes a part of the original building. To be an annexe there needs to be a significant degree of separation, a separate building that happens to have a link with the original building. Too often buildings are called annexes that are extensions; a separate entrance is insufficient for an extension to be an annexe. An annexe may be a separate building.[61]

The activities in the annexe may be different from those undertaken in the main building and this may in fact help distinguish the annexe from the main building. Although the annexe must be able to function independently of the main building it does not need to have its own supply of electricity or other services, although the provision of separate utilities does emphasize the separateness of the annexe.

---

[60] [2003] STC 486, [2003] EWHC 404 (Ch D) (applied in *Chacombe Park Development Services Ltd* (VTD 1414))

[61] See *Stephen Colchester* [2014] UKUT 0083 (TCC)

HMRC's views on what is an annexe are set out in VAT Notice 708 'Buildings and construction'[62] at paragraph 3.2.6:

'An annexe can be either a structure attached to an existing building or a structure detached from it. A detached structure is treated for VAT purposes as a separate building. The comments in this section only apply to attached structures.

There is no legal definition of 'annexe'. In order to be considered an annexe, a structure must be attached to an existing building but not in such a way so as to be considered an enlargement or extension of that building.

An enlargement or extension would involve making the building bigger so as to provide extra space for the activities already carried out in the existing building. Examples of an enlargement or extension are a classroom or a sports hall added to an existing school building or an additional function room (or kitchen or toilet block) added to an existing village hall.

On the other hand, an annexe would provide extra space for activities distinct from but associated with the activities carried out in the existing building. The annexe and the existing building would form two separate parts of a single building that operate independently of each other.

Examples of an annexe are a day hospice added to an existing residential hospice, a self-contained suite of rooms added to an existing village hall, a church hall added to an existing church or a nursery added to a school building'.

6.3.4   Solely

HMRC had published an Extra-Statutory Concession for small business use by charities, ESC 3.29, which permitted zero-rating of a building which was used for at least 90 per cent of the time for non-business purposes, or where 90 per cent. of the area was used for non-business purposes. This ESC was withdrawn with effect from 1 July 2010. However, HMRC have confirmed[63] that, from that date, they will regard the test of use 'solely' for a relevant charitable purpose as satisfied provided that the relevant use is 95% or more. Qualifying use can be calculated by any method that is fair and reasonable.

6.4   Certificates
Note (12)(b), Group 5, Schedule 8

---

[62] August 2014

[63] In Revenue & Customs Brief 32/10 'VAT – changes to the application of the zero-rate to new buildings used for a relevant charitable or residential use' (3 August 2010)

Where all or part of a building is intended solely for use for a relevant residential or charitable purpose, the first grant of a major interest in it cannot be zero-rated unless, *before* the supply is made,[64] a certificate in the form specified by HMRC has been given by the person receiving the supply to the supplier. The form of the certificate in relation to the zero-rating of supplies of a major interest in such a building is set out at paragraph 18.2 of VAT Notice 708[65] which has the force of law.

The provision of a certificate is not conclusive of qualifying use but it is a pre-requisite. The supplier should therefore take reasonable steps to ensure that the use of the building will be as described on the certificate. Evidence of this, and correspondence with the recipient of the supply should be retained to show that such efforts have been made. To safeguard their position, the supplier should seek to include a contractual provision that VAT will be paid if it is due because of intended non-qualifying use.

The certificate should strictly be issued before the supply is made, but HMRC, it seems, will, by 'allow your supplier to adjust his VAT charge on receipt of a belated certificate'[66], if:

- the recipient of the supply can demonstrate that at the time of supply he intended the building to be used in the way certified; and
- all other conditions for zero-rating (or the reduced rate[67]) are met.

This is contrary to the express wording of Note (12)(b).

Section 62 provides for a VAT-geared penalty where an incorrect certificate is given. The defence of reasonable excuse is available. The penalty is not VAT and so is not recoverable as input tax.

6.5   Claw-back on change of use

A charge to VAT arises where the construction of, or grant of an interest in, a building has been zero-rated on the basis of its intended use (a relevant residential or charitable purpose) and that use changes after the grant has been made. This, therefore, covers not only cases where the zero-rated supply of the completed or uncompleted buildings and construction services falling within Item 1 and 2, Group 5, Schedule 8 but also supplies of conversion services falling within Item 3 (supplies to relevant housing associations of the services of converting non-residential building into a

---

[64] For **time of supply** see **Chapter 2**
[65] 'Buildings and construction' (August 2014)
[66] See paragraph 17.6 VAT Notice 708 'Buildings and construction' (August 2014)
[67] See **Chapter 10**

building intended for use solely for a relevant residential purpose)[68] and building materials falling within Item 4.

Before 1 March 2011, the charge to tax and the method of calculating it differed depending on whether or not the recipient of the zero-rated supply subsequently granted an interest to a third party. Where a change in use occurred in an unidentifiable part of the premises, the charge arose on the entire premises or part of the premises.

For buildings completed on or after 1 March 2011, and whose use changes on or after 1 March 2011, new measures provide for a uniform application of the charge to VAT and a single method of calculation.

6.5.1 The rules for buildings completed on or after 1 March 2011

Part 2, Schedule 10 (as substituted by the Value Added Tax (Buildings and Land) Order 2011[69])

Where one or more 'relevant zero-rated supplies 'relating to' a building or part of a building' have been made to a person and, within ten years of completion of that building[70] and there is an increase in the use of the building for a 'non-relevant purpose[71] a charge arises on each occasion. An increase may be as a result of:

(1) the disposal of the entire interest in the building (or part of the building), or

(2) a change in the use of the entire building (or part of the building); or

(3) an change in the use of specific parts of the building.

A 'relevant zero-rated supply' is defined in paragraph 35(2) of Schedule 10 and is:

'a grant or other supply which relates to a building (or part of a building) intended for use solely for –

(a) a relevant residential purpose, or

(b) a relevant charitable purpose,

and which, as a result of Group 5 of Schedule 8, is zero-rated (in whole or in part).'

---

[68] See **7.1** below

[69] SI 2011/86

[70] Paragraph 36, Schedule 10 – when a building is completed is determined in accordance with Note (2), Group 1, Schedule 9 –see **1.2.6** above

[71] A 'non-relevant purpose' is a purpose that is neither a 'relevant residential purpose' nor a 'relevant charitable purpose'

This, therefore, covers not only the zero-rated supply of the completed or uncompleted building falling within Item 1, Group 5, Schedule 8 but also supplies of construction services and building materials falling within Items 3 and 4.

Where use is made of the building (or part of the building) for both a relevant and a non-relevant purpose, the proportion of use for a non-relevant purpose is to be calculated in the same proportion as if an identifiable part of the building were used for a non-relevant purpose.[72]

Where a charity is using the relevant building (or a part of) as a village hall or similarly in providing social or recreational facilities for a local community, the building (or the part of the building) is treated as being used for a relevant charitable purpose whether or not the occupier is using it for a relevant charitable purpose.[73]

Where the charge applies, the person's interest, right or licence in the relevant building held immediately prior to the time when the increase occurs is treated as supplied to him for the purposes of a business which he carries on; and supplied by him in the course or furtherance of that business[74]. In other words, there is a self-supply immediately before the time of that increase. The supply is taken to be a taxable supply which is not zero-rated, the value of which is taken to be in the case of the first deemed supply, the amount obtained by the formula:[75]

$$R2 \times Y \times ((120 - Z) / 120)$$

In the case of any subsequent deemed supply, the amount obtained by the formula:

$$(R2 - R1) \times Y \times ((120 - Z) / 120)$$

Where:

R2 is the proportion of the relevant building disposed of or used for non-relevant purposes in the 'relevant period'.

R1 is the proportion of the relevant building disposed of or used for non-relevant purposes at an earlier time in the relevant period.

---

[72] Paragraphs 35(4) and (5), Schedule 10
[73] Paragraph 36(6), Schedule 10
[74] Paragraph 37(1), Schedule 10
[75] Paragraph 37(3), Schedule 10

Y is the amount that yields the amount of VAT that would have been chargeable on the relevant supply if it had not been zero-rated (or the aggregate amount of VAT if there was more than one supply).

Z is the number of whole months since the day on which the relevant building were completed.

'Relevant period' means ten years beginning with the day on which the relevant building is completed[76].

Examples[77]

1. A charity constructs/acquires a new building at the zero rate of VAT because they have certified that they intend use the building solely for a non-business purpose. The value of the zero-rated supply was £5 million. The standard rate of VAT at the time of supply was 20%. The building consists of five floors.

During the first five years, the building was used as intended. After five years, the charity decides that they will use the top floor of the building for a business purpose.

VAT of £100,000 on a self-supply charge will need to be accounted for. That has been calculated as follows:

- value of the supply or supplies that would have yielded £1 million VAT = £5 million
- proportion of the building affected by the change = one floor of five, 20%
- number of months remaining in the ten year period that this part of the building will not be used as intended = 60 months out of 120 that is, 50%
- the standard rate of VAT at the time of the 'change in use' is 20%.

Therefore the value of self-supply = £5 million × 20% × 50% = £500,000.

VAT @ 20%

= **£100,000**

2. A charity constructs/acquires a new building at the zero rate of VAT because they have certified that they intend to use the building solely for a non-business purpose. The value of the zero-rated supply was £5 million. The building consists of five floors.

During the first five years, the building was used as intended but at the end of the fifth year, the charity sold its entire interest in the building.

VAT of £500,000 will need to be accounted for on a self-supply charge, calculated as follows:

---

[76] Paragraph 35(2), Schedule 10

[77] Taken from VAT Notice 208 'Buildings and construction' (August 2014) paragraph 19.3.3

- value of the supply or supplies that would have yielded £1 million VAT = £5 million
- proportion of the building affected by the change = 100%
- number of months remaining in the ten year period that this part of the building will not be used for a relevant charitable purpose = 60 months out of 120
- the standard rate of VAT at the time of the disposal is 20%.

Therefore the value of self supply = £5 million × 100% × (60/120) = £2.5 million

VAT @ 20%

= £500,000.

6.5.2   The rules for buildings completed before 1 March 2011

Part 2, Schedule 10 (as it was before the changes made by the Value Added Tax (Buildings and Land) Order 2011[78])

Disposal, part disposal or letting

The claw-back provisions apply where:

(1) one or more 'relevant zero-rated supplies' relating to a building (or part of a building) have been made to a person; and

(2) within the period of ten years beginning with the day on which the building is 'completed', the person grants an interest in, right over or licence to occupy:

   (a) the building or any part of it; or

   (b) the building or any part of it including, consisting of or forming part of the part to which the relevant zero-rated supply or supplies related; and

(3) after the grant:

   (a) the whole or any part of the building or of the part to which the grant relates, or

   (b) the whole of the building or of the part to which the grant relates, or any part of it including, consisting of or forming part of the part to which the relevant zero-rated supply or supplies related,

   is not intended for use solely for a 'relevant residential purpose' or a 'relevant charitable purpose'.

In such circumstances, so far as the grant relates to so much of the building as by reason of its intended use gave rise to the relevant zero-rated supply or supplies, and is not intended for use solely for a relevant residential purpose or a relevant charitable purpose after the grant, it is taken to be a

---

[78] SI 2011/86

taxable supply in the course or furtherance of a business which is not zero-rated.

A 'relevant zero-rated supply' means a grant or other supply which relates to a building (or part of a building) intended for use solely for a 'relevant residential purpose' or a 'relevant charitable purpose' and which, as a result of Group 5, Schedule 8 is zero-rated in whole or in part.

Change of use without disposal
The claw-back provisions apply where:
(1) one or more 'relevant zero-rated supplies' relating to a building (or part of a building) have been made to a person; and
(2) within the period of ten years beginning with the day on which the building is 'completed' the person uses:
   (a) the building or any part of it, or
   (b) the building or any part of it including, consisting of or forming part of the part to which the relevant zero-rated supply or supplies related,

   for a purpose which is neither a 'relevant residential purpose' nor a 'relevant charitable purpose'.

In such circumstances, the person's interest in, right over or licence to occupy so much of the building as by reason of its intended use gave rise to the relevant zero-rated supply or supplies, and is used otherwise than for a relevant residential purpose or a relevant charitable purpose, is treated as supplied to the person for the purposes of a business which the person carries on and supplied by the person in the course or furtherance of the business when the person first uses it for a purpose which is neither a relevant residential purpose nor a relevant charitable purpose.

The supply is taken to be a taxable supply which is not zero-rated as a result of Group 5 of Schedule 8. The value of the supply is calculated by the formula:

$$A \times (10 - B) \div 10$$

where

A = the amount that yields an amount of VAT chargeable on it equal to the VAT which would have been chargeable on the relevant zero-rated supply (or, if there was more than one supply, the aggregate amount of the VAT which would have been chargeable on the supplies) had so much of the building not been intended for use solely for a relevant residential purpose or a relevant charitable purpose.

B = the number of whole years since the day the building was completed for which the building or part concerned has been used for a relevant residential purpose or a relevant charitable purpose.

Example[79]

A charity paid £1 million for a new zero-rated building for its non-business use. After two years and seven months it changes the use of the entire building to business use.

The VAT that would have been payable if the initial supply had been standard-rated is

£1m × 20%* = £200,000

The amount due to HMRC is £200,000 × 80% = £160,000.

*17.5% from 1 January 2010 to 3 January 2011; 15% from 1 December 2008 to 31 December 2009.

Consequences of claw-back

The deemed self-supplies are included in taxable turnover when deciding whether VAT registration is required. The VAT due on the deemed self-supply must be accounted for as output tax on the VAT return for the period in which the use is changed. The VAT can be deducted as input tax on the same return to the extent that it relates to any other taxable supplies made. It may be necessary to make subsequent adjustments to the amount of input tax deducted under the capital goods scheme.

---

[79] Taken from VAT Notice 208 'Buildings and construction' (August 2014) paragraph 19.2.1

7 Property Transactions Involving Housing Associations – the Special Rules

In general, the normal VAT rules apply to property transactions involving housing associations but there are special rules for 'relevant housing associations'[1] for the zero-rating of certain conversion services and in relation to the option to tax. These special rules ensure that housing associations are not charged VAT, as, because they mainly make exempt supplies of residential lettings, they cannot usually recover input tax meaning that there would be an additional cost for the provision of social housing.

7.1 Zero-rating of conversions
Items 3 and 4, Group 5, Schedule 8

Zero-rating relief is available for the supply of certain goods and services:
(1) made directly to a 'relevant housing association'
(2) in the course of the conversion of
(3) a 'non-residential building'[2] or a part of such a building into:
    (a) a building or part of a building 'designed as a dwelling[3]' or dwellings; or
    (b) a building or part of a building intended for use solely for a 'relevant residential purpose.[4]

A non-residential building or a non-residential part of a building does not include a garage occupied together with a dwelling.[5]

The conversion of a non-residential building into a building designed as a dwelling or number of dwellings includes the conversion of a non-residential building to a garage, provided that the dwelling and the garage are converted at the same time, and the garage is intended to be occupied with the dwelling or one of the dwellings.[6]

Where the building being converted already contains a residential part, for zero-rating to apply the conversion must either be to a building for use for a

---

[1] For definition of **'relevant housing association'** see **1.2.29** above
[2] **'Non-residential building'** is defined in Note (7)(A), Group 5, Schedule 8 - see **1.2.20**
[3] For when a **building is designed as a dwelling** see **4.3.2** above
[4] For **'use solely for a relevant residential purpose'** see **0** above
[5] Note (8), Group 5, Schedule 8
[6] Note (3), Group 5, Schedule 8

relevant residential purpose or must create an additional dwelling or dwellings.[7]

Where a service supplied in the course of a qualifying conversion is supplied in part in relation to that conversion and in part in relation to other purposes, an apportionment may be made to determine the extent to which it is to be treated as falling within the zero-rating relief.[8]

To the extent that part of a building that is converted is designed as a dwelling or number of dwellings or is used solely for a relevant residential purpose, and part is not, the building is treated as two separate buildings and an apportionment is made where a supply relates to both parts.[9]

Examples of a non-residential conversion are the conversion into housing of:

- a commercial building such as an office, warehouse, shop
- an agricultural building such as a barn
- a disused school or church

The services must be supplied 'in the course of' the conversion. In *CCE v Rannoch School Ltd*[10] the Court of Session considering the same wording ('in the course of' the construction) in Item 2, Group 5, Schedule 8 said that in the course of' referred to services done 'contemporaneously or consecutively' in relation to the construction of the new building and which had a 'substantial connection' with it. This was a question of degree.

Only services which relate to the conversion are eligible for zero-rating. Specifically excluded (and therefore always taxable at the standard rate) are:
(1) the separate supply of architectural, surveying, consultancy or supervisory services.
(2) the hire of goods on their own (e.g. plant and machinery without an operator, scaffolding without erection/dismantling, security fencing and mobile office); and
(3) the private use of goods.

These excluded services are discussed in more detail in **Chapter 0** below.

---

[7] Note (9), Group 5, Schedule 8
[8] Note (11), Group 5, Schedule 8
[9] Note (10)(b), Group 5, Schedule 8
[10] [1993] STC 389

Building materials and certain electrical goods, supplied by the person providing the above services and incorporated into the conversion are also zero-rated.[11]

The supplier of the conversion services should require evidence to satisfy himself that his customer is a relevant housing association, and, before the supply is made, obtain from that housing association the relevant certificate confirming the intended use of the property. The form of the certificate is set out at paragraph 18.1 of VAT Notice 708.[12] Section 62 *VATA* provides for a VAT-geared penalty where an incorrect certificate is given. The defence of reasonable excuse is available.

Subcontractors' services will not be supplied directly to the relevant housing association and will, therefore, not be eligible for zero-rating.

7.2 Claw-back on change of use
Part 2, Schedule 10

Change of use claw-back provisions can apply where zero-rating has been applied to the supply of services of converting a non-residential building into a building intended for use solely for a relevant residential purpose and certain events occur within ten years of the building's completion. These provisions are described at **6.5** above.

7.3 Disapplication of the option to tax
Paragraph 10, Schedule 10

The option to tax has no effect in relation to any grant made to a 'relevant housing association'[13] where the housing association has given the grantor a certificate stating that the land is to be used (after any necessary demolition work) for the construction of a building or buildings intended for use as a dwelling or number of dwellings or solely for a relevant residential purpose. This has the effect that the supply to the housing association remains exempt.

As a housing association normally grants less than a major interest[14] in its housing stock (for example, a weekly or monthly tenancy), its onward supplies are usually exempt with the result that associated input tax recovery is denied. The purpose of disapplication of the option to tax is to

---

[11] For 'building materials' see **10.7.1** below

[12] 'Buildings and construction' (August 2014)

[13] For definition of 'relevant housing association' see **1.2.29** above

[14] For definition of a 'major interest' see **1.2.16** above

ensure that the housing association does not incur irrecoverable VAT on the acquisition of land on which it is going to build a dwelling or dwellings or a building to be used for a relevant residential purpose. The construction works will, in the main, be zero-rated under the normal rules.[15]

The certificate must be provided by before the time when the price for the grant is 'legally fixed'[16] or, if the seller agrees, at any later time before a supply is made to which the option to tax would otherwise apply is made.[17] The certificate must be on Form VAT1614G.[18] Section 62 provides for a VAT-geared penalty where an incorrect certificate is given. The defence of reasonable excuse is available.

Paragraph 33 of Schedule 10 applies Notes (4), (5) and (12) to Group 5 of Schedule 8 in order to determine the meaning of 'use for a relevant residential purpose' for the purposes of paragraph 10 of Schedule 10 save that paragraph 10(4) excludes the application of Note (12). So, 'use for a relevant residential purpose' means[19] use as:

(a) a home or other 'institution' providing residential accommodation for children;

(b) a home or other institution providing residential accommodation with personal care for persons in need of personal care by reason of old age, disablement, past or present dependence on alcohol or drugs or past or present mental disorder;

(c) a hospice;

(d) residential accommodation for students or school pupils;

(e) residential accommodation for members of any of the armed forces;

(f) a monastery, nunnery or similar establishment; or

(g) an institution which is the sole or main residence of at least 90 per cent of its residents, except use as a hospital, prison or similar institution or a hotel, inn or similar establishment,

except use as a hospital, prison or similar institution or an hotel, inn or similar establishment.

---

[15] See **Chapter 10**

[16] See Box C in paragraph 3.6.3 of VAT Notice 742A 'Opting to tax land and buildings' June 2013) which has the force of law by reason of paragraph 10(2)(a) Schedule 10

[17] For **time of supply** see **Chapter 2**

[18] See paragraph 3.6.3 of VAT Notice 742A 'Opting to tax land and buildings' June 2013) which has the force of law by reason of paragraph 10(5) Schedule 10

[19] See discussion at **0** above

Where a number of buildings are constructed at the same time and are intended to be used for a relevant residential purposes they are to be treated as intended for use solely for a relevant residential purpose even if they would not qualify individually. The buildings must be built at the same time and on the same site and must be intended to be used together as a unit solely for a relevant residential purpose[20].

In *Langstane Housing Association Ltd*[21] a housing association acquired property that was subject to the option to tax, and later issued a certificate purporting to disapply the option. The tribunal dismissed the appeal, holding that 'the certificate seeking disapplication of the 'option to tax' cannot be issued retrospectively'.

---

[20] Note (5), Group 5, Schedule 8
[21] (VTD 19111)

VAT AND PROPERTY

8 Reliefs for Protected Buildings

Group 6, Schedule 8[1]

8.1 Introduction

Before 1 October 2012 there were two zero-rates in relation to 'protected buildings'[2], one for supplies of qualifying services and 'building materials' in the course of an 'approved alteration'[3] of such a building, the other for the first grant of a 'major interest'[4] in a substantially reconstructed protected building by a person substantially reconstructing it.

From 1 October 2012 the first relief was abolished by the amendment of Group 6 to remove Items 2 and 3 and changes were made to the second. There are transitional rules in relation to the removal of the first relief. Supplies of services (other than 'excluded services'[5]) and of 'building materials'[6] made in the course of an approved alteration to a protected building, pursuant to a written contract entered into or a relevant consent applied for before 21 March 2012, continue to be zero-rated until 30 September 2015.[7]

Works on protected buildings may be able to benefit from the reduced rate relief considered in **Chapter 10**. A grant is available to defray the VAT charge on certain repairs to and maintenance of listed buildings that are used as places of worship.[8]

8.2 Zero-rating for substantially reconstructed protected buildings from 1 October 2012

Item 1, Group 6, Schedule 8

The first grant by a person 'substantially reconstructing' a protected building of a 'major interest' in, or in any part of, the building or its site is zero-rated.

From 1 October 2012 to be a substantial reconstruction the reconstructed building must incorporate no more of the original building before the

---

[1] See **1.2.25** for definition of '**protected building**'
[2] Group 6, Schedule 8
[3] See **1.2.1** for the meaning of '**approved alteration**'
[4] See **1.2.16** for the meaning of '**major interest**'
[5] See **10.3.3** for the meaning of '**excluded services**'
[6] See **10.7.1** for meaning of '**building materials**'
[7] Paragraph 7 Schedule 26 *FA 2012*
[8] Details available at www.lpwscheme.org.uk

reconstruction began than the external walls, together with other external features of architectural or historic interest.

Under transitional arrangements[9], the first grant of a major interest in a substantially reconstructed protected building continues to be zero-rated[10] until 30 September 2015 where:

(1) at least three-fifths of the work (measured by reference to cost) would, if supplied by a taxable person, be relevant supplies under the transitional arrangements for approved alterations;[11] or

(2) at least ten per cent of the reconstruction (measured by reference to cost) was completed before 21 March 2012 and at least three-fifths of the work would, if supplied by a taxable person, be relevant supplies under the transitional arrangements for approved alterations but for the requirement for a written contract to have been entered into or relevant consent to have been applied for before 21 March 2012.

---

[9] Paragraph 7(5) Schedule 26 FA 2012

[10] Note (4), Group 6, Schedule 8 as it was before its amendment by paragraph 3, Schedule 26, *FA 2012*

[11] Outlined in **8.1**

9 Supplies of Commercial Property and the Option to Tax

For the purposes of this book a supply of commercial property is any supply of an interest in or right over land other than:

- a supply falling within Items (a) to (n), Group1, Schedule 9;[1] or
- a supply falling within Group 5, Schedule 8.[2]

A 'commercial building' is a building which is neither designed as a dwelling[3] or number of dwellings nor intended for use solely for a relevant residential purpose[4] or a relevant charitable purpose.[5] 'Commercial building' is not a term which is used in the VAT legislation.

The freehold sale of a new or uncompleted commercial building is subject to VAT at the standard rate.[6] Any other supply of commercial property, such as the leasing or letting of a new commercial building, is exempt from VAT[7] subject to the effect of the option to tax which can change the VAT liability of the supply from exempt to standard rated.

The rest of this chapter looks at the option to tax in detail.

9.1 Introduction to the option to tax

In the 1980s the European Commission took action against the UK over its policy of allowing zero-rate relief on the construction of commercial buildings. On 21 June 1988, the European Court gave its decision in the infraction proceedings[8] and agreed with the Commission that the UK's zero-rate relief for construction of commercial buildings was not permissible under EU law.

As a result VAT had to be charged on the construction costs of new commercial properties. To ameliorate the effect of the additional VAT cost on businesses the UK also introduced the option to tax. The option to tax required the business to charge VAT on the supplies made of the property

---

[1] These supplies are always taxable at the standard rate - see **3.2.14** above

[2] These supplies are zero-rated – see **Chapters 0** and **1**

[3] For the meaning of '**dwelling**' see **1.2.7**

[4] For the meaning of '**relevant residential purpose**' see **1.2.29** above

[5] For the meaning of '**relevant charitable purpose**' see **1.2.28** above

[6] Item 1(a)(i) and (ii), Group 1, Schedule 9

[7] Section 31 and Item 1, Group 1, Schedule 9

[8] In *EC Commission v United Kingdom* (Case C-416/85) [1988] STC 456 (ECJ)

but enabled that business to recover the VAT it had incurred on acquisition or construction.

The option to tax will, subject to the exceptions set out below, remove a supply of the land and/or building over which it has been exercised from the scope of the exemption in Group 1, Schedule 9. In other words, it allows a person to tax certain supplies which would otherwise be exempt. A person does not need to own the land in order to opt to tax it.[9]

The option to tax is a form of relief as its exercise prevents irrecoverable input tax being incurred by the person making the supply. Changing the VAT liability of a supply from exempt to taxable at the standard rate allows VAT charged to the supplier to be recovered in most cases[10]. Where VAT is chargeable on a property transaction as a result of the exercise of the option to tax it will increase the chargeable consideration for stamp duty land tax purposes.

Some of the issues to consider when deciding whether to exercise the option to tax are:

- What VAT is it expected will become recoverable?
- If there are existing tenants, can VAT be added to the rent under the terms of the lease or will the rent be inclusive of VAT?
- What effect will an exercise of the option to tax have on the marketability of the property in the future?

The option to tax is also referred to as the 'election to waive' exemption. The terms are interchangeable. The EU vires for the option to tax is found in article 137.1(b)-(d) of the VAT Directive which provides that Member States 'may allow taxable persons a right of option for taxation' in respect of:

- the supply of a building or of parts thereof, and of the land on which the building stands, other than the supply the supply, before first occupation, of a building or parts of a building and of the land on which the building stands;
- the supply of land which has not been built on other than the supply of building land; and
- the leasing or letting of immovable property.

Article 12.3 provides that 'building land' means 'any unimproved or improved land defined as such by the Member States'. A Member State introducing an option may restrict its scope.

---

[9] This can be important where property is bought at auction – see discussion at **9.16**
[10] See **9.13** below

A word of warning:
For supplies made on or after 1 June 2008, the provisions relating to the option to tax in Schedule 10 *VATA* were completely rewritten.[11] There have also been numerous changes in the rules since then.

9.2 Overview of the main points about the option to tax

(1) The option is unilateral, and personal to the person exercising it. It does not normally bind anyone else, although there are special rules for members of VAT groups.

(2) There are rules about the extent of the option. For example, it is not possible to opt on only part of a building.

(3) Some types of land or buildings, such as dwellings, are not affected by the option.

(4) The exercise of the option cannot be retrospective and needs to be notified to HMRC within 30 days. The time limit for notifying an option to tax may be different when it relates to an option to tax that has to be exercised by a purchaser of land for which TOGC treatment is sought.

(5) The exercise of the option may require HMRC's prior permission if the person opting has previously made exempt supplies in relation to the land.

(6) The option is irrevocable, subject to some limited exceptions.

(7) Where an existing lease is affected by the exercise of an option to tax, the rent (and any service charge) will become subject to VAT and the landlord can usually add VAT to the rent.

(8) The exercise of an option can sometimes allow recovery of past input tax.

(9) There are anti-avoidance rules which may be relevant where an anticipated occupier of opted property is not fully taxable, and regardless of whether avoidance is involved.

9.3 The UK legislation relating to the option to tax

The relevant UK provisions are in Part 1, Schedule 10 and the scheme of the legislation is as follows:

(1) The effect of the option to tax is dealt with in paragraph 2 of Schedule 10 (exempt supplies become taxable).

---

[11] Subject to transitional provisions and savings in Schedule 2 Value Added Tax (Buildings and Land) Order 2008 (SI/2008/1146)

(2) 'Grants'[12] are excluded from the effect of paragraph 2 of Schedule 10 by:
- paragraph 5 (buildings designed or adapted, and intended for use, as dwellings etc),
- paragraph 6 (conversion of buildings for use as dwelling etc)
- paragraph 7 (charities)
- paragraph 8 (residential caravans)
- paragraph 9 (residential houseboats)
- paragraph 10 (relevant housing associations)
- paragraph 11 (DIY builders)

(3) Paragraphs 12 to 17 (anti-avoidance) provide for certain supplies resulting from a grant to be excluded from the effect of paragraph 2.

(4) Paragraphs 18 to 30 of Schedule 10 deal with:
- the scope of the option to tax
- the day from which the option to tax has effect
- notification requirements
- elections to opt to tax land which is subsequently acquired (real estate elections)
- revocation of an option
- exclusion of new buildings on opted land
- requirement for prior permission in the case of exempt grants made before the exercise of an option to tax

(5) Paragraphs 31 to 34 of Schedule 10 deal with definitions and supplementary matters.

9.4   Effect of the option to tax

Paragraph 2, Schedule 10

Where a person has exercised the option to tax in relation to any land[13], and:
(1) a 'grant' is made in relation to the land
(2) at a time when the option has effect
(3) by the person who has exercised that option or by a 'relevant associate'[14] of that person,

that grant is taken out of the scope of the exemption in Group 1, Schedule 9 and therefore becomes taxable at the standard rate. Any supplies which are zero-rated would not fall into Group 1, Schedule 9 (as zero-rating takes

---

[12] For the meaning of '**grant**' see **1.2.11** above
[13] See 'Scope of the option to tax' at **9.5** below
[14] Defined in paragraph 3, Schedule 10 – see **9.13.1** below

priority over exemption[15]) and so are unaffected. The option to tax also has no effect in relation to certain supplies[16] and it is disapplied by anti-avoidance provisions in some instances.[17] In those cases the supplies remain exempt.

In *Southport Flower Show Ltd*[18] a registered charity which organised a flower show reclaimed the input tax incurred in relation to it. HMRC rejected the claim on the basis that the holding of the flower show was an exempt supply falling within Item 1, Group 12, Schedule 9 (fund-raising events by charities). The charity appealed, contending that it should be permitted to reclaim input tax because it had opted to tax the relevant land on which the flower show was held. The tribunal rejected this contention and dismissed the charity's appeal on the basis that the exercise of the option to tax does not exclude exemption by virtue of Group 12, Schedule 9, only Group 1.

The option continues until revoked[19] and affects all future supplies made in relation to that property which would otherwise be exempt. It is not possible, for example, to opt to tax rents but then not tax a subsequent sale of the property.

A person may be required to register for VAT as a result of the exercise of the option to tax. Form VAT 5L should be used in these circumstances in addition to Form VAT 1 (application for registration).

It is advisable when acquiring an interest in land over which the option to tax is regarded by the seller as having effect to obtain a copy of the seller's notification of the exercise of the option to tax to HMRC and HMRC's acknowledgment of the notification as only VAT which is properly charged can be recovered as input tax. The same applies to VAT charged on rent. It may also be necessary to seek confirmation that the option to tax has not been revoked under any of the provisions discussed at **9.9** below.

9.4.1 Effect of the option on the consideration for a supply

The normal tax point rules apply to supplies of land or buildings.[20] In a tenanted building, a tax point might not occur until payment is received. In these circumstances, where a business opts to tax after rent becomes due

---

[15] By reason of section 30(1) VATA
[16] By paragraphs 5 to 11, Schedule 10 - see **9.12.** below
[17] In paragraphs 12 to 17, Schedule 10 – see **9.14** below
[18] [2012] UKFTT 244 (TC)
[19] For **revocation** see **9.9** below
[20] These rules are set out in **2.2** above

but before it is paid, it must account for output tax on the rental receipt. This is the case even if the payment covers a period before the option to tax took effect.

Section 89 VATA provides as follows:

'89 *Adjustments of contracts on changes in VAT.*

(1) Where, after the making of a contract for the supply of goods or services and before the goods or services are supplied, there is a change in the VAT charged on the supply, then, unless the contract otherwise provided, there shall be added to or deducted from the consideration for the supply an amount equal to the change.

(2) Subsection (1) above shall apply in relation to a tenancy or lease as it applies in relation to a contract except that a term of a tenancy or lease shall not be taken to provide that the rule contained in that subsection is not to apply in the case of the tenancy or lease if the term does not specifically refer to VAT or this section.

(3) References in this section to a change in the VAT charged on a supply include references to a change to or from no VAT being charged on the supply (including a change attributable to the making of an election under paragraph 2 of Schedule 10).'

This means that where the option to tax is exercised after exchange of contracts (or after agreement for lease) and the terms of that contract (or the agreement for lease) do not either specifically exclude section 89 or state that the agreed consideration is inclusive of any VAT charge arising from the exercise of the option to tax the consideration will be increased by statute to include VAT.

In the case of a lease, where the option is exercised during the term section 89 will apply to payments of rent where the tax point[21] falls after exercise. If an election has been made but, under the terms of the contract, VAT cannot be added, any sum received should be treated as VAT-inclusive and the VAT element calculated by multiplying the sum received by the appropriate VAT fraction.

There is no requirement on the lessor to notify the tenant that he has opted unless the lease includes such a provision. However, it is advisable to inform any tenant of the decision to opt at the earliest opportunity so that

---

[21] For **tax points under leases** see **2.2.2** above

they may safeguard their right to recover input tax by opting to tax, if they should so wish.

Section 89 applies where an election is 'made' under paragraph 2 of Schedule 10. It is not clear from this whether it will apply to supplies made during the option notification period.[22]

9.4.2 Supplies arising from earlier grants

If an option to tax is exercised after the time of a 'grant'[23] relating to land, any supplies arising from that grant which are made after the option takes effect are treated as if the grant had been made after the option had been exercised and so are brought within the effect of the option.[24]

9.5 Scope of the option to tax[25]
Paragraph 18, Schedule 10

The option to tax has effect in relation to 'the particular land specified in the option.'[26] A part of a land holding can be identified. It is not necessary to own an interest in the land to exercise the option to tax in relation to it. The fact that the words 'or of a description specified' in paragraph 3(2) of Schedule 10 as it stood before rewriting in 2008 were not carried over to the rewritten Schedule 10 does not affect the continued operation of an option to tax any land which was made before 1 June 2008 and which specified a description of land.[27]

The legislation provides that where the option is exercised in relation to a building or part of a building it has effect in relation to the whole of the building and 'all the land within its cartilage.'[28] For this reason it is not possible to opt to tax part of a building but where the interest of the person opting[29] extends to only part of the building. For example, where he has a lease of certain floors and no interest in the others, the option can only have effect in relation to any interest he owns after he has opted to tax the building or part of the building.

---

[22] See **9.6.2** below

[23] For meaning of '**grant**' see **1.2.11** above

[24] Paragraph 30, Schedule 10

[25] See also **9.10** below '**Real estate elections**'

[26] Paragraph 18(1), Schedule 10

[27] Schedule 2, Value Added Tax Buildings and Land Order 2008 (SI.2008/1146)

[28] Paragraph 18(2), Schedule 10

[29] Including the interest of any 'relevant associate' (defined in paragraph 3, Schedule 10 – see **9.13.1.**)

If the building is demolished or destroyed then the option will still apply to the land on which the building stood and, subject to the right to exclude a new building[30] discussed below, any future buildings that are constructed.

'Curtilage' is not defined in Part 1, Schedule 10. In *Methuen-Campbell v Walters*[31] the Court of Appeal remarked that whether land fell within the curtilage of other land was a question of fact:

> 'The word "curtilage" is defined in the Oxford English Dictionary as "a small court, yard, or piece of ground attached to a dwelling-house and forming one enclosure with it".
>
> Stroud's Judicial Dictionary suggests that it may be wider than that. We have looked at some of the cases cited in Stroud, but I do not think they afford us any assistance. What is within the curtilage is a question of fact in each case, and for myself I cannot feel that this comparatively extensive piece of pasture ought to be so regarded, particularly where, as here, it was clearly divided off physically from the house and garden right from the start and certainly at all material times[32].'

Where the option is exercised in relation to any land but is not exercised by reference to a building or part of a building it will apply to that land together with any existing building on that land as well as any building constructed on the land after the option is exercised[33]. However, the person opting can exclude a new building from the effect of the option by notifying HMRC to that effect under paragraph 27, Schedule 10 (see below).

There is no such thing as an 'opted building'. Each person with an interest in a property makes his own decision as to whether opting in respect of it is worthwhile. So a landlord may have opted to tax a property, and will charge VAT on the rent to his tenant, but the tenant might decide not to opt and will not charge VAT on the rent to his sub-tenant.

Meaning of 'building'
Paragraphs 18(4) to (7), Schedule 10

Buildings linked internally or by a covered walkway and complexes consisting of a number of units grouped around a fully enclosed concourse

---

[30] In paragraph 27, Schedule 10
[31] [1979] 1 All ER 606
[32] Ibid. per Lord Goff LJ at page 616
[33] Paragraph 18(3), Schedule 10

are treated as a single building.[34] However, where the internal link is created or the covered walkway starts to be constructed after the buildings are completed the linkage is disregarded.[35] A 'covered walkway' does not include a covered walkway to which the general public has access.[36]

'Building' includes and enlarged or extended building, an annexe to a building, and a planned building.[37]

Exclusion of new building from the effect of an option
Paragraph 27, Schedule 10

A new building and all the land within its curtilage can be excluded from the effect of an existing option in the following circumstances[38]:

(1) a person has opted to tax land;
(2) subsequently, the construction of a new building on that land begins;
(3) no land within the curtilage of the new building is within the curtilage of an existing building;
(4) notification of exclusion is given to HMRC.

Notification of exclusion can only be given when construction begins. Construction begins for this purpose when the building progresses above ground level[39].

Notification must be given before the end of the period of 30 days beginning with the day on which it is to have effect or such longer period as HMRC may allow in a particular case[40]. The form of notification of exclusion of a new building is specified in paragraph 2.7.5 of VAT Notice 742A 'Opting to tax land and buildings' (June 2013) which has the force of law[41] and is by completing and submitting Form VAT1614F.

The exclusion (which is permanent) has effect from the earliest of the following times:[42]

---

[34] Paragraph 18(4), Schedule 10
[35] Paragraph 18(5), Schedule 10
[36] Paragraph 18(7), Schedule 10
[37] Paragraph 18(6), Schedule 10
[38] Paragraphs 27(1) and (2), Schedule 10
[39] Paragraph 2.7.2 Box A of VAT Notice 742A 'Opting to tax land and buildings' (June 2013) (Box A is given the force of law by paragraph 27(7), Schedule 10)
[40] See paragraph 20(2), Schedule 10
[41] By reason of paragraph 27(4)(a), Schedule 10
[42] Paragraph 27(3), Schedule 10

(1) the time when a 'grant'[43] of an interest in, or in any part of, the new building is first made;

(2) the time when the new building, or any part of it, is first used; or

(3) the time when the new building is completed.

The extended definition of 'building' in paragraphs 18(4) to 18(6), Schedule 10 set out in **9.5** above also applies here.[44]

For the purposes of paragraph 27, 'construction of a building' is to be read in accordance with Notes (16) to (18) of Group 5 to Schedule 8 but without regard to Notes (17) or (18)(b) which relate to annexes to be used solely for relevant charitable purposes and buildings were only a façade is retained respectively.[45]

Other exclusions from effect of the option to tax

'Grants' are excluded from the effect of paragraph 2 of Schedule 10 by:

- paragraph 5 (buildings designed or adapted, and intended for use, as dwellings etc);
- paragraph 6 (conversion of buildings for use as dwelling etc);
- paragraph 7 (charities);
- paragraph 8 (residential caravans);
- paragraph 9 (residential houseboats);
- paragraph 10 (relevant housing associations); and
- paragraph 11 (DIY builders)

Each of these exclusions is dealt with in section **9.12** below. The exclusion may affect input tax recovery in relation to these supplies.

Scope of the option to tax: a word of warning

The rules relating to the scope of the option to tax have changed over the years. For example, before 1 March 1995, if the option to tax was exercised in relation to agricultural land it had effect in relation to all agricultural land that touched or bordered that land which was in the same ownership. The rules applying to linked buildings have also changed on several occasions and care should be taken to ensure that the legislation in force at the relevant time is identified and applied.

---

[43] For the meaning of '**grant**' see **1.2.11** above
[44] In paragraphs 18(4) to (6), Schedule 10
[45] Paragraphs 27(6) and 33, Schedule 10

9.6 Opting to tax – the two-stage process

Opting to tax is now a two-stage process:

(1) the exercise of the option to tax; and

(2) timely notification of the exercise to HMRC.

The obligation to notify was introduced from 1 March 1995.[46] An option made before 1 March 1995 and having effect before that day continues to have effect notwithstanding that it has not been notified to HMRC.[47]

It is essential that the option to tax is exercised before any exempt supplies of the land or building over which it will have effect are made otherwise permission to opt is required[48]. It is also important to opt (and notify) at the right time important where a property is being acquired for which TOGC treatment is sought.[49]

It is advisable when acquiring an interest in land over which the option to tax is regarded by the seller as having effect to obtain a copy of the seller's notification of the exercise of the option to tax to HMRC and HMRC's acknowledgment of the notification as only VAT which is properly charged can be recovered as input tax. The same applies to VAT charged on rent. It may also be necessary to seek confirmation that the option to tax has not been revoked under any of the provisions discussed at **9.9** below.

9.6.1 Exercise of the option to tax

The option to tax must be exercised by a person who has the necessary authority in the business to take the decision[50]. It can be useful to record a decision to opt, perhaps in board minutes, but there is no requirement to do so, and usually the notification and HMRC's acknowledgment of it provide the only evidence for the option. HMRC's permission may, however, be needed before opting where there have been previous exempt supplies of the property.[51]

---

[46] By article 4, Value Added Tax (Buildings and Land) Order 1995 (SI 1995/279)

[47] By reason of the transitional provisions in Schedule 2, Value Added Tax (Buildings and Land) Order 2008 (SI 2008/1146)

[48] See **9.11** below

[49] For **TOGCs** see **Chapter 1**

[50] See *Hammersmith and West London College* (VTD 17540) where the College's assistant principal and its finance director were found to have the necessary authority to opt to tax on behalf of the College

[51] For when permission is needed before opting see **9.11**

Any person can opt to tax any property, including property they do not own. This allows those buying property at auction to opt to tax before the auction and before they acquire an interest in the property which may be advisable in certain circumstances.[52]

Where there are both legal and beneficial owners of a property it is normally the beneficial owner who can exercise the option to tax as he will be making the supply.[53] Where the beneficiaries are numerous, such as is the case with unit trusts and pension funds, the person making the supply is the trustee who holds the legal interest and receives the immediate benefit of the consideration and so it will be the trustee who opts. [54]

Where property is in joint ownership, all beneficial owners must exercise the option to tax.[55] HMRC would register the joint owners as a partnership for VAT purposes.[56]

9.6.2   Notification of the exercise of the option to tax
Paragraph 20, Schedule 10

For the option to be effective the exercise of it has to be notified in writing to HMRC within the appropriate time limit. The notification must be 'given' within 30 days of the date of exercise or of such later date as HMRC allow in a particular case. Notification is not necessary where an application for prior permission is successfully made under paragraph 29(3), Schedule 10.[57] Paragraph 22(10) sets out certain additional requirements for notifying separate options to tax resulting from the conversion of an option to tax existing at the time a real estate election has been made.[58]

The status of supplies made between any period between opting and notifying while the time limit for notification is still running is not clear.

Notification can be made using Form VAT1614A (which can now be completed and submitted online) or by letter containing all the information

---

[52] See discussion at **9.16** below

[53] See paragraph 40, Schedule 10

[54] HMRC's interpretation of paragraph 40, Schedule 10 - see paragraph 7.2 VAT Notice 742A 'Opting to tax buildings and land' (June 2013)

[55] See paragraph 7.3 VAT Notice 742A 'Opting to tax buildings and land' (June 2013)

[56] See **3.5** above

[57] Paragraph 20(4), Schedule 10

[58] See **9.10.4** below

requested on that form[59] and where the business is already VAT-registered should be sent to:

HMRC Option to Tax National Unit
Cotton House,
7 Cochrane Street,
Glasgow
G1 41GY

Fax 0141 555 3367

Alternatively a scanned copy can be emailed to:

optiontotaxnationalunit@hmrc.gsi.gov.uk.

Where a business becomes liable to be registered for VAT purposes as a result of the option to tax, the application to register for VAT *and* the notification of the option to tax should be submitted together to the appropriate VAT registration unit.

Where the option covers land, it is advisable to provide a detailed plan and the Land Registry title number to identify the land. The importance of specifying the land to which an option applies was illustrated in *Exeter Estates Ltd.*[60] In 2007 a company acquired a large site adjoining a dual carriageway. The site included a petrol station, and several warehouses and offices. The company advised HMRC that it had opted to tax the site. In 2011 HMRC formed the opinion that the company had failed to account for VAT on rental income from several buildings which it had opted to tax, and issued an assessment. The company appealed, contending that in 2007, four weeks after its initial letter to HMRC, it had sent a further letter stating 'option to tax to be limited to area etched red on enclosed plan, excluding buildings etched blue'.

The First-tier Tribunal accepted the company's evidence and allowed its appeal. Judge Gort found that 'it was quite clearly not (the company's) intention to opt to tax the buildings outlined in blue on the Land Registry document' and that it was more likely that the letter had been lost by the Royal Mail or by HMRC than that it was never posted.

---

[59] Paragraph 20(3)(a), Schedule 10 gives HMRC power to specify the form in which a notification must be made and the information it must contain but they have not done so – Form VAT1614A is not compulsory

[60] [2013] UKFTT 218 (TC)

HMRC now accept that where the notification is posted on day 30, the notification is in time.[61] Proof of postage should be retained in case there is a dispute about the date of notification. HMRC should be asked to acknowledge the notification and copies of the notification letter and of HMRC acknowledgement should be retained. These letters will provide evidence that the option has been exercised and has effect.

HMRC will normally acknowledge receipt of notification within 15 working days but this is not necessary for the option to tax to have legal effect and a business should not delay charging VAT just because it has not received acknowledgement.

An appropriate person should sign the notification. Following the decision in *Blythe Limited Partnership*[62] HMRC issued guidance[63] on who should notify the exercise of an option to tax and this is summarised below:

(1) In most cases notification will be made by the sole proprietor, one or more partners (or trustees), a director or an authorised administrator. If a business authorises a third party to notify an option on its behalf, HMRC require confirmation that the third party is authorised to do so. They would also like to be notified if the business withdraws that authority. Other more unusual situations are as follows.

(2) Beneficial owners:

Where there is a beneficial owner and a legal owner of land or buildings (e.g. a bare trust), for VAT purposes it is the beneficial owner who is making the supply of the land or building and who should opt to tax. Where, however, there are numerous beneficiaries (e.g. unit trusts and pension funds) the person making the supply is the trustee who holds the legal interest and receives the immediate benefit of the consideration.

(3) Joint owners should together notify a single option to tax if they want supplies of the jointly-owned land or building to be standard-rated.

(4) Limited partnerships:

The general partner(s) should opt to tax. Where title to the land or building is held jointly in the names of the general partner(s) and the limited partner(s), only the titleholders can make any supplies of that

---

[61] *Chalegrove Properties Limited* [2001] VATDR 316 (VTD 17151)

[62] (VTD 16011)

[63] Paragraphs 7.1-75, VAT Notice 742A, 'Opting to tax buildings and land' (June 2013)

land or building together. That suggests that the limited partner(s) is/are involved in the management and running of the partnership and, as such, HMRC treat them as general partners. If the partnership decides to opt to tax, one or more of the partners should sign the notification.

(5) Limited liability partnerships:

A limited liability partnership is a corporate body and is liable to register for VAT, subject to the normal registration rules. If the partnership decides to opt to tax, one or more members must sign the notification.

Late notification

It is not possible to backdate the exercise of an option to tax. Where the option to tax has been exercised but not notified, it may be possible to notify HMRC outside the 30 day time limit.

HMRC in paragraph 4.2.1 of VAT Notice 742A[64] indicate that that they will usually exercise their discretion to accept late notification where documentary evidence that the option to tax has been exercised is provided. This could be in the form of board minutes, minutes of a management meeting or correspondence referring to the decision. Where this evidence is not available HMRC will accept a statement from the 'responsible person' that they had opted to tax but failed to notify, plus evidence that output tax has been charged on any supplies made and any input tax reclaimed is consistent with the option having been exercised and that all relevant facts have been given.

9.6.3   Exercise and notification – two cases

In *Marlow Gardner & Cooke Ltd Directors' Pension Scheme v HMRC*[65] a company had purchased a property in September 1998 and in October 1998 it had let part of the building. The company charged VAT on the rent, and accounted for this to HMRC, although it did not formally notify HMRC that it had opted to tax the property. In January 2004 the company sold the property to an unrelated buyer, and charged VAT on the sale. The buyer disputed the VAT charge, and in February 2004 the company wrote to HMRC and notified them that it had opted to tax the property in October 1998 when it charged VAT on the rent. HMRC accepted the late notification, and, unusually, the buyer appealed. The tribunal dismissed the appeal,

---

[64] 'Opting to tax buildings and land' (June 2013)
[65] [2006] STC 2014

holding that since the company could not charge VAT on the rent except by opting to tax the property, its initial demand for VAT on the rent had been the exercise of the option to tax its supplies in relation to the property. The Chancery Division upheld the tribunal decision commenting that 'there is nothing ... which renders ineffective a notification of election made after the disposal of the land in question.'

In *Honduras Wharf Ltd*[66] a property development company owned a property called Pace House. On 17 August 2005 its VAT consultants sent HMRC notification of an option to tax for Pace House, effective from 20 July 2005. The notification had been prepared by the VAT consultants but signed by the company's sole director. After the option had been exercised, the company charged VAT on the rent paid by the tenant at Pace House and reclaimed the related input tax. In 2009 the company sold Pace House. HMRC assessed the company to VAT on the sale. The company appealed, arguing that VAT was not payable on the sale because no valid option to tax had been made. The company contended that making a valid option to tax was a two part process, there had to be an intention to opt and the option had to be made in writing, and in this case there was no intention on the company's part to make the option to tax.

The tribunal said that the onus was on the company to demonstrate, despite the documentary evidence and the fact that VAT was subsequently charged on rents on Pace House and input tax reclaimed, that this did not reflect the company's intention at the time when the election was made. It was clear, on the evidence provided, that the company, acting through its sole director, had a positive intention to make the option to tax on Pace House at the time the option was made in 2005. The company's appeal was dismissed.

9.7 Day from which the option takes effect

Paragraph 19 Schedule 10

Subject to the requirement to notify[67] and the requirement in certain cases for prior permission from HMRC,[68] an option to tax has effect from the start of the day of exercise or the start of any later day specified in the option.

---

[66] [2014] UKFTT 581 (TC)

[67] **Under paragraph 20, Schedule 10 - see 0**

[68] Under paragraph 28(2), Schedule 10 where there has been a prior exempt grant- see **9.11**

Where an option is revoked during the cooling-off period[69] it is treated as if it had never been exercised.

9.8 Duration of option to tax

The option lasts until it is revoked, either during the three month cooling-off period or after 20 years.[70] This is the case even if the person exercising the option to tax has no interest in the land or building in question.

Deregistration will not end the option to tax. There is also a deemed supply of goods which are business assets on deregistration.[71]

9.9 Revocation of the option to tax[72]

Paragraphs 23 to 26, Schedule 10

Once made, the option to tax can be revoked in the following three circumstances:

(1) during a six-month 'cooling-off' period by the person who made it;
(2) automatically where no interest has been held in the property for over six years; and
(3) by the person who made it where more than 20 years has lapsed since it first had effect.

Each of these is discussed below.

The special rules for revocation of a real estate election are covered in **9.10.7** below. The rules in paragraph 22 of Schedule 10 (revocation of earlier option to tax by a real estate election) are considered at **9.10.3** below.

9.9.1 Revocation of an option to tax during the cooling-off period

Paragraph 23, Schedule 10

An option to tax can be revoked with effect from the day on which it was exercised provided that all of the following conditions are satisfied:

(1) The time that has elapsed since the day on which the option had effect is less than six months.
(2) No VAT has become chargeable as a result of the option.

---

[69] See **9.9.1** below

[70] For **revocation of the option to tax** see **9.9** below – the real estate election itself can only be revoked by HMRC in the circumstances set out in **9.10.7**

[71] Paragraph 8, Schedule 4 – there will be no charge if no input tax has been claimed on the supply of those goods or any of the conditions in paragraph 8(1) are fulfilled

[72] For **revocation of a real estate election** see **9.10.7** above

(3) Since the option had effect, no grant in relation to the land has been made which is treated as neither a supply of goods nor a supply of services because the supply is a supply of the assets of a business:

    (a) by the person exercising the option to a person to whom the business (or part of it) is transferred as a going concern[73]; or

    (b) by a person to the person exercising the option to whom the business (or part of it) is so transferred.

(4) Notification of the revocation is given to HMRC on Form VAT1614C and contains the information requested on that form.

(5) Any further conditions set out by HMRC in a notice and falling within the powers given to them by paragraph 23(4) of Schedule 10 are satisfied. HMRC have specified (in Box F in paragraph 8.1.2 of VAT Notice 742A[74]) that either prior permission for the revocation must be sought from them during the six month cooling-off period, or one of the following conditions must be met:

    (a) neither the person exercising the option nor any 'relevant associate'[75] has recovered input tax attributable to supplies which, if made at the time the option has effect, would be taxable supplies by virtue of that option;

    (b) by virtue of the revocation, the person exercising the option and all relevant associates would be liable to account to HMRC for all input tax attributable to supplies which, if made at the time the option has effect, would be taxable supplies by virtue of that option which they have recovered; or

    (c) input tax attributable to supplies which, if made at the time the option has effect, would be taxable supplies by virtue of that option has been recovered entirely on one capital item and amounts to less than 20 per cent of the total input tax incurred on that item.

The cooling-off period revocation provisions do not apply to the options to tax resulting from the conversion of an existing option to tax into several separate options to tax at the time a real estate election is made.[76]

---

[73] See **Chapter 1** for **transfer of a business as a going concern**

[74] 'Opting to tax buildings and land' (June 2013)

[75] For the meaning of **'relevant associate'** see **9.13.1** below

[76] Paragraphs 22(6)-(10), Schedule 10 - see **9.10.4** below

9.9.2 Automatic revocation of option to tax where no interest has been held for more than six years
Paragraph 24, Schedule 10

Subject to the anti-avoidance provisions in paragraph 26 of Schedule 10 (discussed below) an option to tax exercised by any person in relation to any building or land is treated as revoked if that person does not have a 'relevant interest in the building or land' throughout any continuous period of six years beginning at any time after the option has effect. The option to tax is treated as revoked from the end of that period.

'Relevant interest in the building or land' means an interest in, right over or licence to occupy the building or land (or any part of it).[77]

Revocation: anti-avoidance provisions
Paragraph 26, Schedule 10

The revocation provisions in paragraph 24 of Schedule 10 do not apply where any of conditions A, B and C below is met.

Condition A is that the person who has exercised the option to tax or a 'relevant associate' of that person disposes of a 'relevant interest' in the land or building before the 'relevant time' and at the relevant time, a supply is yet to take place or would be yet to take place in relation to that prior disposal of the building or land if one or more conditions were met (for example, overage).

Condition B is that the person who exercised the option was treated as a member of a VAT group[78] at any time before the 'relevant time' and before the relevant time a 'relevant associate' of that person had ceased to be treated as a member of a VAT group, without, at the time they ceased to be so treated, meeting the following conditions:
(1) the relevant associate had no 'relevant interest' in the building or land;
(2) where a relevant interest had been held by the relevant associate and previously disposed of, no supply is yet to take place or would be yet to take place in relation to that prior disposal of the building or land if one or more conditions were met (for example, overage); and
(3) the relevant associate was not connected with any person who has a relevant interest in the property where that person is the person exercising the option or another relevant associate of the person exercising the option.

---

[77] Paragraph 24(3), Schedule 10
[78] Under section 43A to 43D

Condition C is that the person who exercised the option in relation to the building or land was a body corporate and, at the 'relevant time' a 'relevant associate' of that person is treated as a member of the same group as that person and holds a 'relevant interest' in the building or land or has held such an interest at any time within the previous six years.

'Relevant associate' is defined in section **9.13.1**.

'Relevant interest' means[79] an interest in, right over or licence to occupy the building or land or any part of it.

'Relevant time' means[80] the time from which the option to tax under consideration would be treated as revoked but for the provisions of paragraph 26.

9.9.3 Revocation of option where more than 20 years have lapsed since it first had effect

Paragraph 25, Schedule 10

An option to tax any land is revocable after it has had effect for more than 20 years provided that, at the time when the option is to be revoked, either the revocation conditions specified by HMRC are met or prior permission has been obtained from HMRC.

In deciding whether or not to grant permission, HMRC will give particular consideration to whether or not the person exercising the option or a third party has received a VAT benefit as a result of his actions.

Once HMRC have granted permission, the revocation will have effect from the day permission is granted, or such earlier or later day or time specified in their permission[81]. They may specify a time by reference to the happening of a particular event or meeting of a condition, e.g. they may specify that revocation will take effect after the sale of a property has been completed[82]. HMRC can only specify an earlier day if:[83]

(1) the person exercising the option has purported to give notification of the revocation;

(2) the conditions for revocation are not met; and

(3) HMRC consider that the grounds on which the conditions are not met are insignificant.

---

[79] Paragraph 26(7) Schedule 10
[80] Paragraph 26(7) Schedule 10
[81] Paragraph 25(6), Schedule 10
[82] Paragraph 25(8), Schedule 10
[83] Paragraph 25(7), Schedule 10

In granting permission HMRC may specify further conditions subject to which the permission is given. If any of these conditions are subsequently broken, they may treat the revocation as if it had not been made[84].

Where the revocation conditions are met, the revocation nevertheless does not have effect unless notification of the revocation is given to HMRC by completing Form VAT1614J. Application for permission to revoke an option after 20 years is also made by completing Form VAT1614J. Where permission is sought and given separate notification is not required.

There is power in paragraph 25(4) of Schedule 10 for HMRC to treat an option as validly revoked under these provisions where notification of revocation is given on the basis that the revocation conditions are fulfilled but it is subsequently discovered that they were not.

The revocation conditions

The conditions specified by HMRC are set out in Box G in paragraph 8.3.3 of VAT Notice 742A[85] and are that either:

- the relevant interest condition (condition (1) below) is met; or
- all of conditions (2) to (5) below are met,

in relation to:

- the person who exercised the option or who was treated as exercising the option by virtue of a real estate election;
- a 'relevant associate[86]' 'connected with'[87] such a person for the purposes of Part 1 of Schedule 10; and
- in relation to an option to tax treated as exercised by virtue of a real estate election made by a body corporate (other than the person who exercised the option or who was treated as exercising the option by virtue of a real estate election) which is treated as a member of a VAT group, the body corporate whose relevant interest gave rise to that option to tax.

---

[84] Paragraph 25(9), Schedule 10

[85] 'Opting to tax land and buildings' (June 2013) – Box G in paragraph 8.3.3 of VAT Notice 742A has the force of law

[86] In the revocation conditions 'relevant associate' bears the meaning in paragraph 3 Schedule 10 – see **9.13.1**

[87] Any question of whether a person is connected with another person for the purposes of the revocation conditions is to be decided 'as it would be for the purposes of Part 1 of Schedule 10'

(1) The relevant interest condition.

The person has no interest in, right over or licence to occupy the building or land (or any part of it) at the time the option is revoked and, if the person has disposed of such an interest, no supply is yet to take place or would be yet to take place if one or more conditions were to be met.

(2) The 20-year condition.

The person held an interest in, right over or licence to occupy the building or land (or any part of it) after the time from which the option had effect and more than 20 years before the option is revoked. It does not matter whether, at the time the option is revoked, the person exercising the option continues to hold the interest in, right over or licence to occupy the building or land (or any part of it) that meets this condition.

(3) The capital item condition.

Any land or building over which the option has effect at the time when it is revoked is not a capital item in respect of which the person may have to make an input tax adjustment under the capital goods scheme[88].

For the purposes of the capital item condition land and buildings are not to be regarded as giving rise to an input tax adjustment where the total of the amounts that the person would be required to pay to HMRC under regulation 115(2) VAT Regulations in respect of intervals ending after the revocation on the basis that:

- that person was a taxable person during those intervals; and
- the land or buildings concerned was used after revocation of the option only for making supplies that were not taxable supplies

does not exceed £10,000.

(4) The valuation condition.

The person has not made a supply of an interest in, right over or licence to occupy the building or land (or any part of it) in relation to which the option had effect in the ten years immediately before revocation:

- for a consideration less than the open market value of that supply; or
- which arose from a grant that the person exercising the option intends or expects will give rise to a supply made after the option is revoked for a consideration significantly greater than any consideration for any supply arising from the grant before revocation (except as a result of a rent review determined according to normal commercial practice).

---

[88] For the **capital goods scheme** see **Chapter 1**

(5) The pre-payment condition.

No part of a supply of goods or services made for consideration to the person before the option is revoked will be attributable to a supply or other use of the land or buildings by the person more than twelve months after the option is revoked.

9.10 Real estate elections

Paragraphs 21 and 22, Schedule 10

A real estate election is, in effect, a decision to opt to tax all future property acquisitions. If a person makes a real estate election, that person, (and any member of a VAT group of which that person is a member) is (with certain exceptions) treated as having opted to tax every property in which he subsequently acquires an interest. As each property subsequently acquired is treated as separately opted, with effect from the time of acquisition this means that each option generated by a real estate election is capable of being separately revoked provide that the conditions for revocation are met.[89] Interests held before a real estate election is made are not affected by it.

9.10.1   The real estate election

Paragraph 21(1), Schedule 10

A person may make a real estate election to have effect in relation to 'relevant interests' in any building or land which that person acquires after the real estate election is made. That election will also have effect in relation to relevant interests which a body corporate acquires after the election is made at a time when the body is a 'relevant group member'. Where an interest in land is held before a real estate election is made the real estate election does not affect it – the normal option to tax rules apply so an existing option will remain in force or, if no option has been exercised, it can be exercised in accordance with those rules.

A 'relevant interest' in relation to any building or land means any interest in, right over or licence to occupy the building or land (or any part of it).[90]

A 'relevant group member' means a body corporate which is treated as a member of the same VAT group as a person making a real estate election at the relevant time.[91]

---

[89] For **revocation of the option to tax** see **9.9** above – a real estate election can only be revoked by HMRC in the circumstances set out in **9.10.7**

[90] Paragraph 21(12)(b), Schedule 10

The time at which a relevant interest in any building or land is acquired is the time at which a supply is treated as taking place for the purposes of the charge to VAT in respect of the acquisition, or if there is more than one such time, the earliest of them[92]. In deciding on the time of supply the provisions of any Orders made under section 5(3)(c) which treat certain supplies as neither a supply of goods nor a supply of services are ignored.[93]

Any member of a VAT group can make a real estate election although HMRC expect that normally this will be done by the representative member of the VAT group.[94]

9.10.2 Effect of making a real estate election
Paragraphs 21(2)-(6), Schedule 10
After a person makes a real estate election that person is treated for the purposes of Schedule 10 VATA as if he had exercised an option to tax:
- in relation to the building or land in which the relevant interest is acquired; and
- on the day on which the acquisition was made and with effect from the start of that day.

The requirement in paragraph 20 of Schedule 10 to notify HMRC of the exercise of an option to tax is disapplied in relation to options generated by a real estate election but there are separate notification requirements for the real estate election.[95]

A real estate election will not apply in the following circumstances:

(1) Where a person acquires an interest in a building or land and has (or a body corporate that was a 'relevant group member' at the time, has) previously opted to tax the building or land, under the normal rules with effect from a date before the acquisition date (being the day the real estate election would bite).[96]

(2) Where a person who acquires an interest in a property (the 'later interest') after the real estate election is made already held an interest in

---

[91] Paragraph 21(12)(a), Schedule 10

[92] Paragraph 21(13), Schedule 10 – for **time of supply** see **2.2**

[93] Paragraph 21(14), Schedule 10 – for example, the TOGC rules (see **Chapter 1**)

[94] See paragraph 14.14.1, VAT Notice 742A 'Opting to tax land and buildings' (June 2013)

[95] In paragraph 21(7) – see **9.10.5**

[96] Paragraph 21(3), Schedule 10

the same property before the real estate election was made and continues to hold that interest when the later interest is acquired.[97]

This situation can typically arise where a leasehold interest is held before the purchase of the freehold. Alternatively, an interest in part of a building (e.g. one floor) may be held at the time an interest in another part of the same building is acquired.

(3) Any acquisition of a property in relation to which HMRC's prior permission to exercise the option to tax would be required on certain assumptions set out in paragraph 21(6) of Schedule 10.[98]

The normal option to tax rules continue to apply in the above circumstances.

9.10.3 Revocation of earlier option to tax by a real estate election
Paragraph 22, Schedule 10

Any option to tax exercised by the person or by a relevant group member before the making of a real estate election will generally be treated as revoked by the making of a real estate election if neither that person nor any relevant group member holds an interest in the opted land or building at the time the real estate election is made.

In particular,[99] and subject to the anti-avoidance provisions in paragraph 26, Schedule 10:[100]

(1) If the person previously opted to tax a building (or part of a building) and if, at the 'relevant time', neither that person nor any relevant group member holds a relevant interest in that building, that option is treated as revoked from the relevant time.

(2) If the person previously opted to tax land (without reference to a particular building or buildings) and if, at the 'relevant time', neither that person nor any relevant group member holds a relevant interest in the whole of that land, that option is treated as revoked from the relevant time in relation to that land or the parts of that land in which neither that person nor any relevant group member holds a relevant interest at the relevant time.

---

[97] Paragraph 21(4), Schedule 10
[98] Paragraphs 21(5)-(6), Schedule 10 and for **permission to opt** see **9.11**
[99] Paragraphs 22 (2)-(4), Schedule 10
[100] See '*Anti-avoidance*' below

References to 'relevant time' mean the time the real estate election is made.[101] A 'relevant interest' in relation to any building or land means any interest in, right over or licence to occupy the building or land (or any part of it).[102]

A 'relevant group member' means a body corporate which is treated as a member of the same VAT group as a person making a real estate election at the relevant time.[103]

Anti-avoidance
Paragraph 26, Schedule 10

Revocation of an earlier option will not occur at the time a real estate election is made if either Condition A or Condition B below is met.

Condition A is that the person who has exercised the option to tax or a 'relevant associate'[104] of that person disposes of a 'relevant interest' in the land or building before the 'relevant time' and at the relevant time, a supply is yet to take place or would be yet to take place in relation to that prior disposal of the building or land if one or more conditions were met (for example, overage).

Condition B is that the person who exercised the option was treated as a member of a VAT group[105] at any time before the 'relevant time' and before the relevant time a 'relevant associate' of that person had ceased to be treated as a member of a VAT group, without, at the time they ceased to be so treated, meeting the following conditions:

(1) the relevant associate had no 'relevant interest' in the building or land;

(2) where a relevant interest had been held by the relevant associate and previously disposed of, no supply is yet to take place or would be yet to take place in relation to that prior disposal of the building or land if one or more conditions were met (for example, overage); and

(3) the relevant associate was not connected with any person who has a relevant interest in the property where that person is the person exercising the option or another relevant associate of the person exercising the option.

'Relevant associate' is defined in section **9.13.1**.

---

[101] Paragraph 221(1), Schedule 10
[102] Paragraph 21(12)(b), Schedule 10 applied by paragraph 22(12), Schedule 10
[103] Paragraph 21(12)(a), Schedule 10 applied by paragraph 22(12), Schedule 10
[104] For the meaning of 'relevant associate' see **9.13.1**
[105] Under section 43A to 43D

'Relevant interest' means[106] an interest in, right over or licence to occupy the building or land or any part of it.

'Relevant time' means[107] the time from which the option to tax under consideration would be treated as revoked but for the provisions of paragraph 26, Schedule 10.

9.10.4 Conversion of a pre-existing single option over land into separate options

Paragraphs 22(6)-(10), Schedule 10

An option to tax (the 'original option') exercised in relation to any land (otherwise than by reference to any building or part of a building) by a person who makes a real estate election, or any 'relevant group member' before the making of the real estate election may, in certain circumstances, be converted by the person making the real estate election into separate options to tax different parcels of land. This choice is only available in relation to land or buildings in which that person or any relevant group member has a relevant interest at the time of making the real estate election. (If there is no relevant interest in the property at that time, the pre-existing option is treated as revoked[108]).

A 'relevant group member' means a body corporate which is treated as a member of the same VAT group as a person making a real estate election at the relevant time[109]. References to 'relevant time' mean the time the real estate election is made[110].

The circumstances in which conversion can take place are set out in Box B at paragraph 14.8.3 of VAT Notice 742A[111] (which has the force of law by reason of paragraph 22 (6) of Schedule 10) and are that:

Each parcel of land that is to be treated as being separately opted must be identified by at least one of the following:

- its postal address; or
- land registry title number, map or plan or other description,

and must meet the conditions relating to the scope of an option in paragraph 18, Schedule 10.[112]

---

[106] Paragraph 26(7) Schedule 10
[107] Paragraph 26(7) Schedule 10
[108] See **9.10.3**
[109] Paragraphs 22(11) and (12), Schedule 10
[110] Paragraph 22(1), Schedule 10
[111] 'Opting to tax land and buildings' (June 2013)

The separate options to tax are treated as if they had been exercised by the person making the real estate election (in the case of a VAT group, irrespective of which member of the group made the original option) and as if they had effect from the time from which the original option had effect. The cooling-off period for revocation of an option[113] does not apply to the separate options to tax resulting from a conversion.[114]

Paragraph 22(10) of Schedule 10 provides that the notification given must identify the separate options treated as exercised and the different parcels of land in relation to which those separate options to tax are treated as having effect.

9.10.5   Notifying a real estate election
Paragraph 21(7), Schedule 10

A real estate election has effect only if notification of the election is given to HMRC before the end of the period of 30 days beginning with the day on which it was made (or such longer period as the HMRC may in any particular case allow). The notification must be made on Form VAT1614E and contain the information requested on that form.

Where the person making the real estate election holds relevant interests in any property other than in dwellings or buildings designed or adapted for use as a dwelling, in addition to notifying the real estate election, he must also provide a list of all properties in which he holds a relevant interest at the time of notifying the real estate election.[115] This list must be sent to HMRC within the time specified for notifying the real estate election; otherwise the real estate election will not have effect.

The list must contain the following information in respect of each property (other than dwellings or buildings designed or adapted for use as a dwelling) in which the person holds a relevant interest:

• description of the land or buildings, identified by reference to postal address, land registry title number, map, plan or other description;
• in the case of land or buildings in respect of which no option to tax made by the maker of a real estate election has effect, the date of acquisition of a relevant interest in that land or buildings;

---

[112] See **9.5** above

[113] See **9.9.1** above

[114] Paragraph 22(9), Schedule 10

[115] Box K, paragraph 14.9, VAT Notice 742A 'Opting to tax land and buildings' (June 2013) – Box K has the force of law by reason of paragraph 21(7), Schedule 10

- in the case of land or buildings in respect of which an option to tax made by the maker of a real estate election has effect, the date when the relevant interest in the land or building was first acquired or, if later, the date when the option first had effect; and
- where an option has effect in relation to two or more separately listed parcels of land or buildings, they must be identified as being subject to the same option.

For these purposes, if the person making a real estate election:
- has more than one relevant interest in a parcel of land or a building acquired at different times, only the date of acquisition of the most recently acquired relevant interest is to be provided; and
- is required to provide the date when an option first had effect in relation to a parcel of land or a building and that date is unknown, that person should record that fact and enter an approximate date, using best judgement, and provide a written explanation of why that date is considered reasonable.

9.10.6 Information requirements after a real estate election has been made

Paragraphs 21(8) and (9), Schedule 10

HMRC may at any time require a person who has made a real estate election to give them certain information specified in a public notice within 30 days (or such longer period as they in any particular case allow). The information which may be required is set out in Box L in paragraph 14.12 of VAT Notice 742A.[116]

If a person does not comply, HMRC have the power to revoke the real estate election, in which case that revocation has effect in relation to relevant interests in any building or land acquired after the 'notified time' by that person or by a body corporate which is a relevant group member at the time of acquisition. The 'notified time' means the time specified in a notification given by HMRC to that person and may not be before the notification is given.[117]

If required to do so, the maker of a real estate election must provide to HMRC the specified information in relation to any land or buildings (other than buildings designed or adapted for use as a dwelling) in which that

---

[116] 'Opting to tax land and buildings' (June 2013) – Box L has the force of law by reason of paragraph 21(8), Schedule 10
[117] Paragraph 21(9), Schedule 10

person or a relevant group member holds a relevant interest at the time of providing the required information; or has ceased to hold a relevant interest since making a real estate election or, if later, since the last occasion on which the maker of the real estate election provided such information to HMRC.

The specified information is, in respect of every such property:

- the description of the land or buildings identified by reference to its postal address, land registry title number, map, plan or other description;
- in the case of land or buildings in respect of which no option to tax made by the maker of a real estate election or relevant group member has effect, the date of acquisition of the relevant interest in the land or buildings;
- in the case of land or buildings in respect of which an option to tax made by the maker of a real estate election or a relevant group member has effect, the date when the relevant interest in the land or building was acquired or, if later, the date when the option first had effect; and
- where an option has effect in relation to two or more separately listed parcels of land or buildings, they must be identified as being subject to the same option.

In respect of every property in which a relevant interest has been acquired or disposed of by the maker or the real estate election or a relevant group member since the date of the last such list (if any) the specified information is, as appropriate, the date of the maker of the real estate election or a relevant group member:

- acquiring a relevant interest in land or buildings in which that person has no other relevant interest;
- ceasing to hold a relevant interest in land or buildings without retaining another relevant interest in that property;
- opting to tax land or buildings otherwise than by virtue of a real estate election;
- converting a building or buildings into a dwelling or dwellings;
- excluding a new building from the effect of an option;
- revoking an option to tax in relation to land or buildings,

identifying in each case the land or building to which each occurrence relates.

- the VAT-exclusive value of the supply of a relevant interest acquired or disposed of by the maker of a real estate election or relevant group member;

- the VAT (if any) charged on the supply of a relevant interest by the maker of a real estate election or, where the supply occurred before its admission to the group, the relevant group member.

For these purposes, where the maker of a real estate election or relevant group member has more than one relevant interest in the same land or building that were acquired at different times, only the date of acquisition of the most recently acquired relevant interest is to be provided. In the case of land or a building in which an interest has been held before the date of a real estate election, the date of the occurrence of the making of an option to tax by the person making a real estate election or a relevant group member is the date when that option first has effect; and the date of the occurrence of the revocation of an option is the date from which the revocation has effect.

9.10.7   Revocation of a real estate election
Paragraphs 21(10) and (11), Schedule 10

Once made, a real estate election may not be revoked except by HMRC for failure to provide specified information.

Where a real estate election made is revoked by HMRC, another real estate election may be made at any subsequent time by the person who made it or any body corporate which is a relevant group member at that subsequent time, but only with the prior written permission of HMRC. In such a case, the provisions allowing conversion of a single option into a number of options[118] do not apply.

9.11 Cases where HMRC's permission is required before exercising the option
Paragraphs 28 to 30, Schedule 10

When the option to tax was first introduced, it was not possible to reclaim input tax incurred before the option was exercised. This was changed on 1 January 1992 but only where HMRC gave permission and agreed to the amount of VAT that could be reclaimed.

The current position is that where exempt supplies have been made or it is intended that exempt supplies will be made in relation to the property in the ten year period ending with the day on which the option to tax is to have effect, HMRC's permission to opt to tax is required. There are two

---

[118] See **9.10.4** above

types of permission, automatic permission and specific permission. Each is dealt with below.

Permission cannot be granted retrospectively but where an option to tax is purportedly exercised in a case where prior permission is required but was not obtained, and that exercise was notified to HMRC within the 30 day time limit, paragraph 30 of Schedule 10 gives HMRC the power to dispense with the requirement for prior permission and to treat the option as validly exercised. Paragraph 5.9 of VAT Notice 742A[119] states that HMRC will generally only exercise this power where:

    (a) tax would otherwise be at risk, or

    (b) you took reasonable steps, before notifying the option, to determine whether permission was required, but failed to realise it was required due to a minor error or oversight. For example, you might have made a one off exempt supply which you had overlooked.

9.11.1 Automatic permission to opt to tax
Paragraphs 28(2)(a) and 29, Schedule 10

The conditions for automatic permission are set out in paragraph 5.2 of VAT Notice 742A. Paragraph 5.2 has the force of law.

Permission is automatic where any one of the following conditions are met:

(1) It is a mixed-use development and the only exempt supplies have been in relation to the dwellings.

(2) The person does not wish to recover any input tax in relation to the land or building incurred before the option to tax has effect; and both of the following additional conditions are satisfied:

    (a) The consideration for exempt supplies has, up to the date when the option to tax is to take effect, been solely by way of rents or service charges and excludes any premiums or payments in respect of occupation after the date on which the option takes effect. Regular rental and/or service charge payments can be ignored for the purposes of this condition. Payments are considered regular where the intervals between them are no more than a year and where each represents a commercial or genuine arms-length value.

    (b) The only input tax relating to the land or building that the person expects to recover after the option to tax takes effect will be on overheads, such as regular rental payments, service charges, repairs and maintenance costs. If he expects to claim input tax in relation to

---

[119] 'Opting to tax land and buildings' (June 2013)

refurbishment or redevelopment of the building, he will not meet this condition.

In deciding whether this condition is met, a person should disregard:

- any VAT refundable to a local authority or similar body under section 32(2)(b) VATA;
- any input tax he can otherwise recover by virtue of the partial exemption de minimis rules;
- any input tax he is entitled to recover on general business overheads not specifically related to the land or building, such as audit fees.

(3) Condition A and, if applicable, Condition B, are satisfied (see below).

(4) The exempt supplies have been incidental to the main use of the land or building. For example, where the person has occupied a building for taxable purposes, the following would be seen by HMRC as incidental to the main use enabling this condition to be met:

- allowing an advertising hoarding to be displayed;
- granting space for the erection of a radio mast;
- receiving income from an electricity sub-station.

The letting of space to an occupying tenant, however minor, is not incidental.

Condition A:

The person opting to tax does not intend or expect that any supply which is taxable as a result will:

(1) be made to a connected person, unless that person will be entitled to recover by way of credit or refund at least 80 per cent. of the VAT chargeable on that supply; or

(2) arise from an agreement under which an exempt supply in respect of a right to occupy the property has been or will be made, and that right begins or continues after the effective date of the option.

'Permissible exempt supplies' may be disregarded.

For the purposes of Condition A:

'Property' includes land, buildings and civil engineering works.

The question of whether a person is connected with another person is to be decided as it would be for the purposes of Part 1 of Schedule 10.

'Permissible exempt supplies' means the following exempt supplies arising from a grant in relation to the land:

(1) Supplies for which the consideration solely represents legal and/or valuation costs reimbursed under the agreement for the grant.

(2) Supplies where the consideration is regular rents and/or service charges, and that consideration:

    (a) relates to a period of occupation of the property ending no later than 12 months from the date on which the option first takes effect; and

    (b) where no opted supply, other than an opted supply relating solely to the same period of occupation as an exempt supply under b) above, will be reduced in value as a result of the consideration payable for these exempt supplies.

Condition B

This condition applies where the person has been, or expects to be, entitled to credit for any input tax incurred on capital expenditure on the property by virtue of the option and is as follows:

The person does not intend or expect to use any part of the capital expenditure for the purposes of:

(1) making exempt supplies which do not confer a right to credit under section 26(2)(c) VATA unless:

    (a) all the exempt supplies fall paragraphs 5 to 11, Schedule 10 VATA (exclusions from the effect of the option to tax[120]); or are permissible exempt supplies; or are incidental supplies falling within Group 5 of Schedule 9 to VATA (finance); or

    (b) exempt supplies are made but it is intended or expected that input tax on capital expenditure on the property which is attributed to those exempt supplies will not exceed £5,000; or

    (c) the person expects to be entitled to full credit for all input tax incurred on capital expenditure on the property under *VATA* s 33(2) (statutory bodies: insignificant exempt input tax); or

(2) private or non-business purposes, other than those giving right to a refund under section 33 (statutory authorities), section 33A (museums and galleries) or section 41(3) (Government departments) *VATA*.

For the purposes of Condition B:

'Capital expenditure' is expenditure on goods or services used in connection with the acquisition of, building works on, construction

---

[120] See **9.12** below

works on or the fitting out of, the property. Capital expenditure does not include expenditure on routine repairs and maintenance.

'Entitled to credit' includes entitlement to a deduction or credit arising as a result of the application of Regulation 109 or Part XV of the VAT Regulations.

'Permissible exempt supplies' has the same meaning as for Condition A.

If one of the above conditions is met, the person must still notify HMRC of the option by completing Form VAT1614H (which can be done online although it must be printed out, signed and sent to HMRC). The notification should state that, although the business has made previous exempt supplies of the land or building, it satisfies the conditions for automatic permission.

9.11.2   Specific permission to opt to tax
Paragraphs 28(2)(b) and 29, Schedule 10

If a person who requires HMRC's permission before he can opt to tax does not meet any of the conditions for automatic permission he must obtain specific permission from:

HMRC – Option to Tax Unit
Cotton House
7 Cochrane Street
GLASGOW
G1 1GY

The application must be made on Form VAT1614H (which can be completed online although it must be printed out, signed and sent by post) and contain the information requested on the form.[121] The person wishing to opt must let HMRC know the date from which it would like the option to have effect (which can be any date on or after he makes the application).

HMRC cannot grant permission to opt to tax unless the relevant person has provided all the specified information, and any additional information requested. They must refuse their permission if they are not satisfied that there would be a fair and reasonable attribution of relevant input tax.[122] In deciding this, they must have regard to all the circumstances of the case,[123] but they must have regard, in particular, to:[124]

---

[121] Paragraph 29(1), Schedule 10
[122] Paragraph 28(3), Schedule 10
[123] Paragraph 28(5), Schedule 10
[124] Paragraph 28(6), Schedule 10

(1) the total value of any exempt supply to which any grant in relation to the land gives rise and which is made or to be made before the day from which the person wants the option to have effect;
(2) the expected total value of any supply to which any grant in relation to the land gives rise that would be taxable (if the option has effect); and
(3) the total amount of input tax incurred, or likely to be incurred, in relation to the land.

'Relevant income tax' means input tax incurred, or likely to be incurred, in relation to the land.[125]

'Relevant supplies' means supplies to which any grant in relation to the land gives rise which would be taxable if the option had effect.[126]

If HMRC are satisfied, permission is granted and the option takes immediate effect from the start of the day on which the application was made or the start of any later day specified in the application.[127] There is no requirement for separate written notification of the exercise of the option to tax after permission is granted. Permission may be give subject to conditions and, if these are broken HMRC can treat the application as if it had not been made.[128]

9.12 Exclusions from the effect of the option to tax

There are a number of situations in which an option to tax although exercised and subsisting will have no effect and these are where the grant is in relation to:
(1) a building designed or adapted, and intended for use, as a dwelling or certified as intended for use solely for a relevant residential purpose;
(2) a building certified as intended for use as a dwelling or for a relevant residential purpose (conversions) ;
(3) a building certified as intended for use solely for a relevant charitable purpose but not as an office;
(4) a pitch for a residential caravan;
(5) facilities for mooring a residential houseboat;
(6) land certified by a relevant housing association as to be used for the construction of a building intended for use as a dwelling or for a relevant residential purpose; and

---

[125] Paragraph 28(4), Schedule 10
[126] Paragraph 28(4), Schedule 10
[127] Paragraph 29(3), Schedule 10
[128] Paragraph 29(2), Schedule 10

(7) land to be used for the construction of a dwelling by a DIY builder who is an individual and intends to use that dwelling himself.

Exclusions 1 to 7 are dealt with in turn below. Where a grant gives rise to supplies made at different times after the making of the grant (for example, where rent is paid under a lease), the liability of each of those supplies (in other words, whether any of the exclusions applies) is determined at the time of each supply is made rather than by reference to the time of the original grant.[129]

Paragraphs 12 to 17 of Schedule 10 (anti-avoidance) provide for certain supplies resulting from a grant to be excluded from the effect of paragraph 2, Schedule 10.[130] In addition a person can exclude a new building from the effect of the option. This is dealt with at **9.5** above.

Exclusion (1): Building designed or adapted and intended for use as a dwelling or certified as intended for use solely for a relevant residential purpose - paragraph 5, Schedule 10

Where the option to tax has been exercised and a grant is made in relation to a building or part of a building which is designed or adapted *and* intended for use as a dwelling or number of dwellings the option has no effect and that grant remains exempt. Note (2) to Group 5 of Schedule 8[131] applies to determine whether a building is 'designed or adapted for use as a dwelling.'[132] There is no requirement for a certificate as to intended use as a dwelling and this can give rise to difficulties (see below).

Where the building or part of a building is designed or adapted for use for a relevant residential purpose the option has no effect. Paragraph 33 of Schedule 10 applies Notes (4), (5) and (12) to Group 5 of Schedule 8 in order to determine the meaning of 'use for a relevant residential purpose' for the purposes of Exclusion (1). This means that 'use for a relevant residential purpose' means[133] use as:

(a) a home or other institution providing residential accommodation for children;

(b) a home or other institution providing residential accommodation with personal care for persons in need of personal care by reason of old age, disablement, past or present dependence on alcohol or drugs or past or

---

[129] Section 96(10A) *VATA*
[130] See **9.14** below
[131] See **1.2.7** above
[132] Paragraph 33 Schedule 10
[133] Note (4), Group 5, Schedule 8 – see discussion at **0** above

present mental disorder;

(c) a hospice;

(d) residential accommodation for students or school pupils;

(e) residential accommodation for members of any of the armed forces;

(f) a monastery, nunnery or similar establishment; or

(g) an institution which is the sole or main residence of at least 90 per cent of its residents, except use as a hospital, prison or similar institution or a hotel, inn or similar establishment,

except use as a hospital, prison or similar institution or an hotel, inn or similar establishment.

Where a number of buildings are constructed at the same time and are intended to be used for a relevant residential purpose they are to be treated as intended for use solely for a relevant residential purpose even if they would not qualify individually. The buildings must be built at the same time and on the same site and must be intended to be used together as a unit solely for a relevant residential purpose[134].

The supply must be made to a person who intends to use the building or part of the building solely for a relevant residential purpose.[135] The certification requirement in Note (12)(b) to Group 5 of Schedule 8 applies[136]. Until a certificate is provided by the recipient of the supply to the person making the supply the option is not disapplied.

In *Ebley House Ltd*[137] the tribunal decided that the option had been disapplied in a case where no certificate had been provided saying:

'Clearly it would have been preferable if the Appellant had obtained a certificate or other documentary evidence from the purchaser at the time of sale as to the intended use of the property. However, nothing in the legislation or Public Notice suggests that this is necessary, nor did Mr Bingham [appearing for HMRC]. In the circumstances, the Tribunal must determine the purchaser's intention as a matter of fact, on a balance of probability, based on the evidence before it.'

The decision in *Ebley House Ltd* must be regarded as given per incuriam.

In *SEH Holdings Ltd*,[138] a case relating to paragraph 2(2)(a) of Schedule 10

---

[134] Note (5), Group 5, Schedule 8

[135] Note (12)(a), Group 5, Schedule 8.

[136] See **6.3.3** above

[137] [2013] UKFTT 422 (TC)

[138] [2000] VATDR 324 (VTD 16771)

(the predecessor to paragraph 5, Schedule 10 which did not require the building to be designed or adapted for use as a dwelling) the option to tax was not disapplied on the sale of a disused public house where the intended use of the property as a dwelling was to be by a third party. The tribunal held that it was necessary for the seller to be aware of the buyer's intention to use the property at the time of the sale and, on the evidence, the buyer had not shown that the seller was aware of the intended use of the property at the time of the sale. The tribunal observed that 'normally the rate of value added tax applicable to any transaction is determinable by the application of objective criteria. However, in this appeal the rate depends, unusually, on the intention of someone other than the supplier'. On that basis, the tribunal concluded that 'the legislation which refers to such intention should be narrowly construed', since 'any move away from the contractual link between the seller and the buyer would create many difficulties'.

In *PJG Developments Ltd*[139] a disused public house was sold and the seller who had opted to tax charged output tax on the sale. The seller had obtained planning permission to convert the building into two semi-detached houses and had advertised it as a 'delightful residential opportunity'. The buyer appealed, contending that the effect of paragraph 2(2)(a) of Schedule 10 (the predecessor to paragraph 5, Schedule 10 which did not require the building to be designed or adapted for use as a dwelling) was that output tax should not have been charged as the building was intended for use as a dwelling or a number of dwellings. The tribunal allowed the appeal and distinguished the earlier decision in *SEH Holdings Ltd*, finding that seller 'was aware of the intention that the whole building was to be used as dwellings'.

Exclusion (2): Building certified as intended for use as a dwelling or solely for a relevant residential purpose (conversions) - paragraph 6, Schedule 10

An option to tax has no effect on a grant made to a person in relation to a building or part of a building if the grantee certifies that the building is intended for use as a dwelling or number of dwellings or solely for a relevant residential purpose. The grantee must give a certificate to this effect to the grantor within the period specified in a public notice or, if the seller agrees, at any later time provided that it is before the supply is made[140]. The certificate must be provided on Form VAT1614D.[141] Section 62

---

[139] [2005] VATDR 215

[140] For the **time of supply** see 2.2 above

provides for a VAT-geared penalty where an incorrect certificate is given. The defence of reasonable excuse is available. The conversion works may benefit from relief.[142]

HMRC specify the time limit for providing a certificate in Box B of section 3.4.3. of VAT Notice 742A[143] (which has the force of law). The certificate must be given before the price for the grant of the land interest is 'legally fixed'. HMRC go on to provide examples of what is meant by legally fixed: exchange of contracts, letters or missives, or the signing of heads of agreement.

> 'As a supplier, if you receive a certificate by the time set out in box B below, you must exempt your supply of the building or part of the building to which the certificate relates.'[144]

Although paragraph 6(3) of Schedule 10 provides that the grantee may only give a certificate to the grantor if he:
(1) intends to use the building or part of the building as a dwelling or number of dwellings or solely for a relevant residential purpose[145];
(2) has the 'relevant conversion intention'[146]; or
(3) is a 'relevant intermediary'[147]

There is no suggestion of the grantor having to undertake any due diligence as to whether the grantee actually intends to do what they have certified. Section 62 VATA provides for a VAT-geared penalty where an incorrect certificate is given. The defence of reasonable excuse is available.

A 'relevant intermediary' is a grantee who intends to dispose of the 'relevant interest' to another person who gives the grantee a certificate (on Form VAT1614D) that he has the 'relevant conversion intention' or the 'relevant disposal intention'.[148]

---

[141] Paragraph 6(10)(b) Schedule 10 and paragraph 3.4.2 VAT Notice 742A 'Opting to tax land and buildings' (June 2013)

[142] See **Chapter 10**

[143] 'Opting to tax land and buildings' (June 2013)

[144] See section 3.4.3 of VAT Notice 742A 'Opting to tax land and buildings' (June 2013)

[145] Condition 1 on Form 1614D

[146] Condition 2 on Form 1614D

[147] Condition 3 on Form 1614D

[148] Paragraph 6(4) Schedule 10

The 'relevant interest' in relation to any interest in the building or part of the building to which the grant gives rise means the whole of that interest.[150]

The 'relevant conversion intention' means an intention to convert the building for use as a dwelling or number of dwellings or solely for a relevant residential purpose.[151]

A person has a 'relevant disposal intention' if he intends to dispose of the 'relevant interest' to a third person and that third person gives a 'qualifying certificate' to the person intending to make the disposal.[152]

A person gives a 'qualifying certificate' to another if he gives a certificate (on Form VAT1614D) that:
- he has the 'relevant conversion intention' (Condition 2 on Form VAT1614D); or
- he intends to dispose of the relevant interest to another person who has given a qualifying certificate to him, in other words, that he is a relevant intermediary (Condition 3 on Form VAT1614D),

and so on in the case of further disposals of the relevant interest.[153]

So, for a 'relevant intermediary', a certificate received from a prospective buyer serves two purposes:
(1) it allows that relevant intermediary to issue a certificate disapplying his supplier's option to tax (so that the purchase of the building, or relevant part, is exempt), and
(2) it disapplies the relevant intermediary's own option to tax when he comes to supply the building on to his buyer (so that his sale of the building, or relevant part, is exempt).

A building or part of a building is not regarded as intended for use as a dwelling or number of dwellings at any time if there is intended to be a period before that time during which it will not be so used (but disregarding use for incidental or other minor purposes).[154]

Where only part of a building is intended to be for used as a dwelling or number of dwellings or solely for a relevant residential purpose above, the certificate must make it clear that this is the case and must contain a description of the qualifying part. The option to tax will apply to the part of

---

[150] Paragraph 6(7) Schedule 10
[151] Paragraph 6(7) Schedule 10
[152] Paragraph 6(5) Schedule 10
[153] Paragraph 6(6) Schedule 10
[154] Paragraph 6(8) Schedule 10

the building that is not intended for qualifying use and the grantor must apportion his supply between the exempt and taxable elements.

Notes (4) and (5) to Group 5 of Schedule 8 apply in order to determine the meaning of 'use for a relevant residential purpose' for the purposes of Exclusion (2).[155] This means that **'use for a relevant residential purpose'** is as set out at on page 155 above.

Where a number of buildings are constructed at the same time and are intended to be used for a relevant residential purpose they are to be treated as intended for use solely for a relevant residential purpose even if they would not qualify individually. The buildings must be built at the same time and on the same site and must be intended to be used together as a unit solely for a relevant residential purpose.[156]

Exclusion (3): Building certified as intended for use solely for a relevant charitable purpose but not as an office- paragraph 7, Schedule 10

Paragraph 33 of Schedule 10 applies Notes (6), and (12) to Group 5 of Schedule 8 in order to determine the meaning of 'use for a relevant charitable purpose[157]' in Exclusion (3). This means that the supply must be made to a person who intends to use the building or part of the building solely for a relevant charitable purpose[158].

The certification requirement in Note (12)(b) to Group 5 of Schedule 8 applies by reason of paragraph 33 of Schedule 10. Unless a certificate is provided by the recipient of the supply to the person making the supply the option is not disapplied. The form of the certificate is discussed at **6.4** above.

There is no definition of office use.

Exclusion (4): Pitch for a residential caravan - paragraph 8, Schedule 10[159]

An option to tax has no effect in relation to any 'grant'[160] made in relation to a pitch for a 'residential caravan'. A caravan is not a 'residential caravan' if 'residence in it throughout the year is prevented by the terms of a covenant, statutory planning consent or similar permission.'[161]

---

[155] Paragraph 33 Schedule 10 as modified by paragraph 6(9) which excludes the application of Note (12) to Group 5, Schedule 8

[156] Note (5), Group 5, Schedule 8

[157] For **'use solely for a relevant charitable purpose'** see **6.3**

[158] Note (12)(a), Group 5, Schedule 8.

[159] For more on caravans see **Chapter 13**

[160] For meaning of 'grant' see **1.2.11** above

[161] Paragraph 8(2) Schedule 10

Exclusion (5): Facilities for mooring a residential houseboat - paragraph 9, Schedule 10

An option to tax has no effect in relation to any grant made in relation to facilities for mooring a 'residential houseboat'. Mooring includes anchoring or berthing.[162]

The definition of 'houseboats' in Group 9 of Schedule 8 applies:

'boats or other floating decked structures designed or adapted for use solely as places of permanent habitation, and not having the means of, or not capable of being readily adapted for, self propulsion'.

A houseboat is not a 'residential houseboat' if 'residence in it throughout the year is prevented by the terms of a covenant, statutory planning consent or similar permission.'[163]

Exclusion (6): Land certified by a relevant housing association as to be used for the construction of a building intended for use as a dwelling or for a relevant residential purpose - paragraph 10, Schedule 10
See Section **7.3** above.

Exclusion (7): Land to be used for the construction of a dwelling by an individual who is a DIY builder - paragraph 11, Schedule 10
An option to tax has no effect in relation to any grant made to an individual[164] if the land is to be used for the construction of a building intended for use by the individual as a dwelling provided that the construction is not carried out in the course or furtherance of a business carried on by the individual.

Notes (3) and (16) to (18) to Group 5 of Schedule 8 are applied by paragraph 33 of Schedule 10 in construing the meaning of paragraph 11 so:
(1) A garage built at the same time as a dwelling and intended to be occupied with the dwelling is included in the dwelling. It is insufficient for the planning permission to have been obtained at the same time as the dwellings and for the garages to be built at a later date.[165]
(2) Note (16) to Group 5 of Schedule 8 specifically excludes from the construction of a building any extension, alteration or reconstruction of a building or the construction of an annexe.

---

[162] Paragraph 9(1) Schedule 10
[163] Paragraph 9(2), Schedule 10
[164] This differs from the **DIY builder's scheme** which is not restricted to individuals – see **5.1** above
[165] Note (3), Group 5, Schedule 8

(3) A building that is reconstructed retaining a single or double facade of an old building will be regarded as a new building only if the retention of the facade is required by planning permission or similar permission, such as listed building consent.

9.13 The option to tax and VAT groups

An option to tax made by a member of a VAT group is generally binding upon other members of the same VAT group.[166] A body corporate bound by another group member's option to tax under these rules is known as a 'relevant associate' of that other group member. If a body corporate is a relevant associate, it must normally charge VAT on any supplies it makes of the property in respect of which the option to tax has been exercised, even after it has left the VAT group.

9.13.1 Relevant associate
Paragraphs 3(1) and 3(2), Schedule 10

Where a body corporate ('the opter') exercises an option to tax in relation to any building or land, another body corporate is a relevant associate of the opter if:

(1) it was treated as a member of the same VAT group as the opter at the time when the option first had effect; or

(2) it has been treated as a member of the same VAT group as the opter at any later time when the opter had a 'relevant interest in the building or land'; or

(3) it has been treated as a member of the same VAT group as the opter, or a relevant associate of the opter, at a time when either of them had a 'relevant interest in the building or land'.

A 'relevant interest in the building or land' means an interest in, right over or licence to occupy the building or land (or any part of it).[168]

9.13.2 Ceasing to be a relevant associate
Paragraphs 3(4), 3(5) and 4, Schedule 10

A body corporate ceases to be a relevant associate of the opter in relation to the building or land in the following circumstances at the time when all of the following conditions (the 'No Relevant Interest Conditions) are first met:

(a) The body corporate has no relevant interest in the building or land.

(b) Where the body corporate has disposed of a relevant interest in the building or land, it is not the case that a supply for the purposes of the

---

[166] The rules for VAT groups are in sections 43A- 43D VATA
[168] Paragraph 3(6), Schedule 10

charge to VAT in respect of the disposal is yet to take place, or would be yet to take place if one or more conditions (such as the happening of an event or the doing of an act) were to be met.

(c) The body corporate or the opter is no longer a member of the group mentioned in (1) to (3) above.

(d) The body corporate is not connected with any person who has a relevant interest in the building or land where that person is the opter or another relevant associate of the opter.

For these purposes, whether a person is connected with another person is determined in accordance with section 1122 of the *Corporation Tax Act 2010*. However, a company is not connected with another company only because both are under the control of the Crown, a Minister of the Crown, a government department, or a Northern Ireland department.[169]

When the No Relevant Interest Conditions are met, the body corporate automatically ceases to be a relevant associate from that time. There is no need to notify HMRC or to seek HMRC's permission.

When the No Relevant Interest Conditions are not met, a body corporate also ceases to be a relevant associate of the opter in relation to the building or land at a time when it meets all of the conditions set out below[170] (the 'Specified Conditions') and has notified HMRC that it does so on Form VAT1614B.[171]

The Specified Conditions are:

(1) The body corporate has ceased to be treated as a member of the VAT group by virtue of which it became a relevant associate of the opter.

(2) The body corporate has held any relevant interest in the building or land acquired whilst a member of that VAT group for a period of at least 20 years and has been treated as a relevant associate of the opter for a period of at least 20 years.

(3) Any land or building subject to the option is not subject to input tax adjustment as a capital item under the capital goods scheme.

(4) The body corporate, or a person connected with it, has not, within a period of ten years ending on the date that the body corporate ceases to be a relevant associate, made a supply of a 'relevant interest in the

---

[169] Paragraphs 34(2) and (2A), Schedule 10

[170] Set out in Box E of paragraph 6.3.5. of VAT Notice 742A 'Opting to tax buildings and land' (June 2013) – Box E is given the force of law by paragraph 3(5)(b), Schedule 10

[171] Paragraph 4, Schedule 10

building or land'[172] subject to the option for a consideration that was less than the open market value of that supply or that arose from a grant that the grantor intends or expects will give rise to a supply for a consideration significantly greater than any consideration for any earlier supply arising from the grant (except as a result of a rent review determined according to normal commercial practice).

(5) No supply of goods or services has been made for a consideration to the body corporate (or to a person connected with it) which will be wholly or partly attributable to a supply or other use of the land or buildings made by that body (or by a person connected with it) more than twelve months later.

If a body corporate does not meet the no relevant interest or the specified conditions, it may apply for permission from HMRC to cease to be a relevant associate using Form VAT1614B.[173] Permission will not be granted unless both conditions 1 and 2 of the Specified Conditions are met. In deciding whether or not to grant permission, HMRC will give particular consideration to whether or not the applicant or a third party has received a VAT benefit as a result of the applicant's actions.

If HMRC grants permission, the body corporate ceases to be a relevant associate of the opter from the day on which HMRC give their permission or such earlier or later day as is specified in their permission.[174] HMRC may specify an earlier day only if:[175]

(1) the body corporate has purported to give a written notification of its ceasing to be a relevant associate of the opter by meeting the Specified Conditions;

(2) the Specified Conditions are not, in the event, met in relation to the body corporate; and

(3) HMRC consider that the grounds on which the Specified Conditions are not met are insignificant.

In such a case, the day specified may be the day from which the body corporate would have ceased to be a relevant associate of the opter if the Specified Conditions had been met[176].

---

[172] See **9.13.1** above for definition of '**relevant interest in the building or land**'
[173] Paragraph 3(5)(a), Schedule 10
[174] Paragraph 4(5), Schedule 10
[175] Paragraph 4(6), Schedule 10
[176] Paragraph 4(7), Schedule 10

HMRC may specify conditions subject to which permission is given and, if any of those conditions are broken, they may treat the application for permission as if it had not been made.[177]

9.14 Option to tax: anti-avoidance provisions
Paragraphs 12 to 17, Schedule 10

Certain taxable persons, who are not entitled to recover all of the input tax they incur on the purchase of land or buildings or on major construction projects, enter into arrangements designed to either increase the amount of input tax they can claim or to spread the VAT cost of the purchase or construction over a number of years. To counter this, HMRC have introduced anti-avoidance provisions which disapply the option to tax in relation to the supplies arising from that particular grant. A business that normally receives credit for most of the input tax it incurs is unlikely to be affected by these anti-avoidance measures.

The basics of the anti-avoidance rule are in paragraph 12 of Schedule 10. There does not have to be an intention to avoid VAT for a grant to be caught by the anti-avoidance provisions.

A supply is not a taxable supply as a result of the exercise of the option to tax where:

(1) the 'grant' giving rise to the supply was made by a person (the 'grantor') who was a 'developer' of the land; and

(2) at the time when the grant was made (or treated as having been made), the grantor or a 'development financier' intended or expected that the land:

    (a) would become 'exempt land' whether immediately or eventually and whether or not as a result of the grant; or

    (b) would continue, for a period at least, to be exempt land.

If a supply is made by a person other than the person who made the grant giving rise to it then the person making the supply is treated as the person who made the grant giving rise to it; and the grant is treated as made at the time when that person made the first supply arising from the grant.

The provisions do not apply to grants made before 26 November 1996[178] and there is a special rule in paragraph 17 of Schedule 10 for grants made on or after 19 March 1997 and before 10 March 1999.

---

[177] Paragraph 4(8), Schedule 10

The definitions set out below need to be read into the anti-avoidance provisions in paragraph 12 of Schedule 10.

9.14.1 'Grant'

A grant is a sale of a freehold or other interest, or a lease or letting of land. For the purposes of zero-rating under Group 5 of Schedule 8 a grant includes an assignment or a surrender.[179] For the purposes of Group 1 Schedule 9 'grant' also includes the supply made by the person to whom an interest is surrendered when there is a reverse surrender (i.e. where the person to whom the interest is surrendered is paid by the person by whom the interest is being surrendered to accept the surrender).[180] For the purposes of Part 1 of Schedule 10, Note (1), Group 5, Schedule 8 and Notes (1) and (1A), Schedule 9 are applied (by paragraph 33 of Schedule 10) in construing the meaning of 'grant.'

9.14.2 'Grantor'

The grantor is the person who sells, leases or lets any of the land or buildings and can be anywhere in the chain of people who have an interest in the land or buildings concerned. The test must be applied to each grant made.

9.14.3 'Grants made by a developer'[181]

A 'grant' made by any person (the 'grantor') in relation to any land is made by a developer of that land if the following conditions are met.

(1) The land or the building or part of a building on the land is a capital item under the capital goods scheme[182] in relation to the grantor; or the grantor, or a 'development financier' intended or expected that the land, or a building or part of a building on or to be constructed on the land, would become a capital item under the capital goods scheme in relation to the grantor or any 'relevant transferee'.

A person is a 'relevant transferee' if the person is someone to whom the land, building or part of a building was to be transferred in the course of a supply or in the course of a transfer of a business or part of a business as a going concern.

---

[178] Paragraph 12 (8), Schedule 10 – there are savings for certain grants made after 26 November 1996 and before 30 November 1999
[179] Note (1), Group 5, Schedule 8
[180] Notes (1) and (1A), Group 1, Schedule 9
[181] Paragraph 13, Schedule 10
[182] For the **capital goods scheme** see **11.4** below

(2) The 'grant' is made before the end of the period provided for the making of adjustments relating to the deduction of input tax as respects that item under the capital goods scheme (an 'eligible time').

But if a person other than the grantor is treated as making the grant of the land and the grant is consequently treated as made at what would otherwise not be an eligible time the grant is treated instead as if it was made at an eligible time.

9.14.4 'Development financier[183]'

A development financier in relation to the grantor of any land is a person who has 'provided finance for the grantor's development of the land', or has entered into any agreement, arrangement or understanding (whether or not legally enforceable) to provide finance for the grantor's development of the land, with the intention or in the expectation that the land will become 'exempt land' or continue (for a period at least) to be exempt land.

'Providing finance for the grantor's development of the land'

This is widely defined. It covers directly or indirectly 'providing funds' for meeting the whole (or any part) of the cost of the 'grantor's development of the land' or for discharging (in whole or in part) any liability that has been or may be incurred by any person for or in connection with the raising of funds to meet that cost. It also includes directly or indirectly procuring the provision of such funds by another person for those purposes.

'Providing funds'

'Providing funds' means:
- making a loan of funds
- providing any guarantee or other security in relation to such a loan;
- providing any of the consideration for the issue of any shares or other securities issued wholly or partly for raising those funds;
- providing any consideration for the acquisition by any person of shares or other securities issued wholly or partly for raising those funds; and
- any other transfer of assets or value as a consequence of which any of those funds are made available for that purpose.

'Grantor's development of the land'

References to 'the grantor's development of the land' are references to the acquisition by the grantor of the land or a building or part of a building on the land which is, or was intended or expected to be, a relevant capital item under the capital goods scheme in relation to the grantor. The acquisition of

---

[183] Paragraph 14, Schedule 10

the asset includes its construction or reconstruction; and the carrying out in relation to it of any other works by reference to which it is, or was intended or expected to be, a relevant capital item under the capital goods scheme in relation to the grantor.

9.14.5 'Exempt land'[184]

Land is 'exempt land' if, at any time before the end of the adjustment period under the capital goods scheme as respects that land it is occupied by any of the following persons:

(1) the grantor;

(2) a person connected with the grantor;

(3) a development financier;

(4) a person connected with a development financier;

and that occupation is not 'wholly or substantially wholly' for 'eligible purposes'.

The meaning of 'wholly' and 'substantially wholly' is set out in Box I in paragraph 13.9.1 of VAT Notice 742A[185] which is given the force of law by paragraphs 15(5) and 15A(6A) of Schedule 10. 'Wholly' means 100 per cent and 'substantially wholly' means at least 80 per cent.

Where a person in occupation of the land at any time before the end of the relevant adjustment period, he is treated as not in occupation of the land at that time if the 'building occupation conditions' are met at that time; or his occupation of the land arises solely by reference to any automatic teller machine belonging to him.

The 'building occupation conditions'

These conditions are met if:[186]

(1) the grant consists of or includes the grant of a relevant interest in a 'building'; and

(2) the person (or anyone 'connected with' him if that occupation is not 'wholly, or substantially wholly' for 'eligible purposes') does not, at the time in question:

    (a) occupy any part of the land that is not a building, or

    (b) more than the maximum allowable percentage of any 'relevant building'.

---

[184] Paragraphs 15, 15A and 16, Schedule 10
[185] 'Opting to tax land and buildings' (June 2013)
[186] Paragraph 15A, Schedule 10

Sub-paragraphs (4) to (7) of paragraph 18, Schedule 10 apply to determine what is a building for the purposes of the building occupation conditions.[187] Buildings linked internally or by a covered walkway and complexes consisting of a number of units grouped around a fully enclosed concourse are treated as a single building.[188] However, where the internal link is created or the covered walkway starts to be constructed after the buildings are completed the linkage is disregarded.[189] A 'covered walkway' does not include a covered walkway to which the general public has access.[190] 'Building' includes an enlarged or extended building, an annexe to a building, and a planned building.[191]

For the purposes of (2)(a), occupation of land used for parking vehicles or land within the 'curtilage' of a building is disregarded where that occupation is ancillary to the occupation by a person of the building. 'Curtilage' is not defined. Guidance was given by the Court of Appeal in *Methuen-Campbell v Walters*[192] See **9.5 above** on page 127.

'Relevant building' for the purposes of (2)(b) means a building any relevant interest in which is included in the grant, other than any part of such building in which, immediately before the grant, neither the grantor nor any person connected with the grantor held a relevant interest. It does not include any building a person's occupation of the land arises solely by reference to any automatic teller machine belonging to him.

'Relevant interest' in the building occupation conditions means any interest in or right over or licence to occupy the building or part.

The 'maximum allowable percentage' means:
- 2 per cent where the person is (or is connected with) the grantor; or
- 10 per cent where the person is (or is connected with) a development financier (but not also (or connected with) the grantor).

The way in which occupation of a building is to be measured in set out in Box H in paragraph 13.8.61 of VAT Notice 742A.[194] Box H is given the force of law by paragraph 15A of Schedule 10 and reads as follows:

---

[187] Paragraph 15A(7), Schedule 10
[188] Paragraph 18(4), Schedule 10
[189] Paragraph 18(5), Schedule 10
[190] Paragraph 18(7), Schedule 10
[191] Paragraph 18(6), Schedule 10
[192] [1979] 1 All ER 606
[194] 'Opting to tax land and buildings' (June 2013)

'The proportion of a 'relevant building' occupied by any person or persons for the purposes of paragraph 15A(1)(b)(ii) of Schedule 10 to the Value Added Tax Act 1994 is to be calculated using the recommended practices set out in the current version of the 'Code of Measuring Practice' published by the Royal Institution of Chartered Surveyors (the 'RICS Code'), but subject to the following:

1. The following parts of the building must be excluded:
- any part which is not available for exclusive occupation
- any part intended primarily for use for vehicle parking
- any part which is land forming part of the curtilage of the building.

2. Where in relation to any part of the 'relevant building' the RICS Code either:
- does not specify a 'core definition', or
- specifies the use of more than one 'core definition',

the 'core definition' to be used is that applied or expected to be applied by the grantor for the purposes of calculating rent due from letting that part of the building or, if there is no such definition at the time of the grant, NIA (Net Internal Area).

Explanatory Note 1
Current version of the 'Code of Measuring Practice' means the latest published version at the time the grant is made (i.e., the grant that is subject to the anti-avoidance test).'

For these purposes, whether a person is connected with another person is determined in accordance with section 1122 of the *Corporation Tax Act 2010* but with the modifications in paragraph 34(2A) of Schedule 10.[195]

'Occupation for eligible purposes'[196]
This means 'occupation' which is:
(1) Occupation by a taxable person for the purposes of making supplies which are, or are to be, made in the course or furtherance of a business carried on by the person and are supplies of such a description that the person would be entitled to a credit for any input tax wholly attributable to those supplies.
(2) Occupation of land by a body which falls within section 33 *VATA* (local authorities) so far as the occupation is for purposes other than those of a business carried on by the body.
(3) Occupation of land by a Government department which falls within section 41 *VATA*.

---

[195] Paragraph 34(2), Schedule 10
[196] Paragraph 16, Schedule 10

In determining whether land is occupied for eligible purposes, a person occupying land who:

(a) holds the land in order to put it to use for particular purposes; and

(b) does not occupy it for any other purpose,

is treated as occupying the land for the purposes for which the person proposes to use it for so long as the conditions in (a) and (b) continue to be met.

Where land is in the occupation of a person who is not a taxable person, but is a person whose supplies are treated for the purposes of *VATA* as made by another person who is a taxable person, the land is treated as if the two were a single taxable person.[197] This would apply to occupation by a member of a VAT group.

A person occupies land whether the person occupies it alone or together with one or more other persons; and occupies all of the land or only part of it.[198]

HMRC will consider commercial documents and other evidence such as minutes of meetings, business plans and finance requests to establish the intention and expectation of the taxable persons that are involved in the particular development.[199]

Meaning of 'occupation'

In *HMRC v The Principal and Fellows of Newnham College in the University of Cambridge*[200] a university college wished to renovate its library. It opted to tax the library. It then granted a lease to a wholly-owned subsidiary company, and reclaimed input tax on the costs of renovating the library. HMRC issued a ruling that the effect of what is now paragraph 12 of Schedule 10 was that the college's option was ineffective and that the lease to the subsidiary remained exempt, so that the college was unable to recover the input tax. The Court of Appeal allowed the college's appeal, and the House of Lords upheld this decision (by a 3 to 2 majority, Lord Walker of Gestingthorpe and Lord Neuberger of Abbotsbury dissenting). Lord Hoffmann held that 'occupation' should be defined as 'the right to occupy property as if that person were the owner and to exclude any other person from enjoyment of such a right'. In this case, 'the essence of the right

---

[197] Paragraph 16(9), Schedule 10
[198] Paragraph 16(10), Schedule 10
[199] See VAT Notice 742A 'Opting to tax buildings and land' (June 2013) at para. 13.4
[200] [2008] STC 1225

conferred on the college is the right to the use of the books', and this did not amount to occupation of the library by the college. Lord Hoffmann distinguished the earlier decision in *Brambletye School Trust Ltd*[201] holding that 'a decision as to whether acts attributable to a body like the school or college amount to occupation of premises is a question of degree, sensitive to the particular constellation of facts'. Lord Mance observed that 'there is an important distinction between occupation of land and merely using it'.

HMRC's policy after *Newnham* is that:

> 'HMRC now accept that physical presence alone is not the correct test of occupation for the purposes of what is now VATA 1994 Schedule 10 Paragraphs 12 to 17 (the "anti-avoidance test"). Following the House of Lords judgment, a person is considered to be "in occupation" if, in addition to physical presence which occupation normally entails, they have the right to occupy the property as if they are the owner and to exclude others from enjoyment of such a right. This means a person must have actual possession of the land along with a degree of permanence and control. Such a right will normally result from the grant of a legal interest or licence to occupy. Occupation could also, however, be by agreement or de facto and it is therefore necessary to take account of the day to day arrangements, particularly where these differ from the contractual terms. An exclusive right of occupation is not a requirement; an agreement might, for example, allow for joint occupation. Equally, it is not necessary for a person to be utilising all of the land for all of the time for them to be considered as occupying it.

> A person whose interest in land is subject to an inferior interest, such as to prevent him from having rights of occupation for the time being, is not "in occupation" for the purposes of the anti-avoidance test until the inferior interest expires. It should be noted, however, that an important feature of the test is that it is forward looking and takes account of the intended or expected occupation of the building at any time during the capital goods scheme (CGS) adjustment period. As a result, a person who has granted an inferior interest but intends during that adjustment period to occupy the land himself would intend to be 'in occupation' for the purposes of the anti-avoidance test and so must consider whether his intended occupation was for eligible purposes.

> However, a person can ignore the following types of occupation for the purposes of the test:

> (1) Occupation which is purely for the purpose of making his rental supplies under the grant, since those are the very supplies whose liability he is trying to determine by applying the test. For example:

---

[201] [2002] VATDR 265

(a) occupation by the grantor between the date of the grant and the start of occupation by the tenant which is for the purpose of undertaking refurbishment or repairs,

(b) occupation by maintenance, security or reception staff (or similar), unless it is for the purpose of providing ongoing services separate from the letting itself.

(2) Occupation at a future date, but within the capital goods scheme adjustment period, which is solely for the purpose of re-letting the property or making a fresh grant.'[202]

9.15 Effect of the option to tax on input tax recovery

9.15.1 Input tax incurred on or after the date of the option

Once the option to tax has been exercised, a business can recover input tax on any related expenditure subject to the normal rules:[203]

(1) Where taxable supplies of the land or buildings are made, any input tax relating to those supplies can be recovered.

(2) Where wholly exempt supplies of the land or building are made (because the supplies are not affected by the option to tax), any input tax relating to those supplies cannot be recovered.

(3) Where supplies that are both taxable and exempt are made (e.g. where an opted building is to be used for both commercial and residential purposes), the input tax relating to the taxable supplies can be recovered under the partial exemption rules.

9.15.2 Input tax incurred before the option to tax has effect

Input tax incurred before the option to tax has effect can be recovered where the supply of land or buildings is taxable in its own right (for example, a freehold sale of a commercial building within three years of its completion which is always taxable at the standard rate).

Input tax incurred before the making of supplies can be recoverable where there is an intention, at the time the costs are incurred, that the supplies of the buildings or land will be taxable. The exercise of the option to tax is the best evidence of an intention to make taxable supplies for land and property transactions.

Following the tribunal decisions in *Trustees of Park Avenue Methodist Church*[204] and *Beaverbank Properties Ltd*[205] HMRC accept that objective

---

[202] See Revenue & Customs Brief 33/09 'VAT – clarification of HMRC's policy following the House of Lords' judgment in Newnham College' (8 June 2009)

[203] The input tax recovery rules are outlined in **Chapter 1**

[204] (VTD 17443)

evidence, other than the exercise of an option to tax, can be used to demonstrate an intention to make taxable supplies. This means that where a business wishes to delay exercising the option, it may still be able to recover input tax relating to supplies which will follow the option if it can produce unequivocal documentary evidence that, at the time it seeks to reclaim the input tax, it intends the supplies to be taxable.[206]

HMRC give the following as examples of the types of documents that may contain evidence of intention:[207]

- A signed agreement/contract that specifies that the seller will opt to tax before the sale.
- An investment appraisal or business plan accepted by a bank that confirms that supplies will be treated as taxable.
- Marketing literature that has been distributed to the public and where the scale and type of distribution, together with the nature of the advertisement itself, makes it clear that taxable supplies will be made.
- Instructions or advice from professional advisers that specifies the VAT treatment, together with confirmation of acceptance of the advice by the business.
- Any other similar document that shows that the intention is to make taxable supplies.

The list is not exhaustive and whether a particular document provides the evidence will depend largely upon its content. It is unlikely that any single document will provide sufficient evidence and a business is advised to hold a number of separate documents to prove its intention. HMRC will normally consider evidence as satisfactory where it involves third parties and shows a firm commitment to the making of taxable supplies. A document that merely sets out an option or number of options will not be acceptable.

Where input tax relating to future taxable supplies has been recovered, a business should retain any documents used as evidence of intention and make them available to HMRC on request. If there is any change in the intention to make taxable supplies, a record must be kept of the date of change (together with appropriate evidence) and HMRC must also be informed of the change as soon as possible.[208] Any VAT previously

---

[205] (VTD 18099)
[206] VAT Notice 742A 'Opting to tax buildings and land' (June 2013) at para. 9.2.2
[207] VAT Notice 742A 'Opting to tax buildings and land' (June 2013) at para. 9.2.3
[208] VAT Notice 742A 'Opting to tax buildings and land' (June 2013) at para. 9.2.4

deducted before the intention changed may need to be adjusted and repaid to HMRC.

Where, before supplies are made, the intention to make exempt supplies changes to an intention to make taxable supplies, a business may be able to recover previously exempt input tax under the 'payback rule'. But where the change of intention is not accompanied by the exercise of an option to tax, the business will need to retain suitable evidence of its new intention.[209]

The 'payback rule' is in regulation 109 of the VAT Regulations and allows a business to recoup input tax on costs that are incurred to make exempt supplies, but are instead used wholly or partly to make taxable supplies. Payback also applies to costs incurred for both taxable and exempt purposes, but actually used to make wholly taxable supplies.

Where exempt supplies of the land or building have been made before opting to tax and exempt input tax has been incurred that input tax may be recoverable by making a 'longer period adjustment' under the partial exemption rules.[210]

Where exempt supplies of the land or building have been made before opting to tax and exempt input tax has been incurred that input tax be recoverable by way of adjustments under the capital goods scheme to reflect taxable use after the option has been exercised.[211]

Where a business made exempt supplies of the land or building before opting to tax and incurred exempt input tax, it may be able to recover this under the permission procedure discussed at **9.11** above.

Pre-election input tax: Royal & Sun Alliance Insurance Group plc v CCE[212]
Royal Sun Alliance Group plc ('RSA') held the leasehold interests in a number of properties. RSA had originally occupied the properties for the purposes of its insurance business, but subsequently vacated them, and decided to sublet them. In 1995 it opted to tax the properties. It subsequently claimed a repayment of input tax incurred on rents and service charges relating to the properties before exercising the option (and when the properties were vacant). It had initially attributed this input tax to exempt supplies. HMRC rejected the claim and the representative member

---

[209] VAT Notice 742A 'Opting to tax buildings and land' (June 2013) at para. 9.2.5
[210] The **partial exemption** rules are outlined in **Chapter 1**
[211] For the **capital goods scheme** see **11.4**
[212] [2003] STC 832

of the RSA group appealed, contending that it was entitled to make an adjustment under regulation 109 of the VAT Regulations.

The tribunal dismissed the appeal, finding that the input tax in dispute related to a period when RSA was actively seeking to sublet the properties, and holding that any such supplies would be exempt, because the option to tax had not been exercised at the relevant time. The Chancery Division (Park J) reversed the tribunal decision and that decision was upheld by the Court of Appeal. The House of Lords reversed the decision of the Court of Appeal (by a 3 to 2 majority, Lord Woolf and Lord Clyde dissenting), overturned Park J and restored the tribunal decision in HMRC's favour.

The House of Lords held that the plain effect of regulations 85 and 90 of the VAT Regulations[213] was to treat each successive supply as different from the one before. In relation to the grant of a time-limited interest in land, such as a lease or licence, VAT law treated the superior owner as granting rights of occupation in successive units of time, depending upon the stipulated intervals for payment of the rent. Thus the goods and services supplied during the vacant unopted period were different from those supplied afterwards, and a change of plan about the use to be made of the leases in the future was not a change of intention about the use of the leases in the past. Moreover, an activity that was taxable was not the same for VAT purposes as an activity that was exempt, and, while the nature of the activity usually determined whether it was taxable or exempt, letting land could be two different activities according to whether or not an election had been made. Here RSA had been engaged in one economic activity in the vacant unopted periods, in respect of which it had no outputs, and a different economic activity following its exercise of the option to tax the properties. In deciding to opt and make taxable supplies, RSA was in a position no different from a person who decided to change from an activity which involved making exempt supplies to a different activity which involved making taxable supplies. If there were still inputs from the previous available to be used in the new taxable activity, RSA would be entitled to an adjustment. It could not, however, rewrite history. It had been impossible for RSA, in or about November 1995, to use or form an intention to use supplies of accommodation for successive periods which were then past history.

Lord Hoffmann observed that in order to come within regulation 109, RSA must first have had an intention to use the inputs in supplying exempt sub-

---

[213] Discussed at **2.2.2** above

leases and then used them, or formed an intention to use them, in supplying taxable sub-leases. On the evidence, RSA 'was not carrying on an economic activity for the purpose of making taxable outputs'. Applying the principles in *Belgium v Ghent Coal Terminal NV*[214], 'just as a failure to make taxable supplies does not destroy a right of deduction, so a failure to make exempt supplies does not create one'. RSA was in the same position as someone 'who decided to change from an activity which involved making exempt supplies to a different activity making taxable supplies. If there are still inputs around from the previous activity which can be used in the new taxable activity, like a building which has been constructed for exempt letting and is then used, after an election, for taxable letting, the taxpayer will be entitled to an adjustment', but 'he cannot rewrite history'.

Lord Walker of Gestingthorpe observed that 'it is an inescapable consequence of the general structure of VAT that a trader who makes partially exempt and partially taxable supplies (or who switches from exempt to taxable supplies) cannot expect precisely the same treatment as one who makes taxable supplies throughout. That would be pressing the principle of fiscal neutrality too far.'

9.16 Timing of the exercise of the option to tax – some practical points

Retrospective exercise of the option to tax a property is not possible, timing can be crucial. Many property owners wait to see if their prospective tenant or buyer can reclaim any VAT charged before opting. This is so that the best price can be obtained as irrecoverable VAT will be a cost to the buyer.

It is essential to opt to tax before any exempt supplies are made to avoid the requirement to get HMRC's prior permission to exercise the option. It is also advisable to opt before any input tax is incurred to ensure that that input tax can be recovered.

The grant of a put option in respect of land (the right to require someone to purchase an interest in the land) is not a relevant grant as that grant is not the supply of an interest in the land (and is, in any event, a supply by the prospective buyer).[215]

A transfer of a business as a going concern is not subject to VAT.[216] Where a property is being acquired as part of the TOGC, it will be excluded from the

---

[214] Case C-37/95 [1998] STC 260
[215] Confirmed at paragraph 7.4, VAT Notice 742 'Land and property' (June 2012)
[216] For **TOGCs** see **Chapter 1**

VAT-free transfer if it is a property in respect of which the option to tax has been exercised or it is the grant of a fee simple falling within Item 1(a) of Group 1 of Schedule 9[217] (which are supplies taxable at the standard rate) unless the buyer opts and notifies HMRC before any supply of the property is made to him.

The receipt of a deposit by the seller triggers a supply (tax point) for VAT purposes. This normally impacts where properties are bought at auction because a deposit must be paid when a bid is successful. A buyer could take either of two actions under such circumstances:

(1) opt to tax and notify HMRC before bidding for the property and revoke the option (under the cooling-off provisions[218]) should the sale fall through; or

(2) pay the deposit over to a third party as a stakeholder.

An illustration: *Higher Education Statistics Agency v CCE*[219]

A company purchased a let property at auction. The seller had opted to tax the property, and it was accepted that the letting of the property constituted a business. Following exchange of contracts, the company also opted to tax the property. HMRC issued a ruling that tax was chargeable on the transfer as it was not a TOGC. The effect of this ruling was that, by virtue of the transfer, the property became a capital item within the capital goods scheme,[220] so that if the property were to be used for exempt or non-business purposes within the following ten years, there would be a charge to tax by means of an adjustment to the initial deduction of input tax.

The company appealed, contending that the effect of article 5 of the Value Added Tax (Special Provisions) Order 1995[221] was that the transfer should not be treated as a supply. The tribunal rejected this contention and dismissed the appeal. The effect of article 5(2) of the Order was that the transfer was to be treated as a supply, unless the transferee had opted to tax (and given notification to HMRC) 'no later than the relevant date'. Article 5(3) provided that:

---

[217] Item 1(a) covers the 'grant' of the 'fee simple' in a 'new' or 'uncompleted' 'commercial building' or civil engineering work – for definitions see **1.2**

[218] See **9.9.1** above

[219] [2000] STC 332 (QBD)

[220] For the **capital goods scheme** see **11.4** below

[221] SI 1995/1268

'"relevant date" means the date upon which the grant would have been treated as having been made or, if there is more than one such date, the earliest of them;'

The effect of article 5(3) was that the relevant date was the date of the contract, rather than the date of completion.

The tribunal observed that conveyancing solicitors were generally aware of HMRC's view that 'where it is intended that the transfer of otherwise taxable property is to be regarded as the transfer of a going concern, then the buyer must opt and notify before the tax point relating to the transfer'. The tribunal also held that the relevant legislation was not inconsistent with the Sixth Directive since article 5 (8) of the Sixth Directive 'provides a specific power to Member States to take the necessary measures to prevent distortion of competition in cases where the recipient of assets is not wholly liable to tax'.

The company appealed. Moses J held that 'the relevant date is the date when the deposit was paid'. Since the company had not opted to tax on or before that date, it was liable to pay output tax on the purchase.

10 Supplies in the Building Industry

10.1 Introduction

The normal rule is that supplies of building work and building materials are taxable at the standard rate. Supplies in the building industry which are relieved by being taxed at either the zero-rate (ZR) or the reduced rate[1] (RR) are outlined in the Table at **10.2** below and are dealt with in this book at the location given in the right-hand column of that Table.

The lowest rate applicable to a supply is chargeable. For example, where works of carrying out an approved alteration to an empty listed dwelling qualifies for zero-rating (as an approved alteration to a protected building) and for the reduced-rate (as an alteration to an empty dwelling), zero-rating applies. The same VAT rate applies to retention payments when they are released as applied to previous payments made under the contract.

In most circumstances sub-contractors can apply the zero-rate or the reduced rate to their supplies in the same way as a main contractor but where the work requires a certificate to qualify for relief (for example, where conversion services are supplied to housing associations), a sub contractor's supplies to the main contractor will be taxable at the standard rate.

Where the developer of a building will be making a zero-rated supply of it, the issue of whether he is charged at the standard rate or a reduced rate on building work will have secondary importance. This is because a person making a zero-rated supply can generally reclaim the related input tax charged to him, although there is, of course, a cash flow cost of paying VAT to the supplier and later reclaiming it from HMRC through the VAT return. In contrast, where the supply of the completed building is by way of the grant of a short-lease which is not eligible for zero-rating[2] the VAT liability of the building work and other supplies made to a developer will become more important. As an exempt supply of the building is being made the developer will not be able to reclaim any attributable input tax and so will

---

[1] The reduced rate also applies to the installation of certain energy-saving materials, heating equipment or security goods and the installation of mobility aids for people over 60 but these are not dealt with in this book

[2] See *CCE v Briararch Ltd; CCE v Curtis Henderson Ltd* [1992] STC 732 (HC) and Revenue & Customs Brief 44/08 'VAT: Partial Exemption – VAT adjustments when house builders let their dwellings before selling them' (16 September 2008)

be concerned to ensure that the supplies made to him are, where possible, charged at the zero-rate or the reduced rate to avoid an additional cost.

One potential solution to the problem of short-term lets may be to sell the property to an associate, by way of a zero-rated supply of a major interest in it. As a zero-rated supply has been made the attributable input tax can be recovered. The associate would then make the exempt onward supplies. If the person making the supply of the major interest, or any body corporate treated as a member of a VAT group of which that person is a member, attributes to that supply input tax incurred in respect of a service charge relating to the building; or in connection with any extension, enlargement, repair, maintenance or refurbishment of the building, other than for remedying defects in the original construction, the transaction will have to be notified to HMRC as a designated avoidance scheme. This does not mean that HMRC will necessarily dispute the VAT consequences of the transaction, but they would certainly examine it to see if there was any potential for dispute.

It is the supplier who must determine whether a relief applies as he will be liable to account for any output tax which should have been charged if a supply has been incorrectly characterised. Strictly, only VAT which was properly charged on a supply can qualify as input tax of the person to whom the supply is made so both parties have an interest in getting the VAT liability right.

Claw-back of relief

Change of use claw-back provisions can apply where zero-rating has been applied to a supply of services on the basis of the use of the building and certain events occur within ten years of the building's completion. These provisions are described at **6.5** above.

10.2 Table outlining reliefs

Supply	Rate	Cross reference
The supply of qualifying services in the course of construction of a building designed as a dwelling or number of dwellings	ZR	10.3
The supply of qualifying services in the course of construction of building intended for use solely for a relevant residential purpose	ZR	10.3
The supply of qualifying services in the course of construction of a building intended for use solely for a relevant charitable purpose	ZR	10.3
The supply of qualifying services in the course of construction of a new permanent residential caravan park	ZR	13.1
The supply of qualifying services to a housing association in the course of conversion of a non-residential building into a dwelling or dwellings or a into a building intended for use solely for a relevant residential purpose	ZR	7.1
The supply of qualifying services in the course of an approved alteration to a protected building under the transitional rules applying until 30 September 2015	ZR	8.1
The supply of building materials incorporated into a building by a builder who is also supplying zero-rated services	ZR	10.7
The supply of qualifying goods and services for a disabled person to that person or to a charity	ZR	10.4
The supply of qualifying services in the course of a qualifying conversion	RR	10.5
The supply of qualifying services in the course of the certain residential renovations and alterations	RR	10.6
The supply of building materials incorporated into a building by a builder who is also supplying services taxable at the reduced rate	RR	10.7

10.3 Zero-rating of the construction of certain buildings
Item 2(a), Group 5, Schedule 8

The supply 'in the course of construction' of a building 'designed as a dwelling or number of dwellings' or intended for use solely for a 'relevant residential purpose' or a 'relevant charitable purpose' of services which relate to the construction, other than:

(1) the separate supply of architectural, surveying, consultancy or supervisory services;

(2) the hiring of goods on their own (for example, the supply of plant and machinery without an operator, or of scaffolding without erection/dismantling); and

(3) the private use of goods;

is zero-rated.

The three types of qualifying buildings are referred to in this section as 'qualifying buildings'.

For a discussion of when a building is 'designed as a dwelling or number of dwellings' see **4.3.2** above.

For buildings used for a 'relevant residential' or a 'relevant charitable purpose' see **Chapter 1**.

For services to be zero-rated they must be supplied 'in the course of' the construction of a zero-rated building. Works supplied after construction has been completed cannot be zero-rated even if they would otherwise qualify.[3] There is no definition of when construction of a building is finished for the purposes of zero-rating of building services[4] so the normal meaning of 'in the course of construction' must be applied. The time of supply of the building services themselves is dealt with at **10.9** below.

Other services essential to the construction of a qualifying building and carried out at the same time as that construction will be subject to the same rate of VAT as the construction services. Thus, if a new dwelling or dwellings is being built associated civil engineering works will also be zero-rated. Should these services be carried out under a separate contract or at a later date, they will be standard rated.

The incorporation of 'extra' facilities into a dwelling during its construction will enable the works to be zero-rated. If an indoor gym, pool or sports facility is constructed as part of a dwelling the works would be zero-rated. It should be noted that some goods installed as part of those works may not be eligible for the zero-rate relief.[5] Another example was where a dock was

---

[3] See, for example, *SA Whiteley* [1993] VATTR 248

[4] The definition of when a building is 'completed' in Note (2),Group 1, Schedule 9 is not applied for this purpose

[5] See **10.7** below

incorporated into a newly constructed riverside house, the works necessary for the dock (the sheet piling that held back the riverbank, dockside, staircase to the house and the work necessary to lift the house to allow the boat to be moored underneath) were zero-rated.[6]

In *St Mary's RC High School*[7] the High Court confirmed that not all works connected to the construction of a zero-rated building could be zero-rated and held that the relief is restricted to works 'where there is a relation between the services and the construction of the building'. St Mary's opened in 1981 and the school buildings had been constructed between 1979 and 1983. In order to comply with certain statutory requirements for recreation areas on school premises, two multi-purpose hard playgrounds were included in the original plans. However, the construction of the playgrounds had to be deferred until a diversion order was made in respect of a right of way which crossed part of the school's land and after further funding had been raised to pay for both the diverted right of way and the playgrounds. Construction of the playgrounds commenced in August 1994 and was completed in November of that year.

St Mary's appealed to the tribunal against HMRC's decision that the construction of the playgrounds was an extension to the original school building and therefore did not qualify for zero-rating as 'the supply in the course of the construction of ... a building ... of any services.' St Mary's contended that the playgrounds were part of the original school building as their construction was planned and intended throughout as an integral part of the school premises; hence their construction was the final completion of, not an extension to, the school building; and that as part of the construction work on the school it was zero-rated.

The tribunal accepted that the construction of the playgrounds was properly to be regarded as completing the original school and not as an extension or an enlargement to it and it allowed the appeal having concluded that if the construction of the playgrounds had been carried out when the school was built, the work would have been zero-rated as a whole. HMRC appealed.

Jowitt J laid down the following principles in construing what was then Item 2 of Group 8 of Schedule 5 to the *Value Added Tax Act 1983*:

---

[6] *Turner Stroud & Burley Construction Ltd* (VTD 15454)
[7] [1996] STC 1091 (QB)

(1) The services had to be connected with the construction of the building in that they had facilitated its construction or produced, in their finished result, one whole with the building. That required a consideration both of the purpose of the building and of the end product of the other services in question to establish whether the additional works helped the building to function in accordance with its purpose. However, it was not sufficient that a functional connection be established. There also had to be a temporal connection between the construction of the building and the provision of the other services.

(2) Where those services were not provided contemporaneously with the construction of the building, it was necessary to consider both the reasons for and the length of the delay before deciding whether or not the temporal connection had been established. A question of degree might be involved and the facts of a case might permit of two different views.

In the *St Mary's Case*, however, the tribunal by failing to consider whether or not a sufficient temporal link had been established between the construction of the school and the playgrounds had misdirected itself in law. Moreover, even if the tribunal had considered such a question, the interval between the completion of the building works on the school and the construction of the playgrounds was far too long to establish the necessary temporal link.

A school that constructed a sewage plant for its new boarding house benefited from the zero-rate relief. This was because the work was a necessary part of the new construction, and was contemporaneous with the construction of a qualifying building[8].

Where a zero-rated building is constructed the following can also be zero-rated:[9]

- ground works, including levelling and drainage;
- site clearance;
- providing access, security services (including fencing), power and water to the site;
- soft landscaping required under planning consent;
- snagging or rectification of faults; and
- first connection of utilities to the building.

---

[8] *CCE v Rannoch School Ltd* [1993] STC 389 (CS)

[9] VAT Notice 708 'Buildings and construction' (August 2014) at paragraphs 3.3.3 and 3.3.4

10.3.1 Demolition services

If demolition services are supplied under a separate contract, they are subject to VAT at the standard rate. However, if they are supplied as part of a contract to construct a building the supply takes the same VAT liability as the overall contract. This rule also applies to construction services benefiting from the reduced rate where demolition services are included in the contract.

10.3.2 Civil engineering work to serviced building plots

Following the decision in *D & S Virtue (t/a Lammermuir Game Services)*[10] that a supply of a serviced building plot is a single exempt supply (and not a mixed supply of exempt land and standard-rated civil engineering work), HMRC accept that the supply of civil engineering works to a landowner to service a building plot is zero-rated where it is clear that construction of a qualifying building will begin as soon as possible.[11]

10.3.3 Excluded services

Supplies by architects, engineers, surveyors and all other consultancy or supervisory services relating to the zero-rated construction are subject to VAT at the standard rate unless they are supplied as part of a design and build contract, when the supply takes the same VAT liability as supplies under that contract.

A design and build contract is where a client engages a contractor to carry out both the design and construction elements of the project. Where it is clear in the contract that any services of architects, surveyors or others acting as a consultant or in a supervisory capacity are no more than cost components of the contractor's supply, then the whole supply can be treated as being eligible for the zero rate.

Also excluded from zero-rating under Item 2 of Group 5 of Schedule 8 is the hire of goods[12]. There has been some doubts about whether this covers the provision of scaffolding. The tribunal in *Brian Gilbourne*[13] held that the supply of scaffolding was the hire of goods and was therefore excluded from zero-rating. It was found by a later tribunal in *GT Scaffolding Ltd*[14] that

---

[10] [2007] VATDR 308

[11] Revenue & Customs Brief 64/07 'VAT: Changes in the VAT treatment of serviced building plots' (17 October 2007) now replaced by paragraph 3.3.8 VAT Notice 708 'Buildings and construction' (August 2014)

[12] By Note 20, Group 5, Schedule 8

[13] [1974] VATTR 209

[14] (VTD 18226)

a tightening of the legislation regarding scaffolding meant that it could only be erected and dismantled by qualified staff so GT Scaffolding retained possession of the scaffolding throughout. Consequently there was no hiring of goods and the supply could be zero-rated. *GT Scaffolding Ltd* was reversed in part in *R & M Scaffolding Ltd*[15]. HMRC issued a ruling that the company was making standard rated supplies of the hire of the scaffolding (on the basis of the decision in *Gilbourne*). The tribunal allowed the company's appeal in part, holding that 'once the scaffolding had been erected and certified as safe by the appellant, "possession" passed to its customer.' Accordingly 'there should be an apportionment of the price between the erection and dismantling on the one hand, and the use by the customer on the other.'

The following additional provisions apply where all or part of a building is intended for use solely for a relevant residential or relevant charitable purpose:

(1) Where all or part of a building is intended for use solely for a relevant residential or relevant charitable purpose, a supplier of services within these provisions cannot zero-rate the supply until the customer has given him a certificate to that effect.[16]

(2) No supply of services relating to a building (or part of it) can be taken for the above purposes as relating to a building intended for such use unless it is made to a person who intends to use the building (or part) for such a purpose[17]. The main effect of this is that, although the main contractor can zero-rate the construction of such a building, a subcontractor must standard-rate all supplies to the main contractor on such building projects.

10.3.4 Apportionment

Note (11) to Group 5 of Schedule 8 requires the apportionment of any works that partly fall within the relief and partly outside the relief. Where part of a building being constructed qualifies for zero-rating and part does not (for example, flats above shops) then there is a need to apportion. Any works that relate directly to the zero-rated part of the building can be zero-rated. Works that relate only to the non-zero-rated part are taxable at the standard

---

[15] (VTD 18954 and 18955)

[16] Note (12), Group 5, Schedule 8 – the form of the certificate is set out in paragraph 18.1 VAT Notice 708: Notice 708 'Buildings and construction' (August 2014) which has the force of law

[17] Note (12), Group 5, Schedule 8

rate. Works such as roofs, foundations, wiring, plumbing etc. which relate to both parts must be apportioned between the zero-rated and standard rated elements. Apportionment may also be necessary in the case of a mixed development.

University Court of the University of St Andrews[18] illustrates the difficulties that can arise when there is a need to apportion. The university constructed a facilities building including a gym, music room, kitchen and dining room, projection room, bar, shop and common room to support new student accommodation blocks. This would normally be zero-rated if constructed at the same time as the accommodation blocks. However, the inclusion of a bar and shop meant that some of the costs were standard rated, and the construction costs had to be apportioned. This would not have created a problem for the university, as the VAT incurred on the construction would be recoverable by reason of the taxable supplies made in the shop and bar. The problem arose in respect of the communal areas, areas shared by the accommodation and the bar and shop.

HMRC would not permit the application of the zero-rate to the costs of construction of toilets, cupboards, a first aid room, corridors, lobbies, and other mixed use areas even though these would have been included in the building irrespective of the inclusion of the bar and shop in the project. HMRC's view was that the VAT incurred on these areas had to be recovered according to the university's partial exemption method[19]. This represented a cost to the university on the construction of halls of residence as a result of including areas that would be used only for the purposes of generating taxable income. The university had a partial victory at the tribunal, securing zero-rating for the costs of construction of the toilets, the first aid room and a corridor, but lost in respect of other areas, such as the reception and lobby.

Live-work units[20]
A live-work unit is a property that combines a dwelling and commercial or industrial working space as a requirement or condition of planning permission. Zero-rating is only available to the extent of the dwelling element of the unit. Dwellings that contain a home office are not live-work units and no apportionment is needed.

---

[18] (VTD 19054)

[19] For **partial exemption** see **Chapter 1**

[20] VAT Notice 708 'Buildings and construction' (August 2014) at section 16.4

Live-work units where the work area is a discrete area of floor space must be apportioned to reflect the presence of the commercial element. Where planning permission requires that a minimum amount of the unit must be used for commercial or industrial purposes, the remaining amount can be treated as being the dwelling element for VAT purposes. Where a unit has neither an area that must, as a requirement or condition of planning permission, be used for commercial or industrial purposes, nor planning permission requiring a certain percentage of the floor space be used for commercial or industrial purposes HMRC allow it to be treated for VAT purposes as if it were entirely a dwelling and no apportionment is required.

10.4 Zero-rating of certain goods and services supplied to a disabled person

Group 12, Schedule 8

There are specific reliefs for the disabled in the UK VAT legislation. The ones which are covered in this Chapter are the zero-rating of building work for the benefit of people with disabilities which can apply to:

(1) The provision, extension or adaptation of a bathroom, washroom or lavatory.[21]
(2) The provision of ramps or widened doorways or passages to allow access.[22]

For relief to be available, both the goods and/or services and the recipient must qualify.

The relief is for supplies to the 'handicapped' or to a charity for use by the handicapped. Handicapped is defined as 'chronically sick or disabled'.[23] Infirmity due to old age is insufficient grounds to obtain zero-rating.[24]

HMRC recommend that a supplier obtains a written declaration from his customer that he fulfils the criteria for zero-rating. This declaration is not a prerequisite for relief as it is not required by law[25] but extra-statutory concession 3.11 provides:[26]

---

[21] Items 10 to 13, Group 12, Schedule 8
[22] Items 8, 9 and 13, Group 12, Schedule 8
[23] Note (3), Group 12, Schedule 8
[24] *CCE v Help the Aged* [1997] STC 406 (QB)
[25] For the suggested form of the declaration see VAT Notice 701/7, 'VAT reliefs for disabled people' (August 2002) at Section 10.1
[26] See VAT Notice 48: extra-statutory concessions (21 March 2012)

'VAT: incorrect customer declaration

Where a customer provides an incorrect declaration claiming eligibility for zero-rating under Group ... 12 ... of the zero rate Schedule of the VAT Act 1994, ... and where a supplier, despite having taken all reasonable steps to check the validity of the declaration, nonetheless fails to identify the inaccuracy and in good faith makes the supplies concerned at the zero rate, ... HMRC will not seek to recover the tax due from the supplier.'

10.4.1 Bathroom etc. facilities

Items 10 to 13, Group 12, Schedule 8

The supply to a disabled person of the service of providing, extending or adapting a bathroom, washroom or lavatory in that person's private residence is zero-rated, provided that the work is necessary for that person's condition. The relief is frequently applied where a downstairs bathroom is created for a disabled person who can no longer use an upstairs one. The supply of goods in connection with the supply is also zero-rated.

Where the provision is made in, or extended into an existing room, any works necessary to restore that other room (or what is left of it) can also be zero-rated. Conversely, where the facility is provided and at the same time there are other extension works or additional accommodation is created, the work needs to be apportioned between the zero-rated work of providing the bathroom, washroom or lavatory facilities and the other standard rated works.

Supplies to a charity of these services for the use of the disabled in a residential home for handicapped persons are zero-rated[27], as are supplies to a day-centre where 20 per cent of the individuals using the centre are handicapped[28] provided that, in each case, the provision, extension or adaptation is necessary by reason of the condition of the handicapped. The supply of goods in connection with' the supply is also zero-rated.

The supply to a charity of a service of providing, extending or adapting a washroom for use by the disabled in a building primarily used by the charity for charitable purposes is zero-rated[29] but there is no provision zero-rating supplies of goods in this case.

---

[27] Item 11(a), Group 12, Schedule 8
[28] Item 11(b), Group 12, Schedule 8
[29] Item 12, Group 12, Schedule 8

10.4.2 Disabled access

Items 8, 9 and 13, Group 12, Schedule 8

Zero-rating relief exists for the following:

(1) The construction of ramps, alterations to doorways and alterations to passageways in the private residence of a disabled person to that person to facilitate his entry or movement.[30]

(2) The supply to a charity of the construction of ramps, alterations to doorways and alterations to passageways for the purpose of facilitating a disabled person's entry to or movement within any building.[31]

A private residence includes its gardens, yards and outbuildings. Where qualifying works are undertaken the works will be zero-rated by the contractor providing the services, but work by sub-contractors will be subject to VAT at the standard rate.

The construction of a ramp includes raising or lowering of floor levels to match another adjacent floor level to remove steps, the creation of a slope or the reduction of the angle of a slope. Passageway-widening would include associated widening of doorways, widening of a room so that access is provided to another room and the widening of a path across a disabled person's garden but the creation of a new path is standard rated.

In addition to the works of widening or creation of ramps, necessary remedial works or preparatory works are also zero-rated. The supply of building materials can also be zero-rated, when supplied in connection with the zero-rated rated works. It is usually simplest for the contractor to acquire the goods and re-claim the VAT incurred.

10.5 Reduced rate for qualifying conversions

Group 6, Schedule 7A

VAT is charged at the reduced rate of 5 per cent where 'qualifying services' are supplied in the course of a 'qualifying conversion' and those services are related to the conversion.[32] 'Building materials' may also benefit from the reduced rate relief.[33] There are additional requirements which apply before

---

[30] Item 8, Group 12, Schedule 8
[31] Item 9, Group 12, Schedule 8
[32] Item 1, Group 6, Schedule 7A
[33] Item 1, Group 6, Schedule 7A - see below

a supply of services which relates to a special residential conversion can qualify for the reduced rate.[34]

A 'supply of qualifying services' means:[35]

(1) The carrying out of work to the fabric of the building or part of the building of the building being converted (excluding the incorporation, or installation as fittings, in the building or part of the building of any goods that are not 'building materials').

(2) The carrying out of work within the immediate site of the building that are in connection with:

    (a) the means of providing water, power, heat or access to the building or part of the building,

    (b) the means of providing drainage or security for the building or part of the building,

    (c) the provision of means of waste disposal for the building or part of the building.

This includes the repair, maintenance or improvement to the fabric of the building where the work forms an intrinsic part of the conversion.

All other services are standard-rated. Where part of a supply of services qualifies and part does not, the supply can be apportioned to determine the extent to which the reduced rate can be applied.[36]

The relief applies to the main contractors providing the qualifying services. Sub-contractors can also apply the reduced rate to qualifying services where the work is for a changed number of dwellings or a multiple occupancy dwelling conversion. Sub-contractors must charge the standard rate for work done on special residential conversions as they will not be both supplying the services to the person who intends to use the building for the relevant residential purpose after conversion and in possession of the necessary certificate (see below). The main contractor will be able to reclaim the VAT that is charged to him by the sub-contractor.

10.5.1 Qualifying conversion

There are three types of qualifying conversion.[37] In each case any statutory planning consent and/or any statutory building control approval needed for the conversion must have been granted.[38]

---

[34] Note 8, Group 6, Schedule 7A - see **10.5.1** below
[35] Note 11, Group 6, Schedule 7A
[36] Notes 1(2) and 1(3), Group 6, Schedule 7A
[37] Note 2, Group 6, Schedule 7A

Type One - A 'changed number of dwellings conversion[39]'

A 'changed number of dwellings conversion' is a conversion which produces a change in the number of 'single household dwellings' in any type of building or part of a building. The change can be an increase or a decrease but after the conversion there must be at least one 'single household dwelling.' After the conversion, there must be no part of the premises that contains the same number of single household dwellings (including zero) as before the conversion.

A 'single household dwelling' means[40] a dwelling designed (either originally or as a result of adaptation)[41] for occupation by a single household, and, in relation to which the following conditions are satisfied:

(a) it consists of self contained living accommodation;

(b) there is no provision for direct internal access from it to any other dwelling or part of a dwelling;

(c) the separate use of it is not prohibited by the terms of any covenant, statutory planning consent or similar provision; and

(d) the separate disposal of it is not prohibited by any such terms.

The legislation[42] in relation to a changed number of dwellings conversion provides that the reduced rate will not apply to '...a part that after conversion contains the same number of single household dwellings (whether zero, one, two or more) as before'. The *Wellcome Trust* decision[43] illustrates the need to consider whether all of a building benefits from the reduced rate relief, or just part.

Wellcome Trust owned two interconnecting six-storey terraced houses which were divided into six flats. It arranged to convert the two properties into four flats. HMRC accepted that the work to five floors was taxable at the reduced rate, but ruled that the works on the second floor were subject to VAT at the standard rate. This was because the second floor remained a single household dwelling after the conversion. Wellcome Trust appealed on the basis that the footprint of that floor changed due to changes to the stairwells and other minor works. Wellcome argued that there was no legal definition of the term 'part' and that the second floor of the building being

---

[38] Note 10, Group 6, Schedule 7A

[39] Note 3, Group 6, Schedule 7A

[40] Note 4, Group 6, Schedule 7A

[41] Note 4(4), Group 6, Schedule 7A

[42] Note 3, Group 6, Schedule 7A

[43] [2003] VATDR 572

converted formed part of the building as a whole and therefore it followed that the reduced rate should apply.

The tribunal found for HMRC holding that the second floor had to be regarded as a part of a building and that part still only contained a single household dwelling after the conversion. The tribunal commented that a 'part' 'must have some minimum size', and:

> 'Any relevant part of the premises must be capable of being identified by reference to physical boundaries, normally walls, floors and ceilings after the conversion; a notional line in the middle of a room would not suffice.'

The second-floor flat had to be viewed as 'part' of the building so work on that floor failed to qualify for the reduced rate.

Type Two - A 'house in multiple occupation conversion'[44]

A 'house in multiple occupation conversion' is a conversion from any type of building or part of a building that does not contain any 'multiple occupancy dwellings' into a multiple occupancy dwelling or dwellings. After the conversion the premises must contain only a multiple occupancy dwelling or dwellings and the intended use must not, to any extent, be use for a 'relevant residential purpose'.[45]

A 'multiple occupancy dwelling' is, broadly, hostel-type accommodation, and is defined in Note 4(2), Group 6, Schedule 7A as:

(1) a dwelling that is 'designed for' occupation by persons not forming a single household and that is not to any extent used for a 'relevant residential purpose';
(2) in relation to which the following conditions are satisfied:
    (a) it consists of self-contained living accommodation;
    (b) there is no provision for direct internal access from it to any other dwelling or part of a dwelling;
    (c) separate use is not prohibited by the terms of any covenant or planning permission; and
    (d) separate disposal is not prohibited by the terms of any covenant or planning permission.

A dwelling is 'designed for' occupation of a particular kind if it is so designed as a result of having been originally constructed for occupation of

---

[44] Note 5, Group 6, Schedule 7A
[45] See **1.2.29** above for the meaning of '**use for a relevant residential purpose**'

that kind and not having been subsequently adapted for occupation of any other kind, or as a result of adaptation[46].

Type Three - A 'special residential conversion[47]'

A 'special residential conversion' is a conversion of any building or buildings, or part or parts of a building, or any combination of buildings or parts of buildings which were not being used for a 'relevant residential purpose'[48] into premises intended for use solely for such a purpose. Where the intended relevant residential purpose use after conversion is an 'institutional purpose' the premises being converted must be intended to form the entirety of an institution used for that purpose after conversion.

An 'institutional purpose' is use as:[49]

(a) a home or other institution providing residential accommodation for children;

(b) a home or other institution providing residential accommodation with personal care for persons in need of personal care by reason of old age, disablement, past or present dependence on alcohol or drugs or past or present mental disorder;

(c) a hospice;

(d) a monastery, nunnery or similar establishment; or

(e) an institution which is the sole or main residence of at least 90 per cent of its residents, except use as a hospital, prison or similar institution or a hotel, inn or similar establishment.

There are additional requirements which apply before supplies of services which relate to a special residential conversion can qualify for the reduced rate.[50] These are:

(1) The conversion services must be supplied to a person who intends to use the building for the relevant residential purpose after the conversion.

(2) Before the supply is made the recipient of the supply gives the supplier a certificate in the form set out in paragraph 18.1 of VAT Notice 708.[51]

It is, therefore, a requirement that the contractor must obtain a certificate

---

[46] Note 2(4) Group 6, Schedule 7A

[47] Note 7, Group 6, Schedule 7A

[48] See **1.2.29** above for the meaning of '**use for a relevant residential purpose**'

[49] Note 7, Group 6, Schedule 7A

[50] Note 8, Group 6, Schedule 7A

[51] 'Buildings and construction' (August 2014)

from the person intending to put the building solely to relevant residential use before the reduced rate can be applied to the special residential conversion. There is no requirement for certificates to be obtained for the other two types of qualifying conversion.

10.5.2   Garages
Note 9, Group 6, Schedule 7A

A qualifying conversion includes the construction of a garage or the conversion of a 'non-residential' building (or of a 'non-residential' part of a building) that results in a garage provided that:

(1) the garage works are carried out at the same time as the conversion; and
(2) the resulting garage is intended to be occupied:
   (a) where the conversion is a changed number of dwelling conversion, with a single household dwelling that will after the conversion be contained in the building, or part of a building, being converted;
   (b) where the conversion is a house in multiple occupation conversion, with a multiple occupancy dwelling that will after the conversion be contained in the building, or part of a building, being converted; or
   (c) where the conversion is a special residential conversion, with the institution or other accommodation resulting from the conversion.

'Non-residential' means neither designed, nor adapted, for use as a dwelling or two or more dwellings, or for a relevant residential purpose.[52]

10.6 Reduced rate for certain residential renovations and alterations
Group 7, Schedule 7A

Refurbishing existing residential property can create a VAT cost depending on the ultimate use of the property, and whether the property has been empty for any period. Some reliefs do exist and these can significantly reduce the costs of refurbishment. Usually, the sale or letting of a refurbished property will be exempt and, therefore, no VAT recovery is possible. In addition, all the costs of refurbishment bear VAT. Furthermore, VAT is incurred on alterations.

VAT is charged at the reduced rate of 5% on the supply of qualifying services in the course of renovation or alteration of 'qualifying residential premises' that have not been lived in for two years (including works in connection with garages).

---

[52] Note 9(4), Group 6, Schedule 7A

'Alteration' includes extension.[53] 'Qualifying residential premises' means:

(1) a 'single household dwelling'[54]

(2) a 'multiple occupancy dwelling'[55], or

(3) 'a building, or part of a building, which, when it was last lived in, was used for a relevant residential purpose'.[56]

Where a building, when it was last lived in, formed part of a 'relevant residential unit' then, to the extent that it would not be so regarded otherwise, the building is to be treated as having been used for a relevant residential purpose.[57] A building forms part of a 'relevant residential unit' at any time when:[58]

(a) it is one of a number of buildings on the same site, and

(b) the buildings are used together as a unit for a relevant residential purpose.

For the reduced rate to apply the 'first empty home condition' must be satisfied or, if the premises are a single household dwelling, either the first or the 'second empty home condition' must be satisfied[59] and:

(1) any statutory planning consent needed for the renovation or alteration must have been granted;.[60]

(2) any statutory building control approval needed for the renovation or alteration must have been granted;[61]

(3) where the premises in question are a building, or part of a building, which, when it was last lived in, was used for a 'relevant residential purpose':

(a) the building or part must be intended to be used solely for such a purpose after the renovation or alteration[62], and

(b) before the supply is made, the person to whom it is made must give the supplier a certificate the intention referred to in (a).[63]

---

[53] Note 2(1), Group 7, Schedule 7A

[54] Note 2(4), Group 7 provides that this has the same meaning as for Group 6, Schedule 7A (qualifying conversions)

[55] As in **footnote 54** above

[56] As in **footnote 54** above

[57] Note 2(2), Group 7, Schedule 7A

[58] Note 2(3), Group 7, Schedule 7A

[59] Note 3(1), Group 7, Schedule 7A

[60] Note 4(1), Group 7, Schedule 7A

[61] Note 4(2), Group 7, Schedule 7A

[62] Note 4A(1)(a), Group 7, Schedule 7A

Where a number of buildings on the same site are renovated or altered at the same time and intended to be used together as a unit solely for a relevant residential purpose, then each of those buildings is to be treated as intended for use solely for a relevant residential purpose.[64]

'Building materials' supplied by the person providing the services taxable at the reduced rate and incorporated into the qualifying residential premises or their immediate site, are also taxable at the reduced rate.[65]

10.6.1 The empty home conditions

The 'first empty home condition' is that neither the premises concerned, nor where those premises are a building, or part of a building which when it was last lived in formed part of a 'relevant residential unit', any of the other buildings that formed part of the unit, have been lived in during the period of two years ending with the commencement of the 'relevant works'.[66]

It was recognised that the first empty home condition would not benefit those who acquire and a property and live in it whilst it is being renovated. The 'second empty home condition' (applicable only to single household dwellings) is intended to apply to such people. This condition is that the dwelling was not lived in for a period of at least two years and:

(1) the person, or one of the persons, whose beginning to live in the dwelling brought that period of non-occupation to an end was someone who (whether alone or jointly with another or others) 'acquired the dwelling' at a time no later than the end of that period, and when the dwelling had been not lived in for at least two years;

(2) no works of renovation or alteration were carried out to the dwelling during the period of two years ending with the acquisition (although HMRC will ignore any minor works that were necessary to keep the dwelling dry and secure[67]);

(3) the supply of qualifying services is made to a person who:

    (a) is the person, or one of the persons, whose beginning to live in the property brought to an end the period of non-occupation, and

    (b) is the person, or one of the persons, who acquired the dwelling as mentioned in (1); and

---

[63] Note 4A(1)(b), Group 7, Schedule 7A – for the form of the certificate see paragraph 18.1 of VAT Notice 'Buildings and construction' (August 2014)

[64] Note 4A(2), Group 7, Schedule 7A

[65] See **10.7** below

[66] Note 3(2), Group 7, Schedule 7A

[67] See paragraph 8.3.4, VAT Notice 708 'Buildings and construction' (August 2014)

(4) the 'relevant works' are carried out during the period of one year beginning with the day of the acquisition.

For the purposes of the empty home conditions, the 'relevant works' means[68]:

(1) where the supply is of qualifying services within these provisions, the works that constitute the services supplied; and

(2) where the supply is of 'building materials'[69] supplied with those services, the works by which the materials concerned are incorporated in the premises concerned or their immediate site.

References to a person 'acquiring a dwelling' are to that person having a major interest in the dwelling granted, or assigned, to him for a consideration.[70]

To charge tax at the reduced rate on a supply, a supplier should hold evidence showing that the premises have not been lived in during the two years immediately before h work starts. The evidence can include the electoral roll and council tax data, utilities companies, information from empty property officers in local authorities and other sources of reliable information. If a contractor holds a letter from an empty property officer certifying that a property has not been lived in for two years, or will have been when the work starts, no other evidence is needed. If an empty property officer is unsure about when a property was last lived in, he should write with his best estimate. HMRC may then call for other supporting evidence.[71]

In determining whether a property has been lived in:

- illegal occupation by squatters;
- occupation by 'guardians' (persons installed by the owner to deter squatters and vandals); and
- non-residential use, such as storage for a business,

can be ignored. However, if the dwelling has been lived in on an occasional basis (for example, as a second home) in the two years immediately before work starts, the supply cannot be taxed at the reduced rate.[72]

---

[68] Note 3(4), Group 7, Schedule 7A

[69] See **10.7** below

[70] Note 3(5), Group 7, Schedule 7A

[71] See paragraph 8.3.2, VAT Notice 708 'Buildings and construction' (August 2014)

[72] See paragraph 8.3.3, VAT Notice 708 'Buildings and construction' (August 2014)

It can be difficult to prove the length of time the property has been unoccupied HMRC can put the relevant person to proof on the question of the period a property has been unoccupied. The decision in *Gareth Ronald Witherow*[73] outlines the difficulties that can present themselves in such a case.[74]

10.6.2 Qualifying services

The services subject to the reduced rate of VAT are works required of renovation and restoration. This includes work on the fabric of the property (roofing, re-wiring, re-plumbing, removal or addition of walls, replaster etc.). In addition, works of repair and maintenance, improvements, making good and necessary decoration are subject to the reduced rate. Also eligible for the reduced rate are works in the immediate area to the premises or the site. This includes connection of power, water, sewerage and security for the property.

'Qualifying services' means[75]:
(1) Work to the fabric of the premises (excluding the incorporation, or installation as fittings, in the premises of any goods that are not building materials).
(2) Work within the immediate site of the premises in connection with:
    (a) the means of providing water, power, heat or access to the premises;
    (b) the means of providing drainage or security for the premises; or
    (c) the provision of means of waste disposal for the premises.

This includes any work of repair, maintenance (e.g. redecoration) or improvement (e.g. an extension or the installation of double glazing) carried out to the fabric of the premises.

Where part of a supply of services qualifies under these provisions and part does not, the supply can be apportioned to determine the extent to which the reduced rate can be applied.[76]

10.6.3 Related garage works

For the above purposes, a renovation or alteration of any premises includes any 'garage works' 'related to the renovation or alteration'[77].

---

[73] (VTD 20040)
[74] See also *Gurpreet Singh Bhachu* [2012] UKFTT 498 (TC)
[75] Note 5, Group 7, Schedule 7A
[76] Note 1, Group 7, Schedule 7A
[77] Note 3A, Group 7, Schedule 7A

'Garage works' means:
(1) the construction of a garage,
(2) the conversion of a building, or of a part of a building, that results in a garage, or
(3) the renovation or alteration of a garage.

Garage works are 'related to a renovation or alteration' if:
(1) they are carried out at the same time as the renovation or alteration of the premises concerned, and
(2) the garage is intended to be occupied with the premises.

10.6.4 Subcontractors
Subcontractors who carry out some or all of the qualifying renovation or conversion work can apply the reduced rate to their services unless the work is the renovation of an empty single household dwelling where the owner is in residence (as in that case only a person making supplies to the occupier can apply the reduced rate[78]).

10.7 Relief for building materials etc.
Item 4, Group 5, Schedule 8; Item 2, Group 6, Schedule 7A; Item 2, Group 7, Schedule 7A

'Building materials' supplied by the person providing zero-rated services falling within **10.3** (zero-rated buildings) or **7.1** (certain conversions for housing associations) above are also zero-rated where:
(1) the supply is to a person to whom the supplier is supplying zero-rated services; and
(2) those services include the incorporation of the building materials into the relevant building or its site.

'Building materials' supplied by the person providing services taxable at the reduced rate are also taxed at the reduced rate where:
(1) the supply is to a person to whom the supplier is supplying services which are taxable at the reduced rate; and
(2) those services include the incorporation of the building materials into the relevant building or its 'immediate' site.

VAT charged on supplies of 'building materials' to a DIY builder is eligible for refund provided that the building materials are incorporated in the building or its site in the course of works to which section 35 applies[79].

---

[78] Note 3(3)(d), Group 7, Schedule 7A
[79] For **DIY builders** see **5.1** above

A useful test to determine whether a supply of services is integral to the supply of goods or constitutes a separate supply which will support the zero or reduced rate relief is whether the services are in reality no more than builders obligations which attach in every case to a supply of the goods and therefore form part of that supply.[80] In *Jeffs* Ognall J considered this in relation to supplies of joinery and concluded:

> 'It seems to me here that, looking at the nature of such 'services' as it is contended the taxpayers supplied, they do not come even close to fulfilling the definition set out in item 3 of Group 8 of Sch 5 as expanded by item 2 of Group 8A of that schedule. This was no more than in each of the three cases a contract for the supply of goods. The suggested services, which are submitted to form a wholly discrete and separate item, were in reality no more than the 'common or garden' obligations which attach in every case to a supply of goods pursuant for example to both the common law and under the relevant section (section 14) of the *Sale of Goods Act 1979*. Accordingly, on the facts as found, I am driven to the conclusion that, as matter of law and applying the legal principles which I have already identified, such services as were found to have been provided or offered either antecedent to or contingently subsequent to the supply of the articles in question, were in fact nothing more than the normal obligations imposed by law upon any seller of goods'.

10.7.1   Building materials

'Building materials' are defined in Note (22) to Group 5 of Schedule 8 as goods of a description 'ordinarily' incorporated by builders in a building of the same description as the one in question or its site. This generic test means that the goods benefitting from relief will differ depending on the type of building into which they are incorporated. The range of items is also likely to change over time[81] and may be affected by location.[82]

---

[80] See *CCE v M D and J W Jeffs and another (trading as J & J Joinery)* [1995] STC 759 (QBD)

[81] For example, from 14 August 2014 HMRC amended the VAT Construction Manual (at VATCONST13730) and VAT Notice 708 'Buildings and construction' to include intelligent lighting systems (but not the accompanying remote control handsets) as items that could constitute 'building materials'

[82] See *British Airports Authority* (VTD 447) in which the tribunal held that mechanical ventilator units, which were installed for sound-proofing purposes in houses near to an airport, were articles 'of a kind ordinarily installed by builders'

'Incorporation' includes (but is not limited to) installation as a fitting.[83] Note (22) is applied for the purposes of Groups 6 and 7 of Schedule 7A and the DIY builders scheme.[84] The meaning of the expressions 'incorporated' and 'ordinarily incorporated' (and that expression's former iteration, 'ordinarily installed') was considered in detail by the First-tier Tribunal in *Taylor Wimpey*.[85] The tribunal held that 'incorporates' meant anything physically attached to the house, even if merely plugged or plumbed in, to the extent it was a part of the zero-rated supply of the house. It does not only refer to items incorporated as a fixture.

Certain items are specifically excluded[86] from being building materials and these are:

(1) Fitted or pre-fabricated furniture, other than furniture designed to be fitted in kitchens:
'Furniture' is not defined and whether an item is furniture is very much a matter of impression.[87]

(2) Materials for the construction of fitted furniture, other than kitchen furniture;

(3) Electrical or gas appliances (even if required to be incorporated in a building as a result of building Regulations) unless the appliance is:

(a) designed to heat space or water (or both) or designed to provide ventilation, air cooling, air purification or dust extraction;

(b) a door-entry system, waste disposal unit or machine for compacting waste but only if in each case it is intended for use in a building designed as a number of dwellings (for example, a block of flats);

(c) a burglar alarm, fire alarm or fire safety equipment or designed solely for the purpose of enabling aid to be summoned in an emergency;

(d) a lift or hoist;

(4) Carpets or carpeting materials.

One of the issues in *Price*[88] was a claim under the DIY builders' scheme for a VAT refund in relation to roller blinds. HMRC had opined in VAT 431 NB[89]

---

[83] Note (23), Group 5, Schedule 8

[84] By Note 12, Group 6, Note 6, Group 7, Schedule 7A and section 35(4) VATA respectively

[85] [2014] UKFTT 575 (TC)

[86] By Note (22), Group 5, Schedule 8

[87] *CCE v McLean Homes Midland Ltd* [1993] STC 335 (QB)

(and still does) that blinds were not building materials for this purpose (unless they were 'integral, that is, blinds inside sealed double glazing units') but, as the tribunal pointed out, HMRC's opinion is not the law.

The tribunal found the exceptions to the definition of building materials helpful in deciding the scope of the term. On first sight it might be concluded that building materials were bricks, cement and roof tiles etc. However, the tribunal noted, there would be no point in excluding something from the definition that was not within it, which would suggest that without the exclusions, prefabricated furniture, materials to make fitted furniture, and carpeting would be building materials.

The tribunal concluded:

'although as a matter of judicial notice, because there was no evidence on the point, that roller blinds are as much 'goods of a description ordinarily incorporated by builders in a [dwelling house]' as finished or prefabricated furniture, furniture designed to be fitted in kitchens or carpets or carpeting material. In short, there seems to me to be nothing 'extraordinary' about their incorporation into a dwelling house by builders. HMRC's specific exclusion of them in notice VAT 431NB does not in my view affect the legal position.'

The tribunal, therefore, held that roller blinds were building materials and Mr. Price's appeal was allowed to that extent.

Judicial notice refers to facts, which a judge can be called upon to receive and to act upon, either from his general knowledge of them, or from inquiries to be made by himself for his own information from sources to which it is proper for him to refer. Judicial notice is a means of establishing, rather than proving, a fact.[90] Revenue & Customs Brief 02/11[91] states that HMRC intends to ignore the decision in *Price*, and stand by its view that roller blinds are not building materials. The Brief includes the following by

---

[88] [2010] UKFTT 634 – the tribunal in the later case of *Coopers Fire Ltd* [2013] UKFTT 154 (TC) took the view that fire curtains that took the form of roller blinds were eligible for zero-rating

[89] 'VAT refunds for DIY housebuilders - Claim form for new houses and notes' (the current version was issued in June 2014)

[90] *Commonwealth Shipping Representative v P & O Branch Service* [1923] AC 191 (HL) at 212, per Lord Summer.

[91] 'VAT: HM Revenue and Customs' position following the First Tier Tribunal decision in the case of John Price' (25 January 2011)

way of a possible explanation for this seemingly cavalier attitude (when an appeal would have seemed to be the fairer way to proceed):

'The Tribunal chairman did not hear any evidence on the point of what is and what is not a 'building material' for VAT purposes but reached his conclusion as a matter of judicial notice, that is, as a common sense fact.'

HMRC give the following examples of articles which, in their view, are not furniture and therefore can be building materials[92]:

(1) Basic storage facilities formed by becoming part of the fabric of the building, such as airing cupboards and under-stair storage cupboards.

(2) Items that provide storage capacity as an incidental result of their primary function, such as shelves formed as a result of constructing simple box work over pipes, and basin supports which contain a simple cupboard beneath.

(3) Basic wardrobes installed on their own with all the following characteristics:

(a) The wardrobe encloses a space bordered by the walls, ceiling and floor. But units whose design includes, for example, an element to bridge over a bed or create a dressing table are furniture and are not building materials.

(b) The side and back use three walls of the room (such as across the end of a wall), or two walls and a stub wall. But wardrobes installed in the corner of a room where one side is a closing end panel are furniture and are not building materials.

(c) On opening the wardrobe the walls of the building can be seen. These would normally be either bare plaster or painted plaster. Wardrobes that contain internal panelling, typically as part of a modular or carcass system, are furniture and are not building materials.

(d) The wardrobe should feature no more than a single shelf running the full length of the wardrobe, a rail for hanging clothes and a closing door or doors. Wardrobes with internal divisions, drawers, shoe racks or other features are furniture and are not building materials.

Cookers which are designed to have the dual purpose of heating the room or the building's water are included under (a) above. Telephones or electric gates and barriers are not included under (c) above. Fixed amplification equipment in churches may also be zero-rated. Appliances powered by

---

[92] See paragraph 13.5.2 VAT Notice 708 'Buildings and construction' (August 2014)

other fuels (for example, solid fuel or oil-fired cookers) are building materials when they are ordinarily incorporated in the building.[93]

10.7.2 Builder's block

VAT incurred by a builder on certain goods to which zero-rating does not apply but which are incorporated in a zero-rated building or its site cannot be reclaimed because recovery is prevented by article 6 of the Value Added Tax (Input Tax) Order 1992.[94] This provision, referred to as the 'builder's block', was considered by First-tier Tribunal Judge Mosedale in *Taylor Wimpey*.[95]

Taylor Wimpey claimed a refund of input tax paid on appliances and carpets which it had installed in new homes since 1973. Taylor Wimpey's recovery of the VAT paid was denied by HMRC because of the builder's block. The First-tier Tribunal had to consider whether Taylor Wimpey was able to recover the VAT on the goods basis that:

(1) the goods were not fixtures and were therefore not 'incorporated' within the new homes;

(2) if the goods were 'incorporated', they were 'of a kind ordinarily installed by builders' and therefore excepted from the builder's block; or

(3) alternatively, the block was unlawful and breached EU law to the extent that it had been extended to include additional items.

The First-tier Tribunal found against Taylor Wimpey on the first and second points. In respect of the EU law point, the judge held that the builder's block was 'probably' unlawful in its entirety. In rejecting Taylor Wimpey's argument that the builder's block was unlawfully extended by HMRC from 1990, the Judge took a more fundamental approach which was that article 28(2)(a) of the Sixth Directive was the vires for the maintenance of exemption with a refund (the UK's zero rate). However, where a tax authority has enacted an exemption without a refund (as is the case with the builder's block), the effect is an exemption which was not permitted by article 28(2)(a).

Having concluded that the builder's block was therefore 'probably' illegal, the focus of the case now shifts on to the effect of that on Taylor Wimpey's claim. Whilst Taylor Wimpey can invoke its directly effective right to

---

[93] See paragraph 13.6 VAT Notice 708 'Buildings and construction' (August 2014)
[94] SI 1992/3222
[95] [2014] UKFTT 575 (TC)

recover input tax illegally blocked, the judge has asked for further submissions on whether this gives rise to an output tax liability.

VAT at the standard rate must be accounted for on the supply of goods by the builder which do not qualify for zero-rating or the reduced rate. Zero-rating does not apply where building materials are imported or acquired from another Member State.[96]

10.7.3   Examples of articles 'ordinarily' incorporated in a building[97]
Dwellings:
- air conditioning
- bathroom accessories, such as fixed towel rails, toilet roll holders, soap dishes, etc
- builder's hardware
- burglar alarms
- curtain poles and rails
- decorating materials
- doors
- dust extractors and filters (including built-in vacuum cleaners)
- fencing permanently erected around the boundary of the dwelling
- fireplaces and surrounds
- fire alarms
- fitted furniture (but only kitchen furniture is 'building materials')
- flooring materials (but carpets and carpeting materials are not 'building materials')
- gas and electrical appliances when wired-in or plumbed-in (but only certain gas and electrical appliances are 'building materials')
- guttering
- heating systems (including radiators and controls, ducted warm-air systems, storage heaters and other wired in heating appliances, gas fires and solar powered heating)
- immersion heaters, boilers, hot and cold water tanks
- kitchen sinks, work surfaces and fitted cupboards
- letter boxes
- lifts and hoists
- light fittings (including chandeliers and outside lights)
- plumbing installations, including electric showers and 'in line' water softeners

---

[96] Note (24), Group 5, Schedule 8
[97] See section 13.8 VAT Notice 708 'Buildings and construction' (August 2014)

- power points (including combination shaver points)
- sanitary ware
- saunas
- shower units
- smoke detectors
- solar panels
- solid fuel cookers and oil-fired boilers
- swimming pool inside the house, including water heaters and filters (but not diving boards and other specialist equipment)
- TV aerials and satellite dishes
- ventilation equipment (including cooker hoods)
- warden call systems
- window frames and glazing
- wiring (including power circuits and computer, telephone and TV cabling)

Buildings used for a relevant residential purpose may include (in addition to the list above for dwellings):
- mirrors
- safes
- external lighting systems

Buildings used for a relevant charitable purpose
- blinds and shutters
- mirrors
- safes
- external lighting systems

Schools may include (in addition to the list above for buildings used for a relevant charitable purpose):
- blackboards fixed to or forming part of the wall
- gymnasium wall bars
- notice and display boards
- mirrors and barres (in ballet schools)

Churches may include (in addition to the list above for buildings used for a relevant charitable purpose):
- altars
- church bells
- fonts
- lecterns
- pipe organs
- pulpits

10.8 Self-supply of construction, alteration and demolition services

Value Added Tax (Self-supply of Construction Services) Order 1989[98]

Article 18(1)(a) of the VAT Directive[99] provides that Member States may treat as a supply of goods for consideration 'the application by a taxable person for the purposes of his business of goods produced, constructed, extracted, processed, purchased or imported in the course of such business, where the VAT on such goods, had they been acquired from another taxable person, would not be wholly deductible.' Goods and services are treated for the purposes of VAT as if they are both supplied to a person for the purposes of his business and supplied by him in the course or furtherance of his business where the Treasury make an Order to that effect.[100] The Value Added Tax (Self-supply of Construction Services) Order 1989 is such an Order.

Article 3 of the Order provides that where a person performs specified services in the course or furtherance of a business carried on by him, for the purpose of that business and otherwise than for a consideration, those services are treated as both supplied to him for the purpose of that business and supplied by him in the course or furtherance of that business unless:

(1) the open market value of the services is less than £100,000; or
(2) the services would, if supplied for a consideration in the course or furtherance of a business by a taxable person, be zero-rated.

The specified services are:

(1) constructing a building;
(2) extending, altering, or constructing an annex to, any building such that the floor area of the original building is increased by 10 per cent or more;
(3) constructing any civil engineering work;
(4) carrying out any demolition work contemporaneously with, or preparatory to, the works in heads (1) to (3) and in connection with those works.

VAT must be accounted for on the open market value of the services performed (subject to a de minimis limit of £100,000) in the VAT return for the period in which the services are performed.

---

[98] SI 1989/472
[99] Formerly article 5(7)(a) Sixth Directive
[100] Section 5(5) and 5(6)

The services are treated as if they were supplied to and by the person for the purpose of his business[8]. The resulting input tax cannot be attributed to the deemed supply (which would give full input tax credit), but only to the actual use to which the service was put.[101] Where the value of the self-supply exceeds £250,000, adjustments may be required in future years under the capital goods scheme.[102]

It should be noted that the self-supply charge applies regardless of whether the person would have been entitled to full input tax credit had the building been constructed by a third party.

Where a person not registered for VAT makes a self-supply falling within these provisions, the value of the self-supply will make him liable for registration.

10.9 Time of supply of building services

The rules applying to the time of supply of services by the building industry are outlined below.

10.9.1   Single payment contracts for building work

For single payment contract the normal tax point rules set out at **0** above apply to determine the time of supply.

10.9.2   Retention payments

Building contracts often include retention clauses which allow a proportion of the contract price to be kept back after completion of the work pending confirmation that the supplier has done the work properly and has completed the snagging. There are special tax point rules that apply to a retention 'pending full and satisfactory performance of the contract'. The tax point for the retention element of the contract is the earlier of[103]:

(1)   the time when a payment in respect of any part of a retention made pursuant to the terms of the contract is received by the supplier; or

(2)   the date that the supplier issues a VAT invoice relating to the retention unless the contract is covered by the special anti-avoidance rule in regulation 93 VAT Regulations (see **10.9.4** below).

There is no obligation to issue a tax invoice for a zero-rated supply in the UK.

---

[101] Regulation 104 VAT Regulations
[102] For the **capital goods scheme** see **11.4** below
[103] Regulation 89 VAT Regulations

10.9.3 Stage or interim payment contracts

Where services, or services together with goods, are supplied in the course of the construction, alteration, demolition, repair or maintenance of a building or of any civil engineering work under a contract which provides for payment for such supplies to be made periodically or from time to time, those services (or goods and services) are normally treated as separately and successively supplied at the earlier of the following times:[104]

(1) each time that a payment is received by the supplier; or

(2) each time the supplier issues a VAT invoice.

There is no basic tax point[105] when the work is completed unless the services fall within the special anti-avoidance rule in regulation 93 VAT Regulations (see **10.9.4** below).

10.9.4 Special anti-avoidance rule for supplies in the building industry[106]

The special anti-avoidance rule in regulation 93 VAT Regulations counters the VAT deferral effect of contracts for the supply of building work taxable at the standard or reduced rate made between connected parties under which payment does not become due for many years after completion and no VAT invoice is issued before that time.

Where services, or services together with goods, are supplied in the course of the construction, alteration, demolition, repair or maintenance of a building or any civil engineering work under a contract which provides for payment for such supplies to be made periodically or from time to time, the provisions of regulation 93 VAT Regulations may apply to generate a tax point and crystallise a charge to VAT. The rules are complex but, in summary, do not apply where:

(1) the person who will be occupying the land or building on which certain types of works (referred to in this section as 'relevant services') have been carried out will be doing so wholly or mainly for 'eligible purposes';

(2) the supplier is not connected with the proposed occupier; and

(3) neither the supplier nor any of his subcontractors, is receiving finance from the proposed occupier, nor anyone connected with them.

---

[104] Regulation 90 VAT Regulations

[105] For the basic tax point for services see **0** above

[106] Regulation 93 VAT Regulations

In this connection, finance does not include payments for supplies.[107]

Where the anti-avoidance rule applies then to the extent that relevant services have not already been treated as supplied by reason of the receipt of a payment by the supplier or the issue of a VAT invoice, there is an additional tax point of the day on which the services are performed.[108]

The types of service caught ('relevant services') are services or services together with goods supplied in the course of the construction, alteration, demolition, repair or maintenance of a building or any civil engineering work.

Relevant services fall within regulation 93 if, at the time they were or are 'performed', either of the two conditions set out below is satisfied. The is no definition of when services are performed even though this term is used extensively in the VAT legislation so 'perform' would bear its normal meaning of 'to carry out, execute or fulfil.'[109]

The first condition[110]

The supplier or a 'person responsible for financing the supplier's costs' intends or expects that the land on which the building or civil engineering work in question is situated will be occupied (whether immediately or eventually) or will continue to be occupied (for a period at least) by:

(1) the supplier,

(2) a person responsible for financing the supplier's costs, or

(3) a person connected with either such person within the meaning of section 839 *ICTA 1988* (but a company is not connected with another for these purposes only because both are under the control of the Crown, a Minister of the Crown, a government department or a Northern Ireland department)[111]

other than where that occupation is wholly or mainly for 'eligible purposes'.

'Occupation for eligible purposes' means[112]:

(1) occupation by a taxable person for the purpose of making supplies which are in the course of furtherance of a business and are supplies of

---

107 Regulation 93(6) VAT Regulations

108 Regulation 93(1) VAT Regulations

109 See Oxford English Dictionary

110 Regulation 93(2)(a) VAT Regulations

111 Regulation 93(15) and 93(16) VAT Regulations

112 Regulation 93(10) VAT Regulations

such a description that any input tax wholly attributable to those supplies would be input tax for which he would be entitled to credit;

(2) occupation by a body to which section 33 applies (local authorities and certain other public bodies) to the extent that the body occupies the land for non-business purposes; and

(3) occupation by a government department falling within section 41.

Where occupation is by a person who is not a taxable person but whose supplies are treated for VAT purposes as made by another person who is a taxable person, those two persons are to be regarded as a single taxable person.

HMRC take the view[113] that a building is used 'wholly or mainly' for eligible purposes if the occupier can recover 80% or more of the VAT relating to that building. It does not matter whether their overall ability to recover VAT is greater or less than 80%.

Buildings that are not normally regarded by HMRC[114] as being 'wholly or mainly for eligible purposes' include those used:

- as a bank, or the headquarters of a banking group;
- as an insurance broker's office, or the office of an insurance company;
- as a school, college or university;
- as an office for a charity (but the special anti-avoidance rules do not apply if the work for a charity is zero-rated);
- as a private hospital, or the head office of a private healthcare business; or
- for any purpose if the occupier is not registered for VAT (but the special anti-avoidance rules do not apply if the work is zero-rated, such as constructing a house)

Buildings that are normally regarded by HMRC[115] as being 'wholly or mainly for eligible purposes' include those used:

- as the head office of a fully taxable business
- for any purpose where the occupier is a government department;
- by a local authority for carrying on its statutory functions;
- as a retail shop;
- as a wholesale outlet;
- as a factory or workshop;

---

[113] VAT Notice 708 'Buildings and construction' (August 2014) at paragraph 24.7
[114] VAT Notice 708 'Buildings and construction' (August 2014) at paragraph 24.7.1
[115] VAT Notice 708 'Buildings and construction' (August 2014) at paragraph 24.7.2

- as an importer's office or warehouse; or
- as a charity shop,

provided, in the case of the last five, that the retailer, etc. is registered for VAT.

A 'person responsible for financing the supplier's costs' is a person who has either provided finance for the supplier's costs, or entered into an agreement or understanding (whether or not legally enforceable) to provide finance for the supplier's costs.[116]

'Providing finance' is widely defined.[117] It includes directly or indirectly providing funds *either* to meet the whole or part of the supplier's costs *or* to discharge the whole or part of any liability incurred in raising funds to meet those costs. It also includes directly or indirectly procuring the provision of funds by another person for either of those purposes. The funds may be provided by way of loan, guarantee or other security, consideration for a share issue used to raise the funds or any other transfer of assets or value as a consequence of which the funds are made available. Providing funds does not include making interim payments for construction work on which VAT is accounted for.

A 'supplier's costs' are his costs of supplying the services, or services together with goods, and consist of any amounts payable by the supplier for supplies to him of goods and services used in making his supply; and the supplier's staff costs and other internal costs of making his supply.[118]

The second condition[119]

The supplier has received (and used in making his supply) any supply of services, or services together with goods, from a subcontractor the time of supply of which was determined under the anti-avoidance provisions in regulation 93 (or would have been but for the issue by that subcontractor of a VAT invoice other than one which has been paid in full). Thus a main contractor is affected by the anti-avoidance rules if any of his subcontractors are affected by it.

HMRC say that they will not be seeking to catch a contractor out on a technicality in this area, and if it does come to their attention that a

---

[116] Regulation 93(4) VAT Regulations
[117] Regulation 93(5) and 93(6) VAT Regulations
[118] Regulation 93(7) VAT Regulations
[119] Regulation 93(2)(b) VAT Regulations

contractor is inadvertently affected by the rule because of his subcontractors, they will look at his case sympathetically.[120]

10.9.5   Accounting for VAT[121]

Where the anti-avoidance rule in regulation 93 applies, VAT must be accounted for on the full value of the contract, less any amounts on which VAT has already become due because a payment has been received or a VAT invoice issued. The full value of the contract includes retentions and disputed amounts.

Where there is a dispute, or where it is not possible to know the exact value of the contract for any other reason, a reasonable estimate of the value must be made. In cases of dispute, a supplier need not account for VAT on the full amount he is claiming from the customer if he feels that he will most likely be forced in the end to settle for a lower amount. He should account for VAT on his best estimate of the amount that will eventually be agreed. (HMRC recommend that the supplier documents the basis of his estimate, so that he can later show that it was reasonable.) Subsequently, when the value of the contract is finalised, the supplier may need to make an adjustment to the VAT paid.

10.9.6   Public/Private Partnership (formerly Private Finance Initiative)[122]

If a PPP or PFI arrangement relates to a building that will be occupied exclusively by a government department (including an NHS hospital), the anti-avoidance rules do not apply. However, some PPP and PFI arrangements relate to buildings that will be occupied by private sector businesses as well as government departments. In such cases, the part of the building occupied by the private sector business may be caught by the special anti-avoidance rules. If so, there is no need to account for VAT on the entire building on completion, only on a proportion of the overall price that fairly reflects the part of the building that will be occupied by private companies.

10.10 Self-billing and authenticated receipts

Self-billing[123]

Under a self-billing arrangement, the customer makes out VAT invoices on behalf of the VAT-registered supplier (for example, a main contractor

---

[120] VAT Notice 708 'Buildings and construction' (August 2014) at paragraph 24.8
[121] VAT Notice 708 'Buildings and construction' (August 2014) at paragraph 24.10
[122] VAT Notice 708 'Buildings and construction' (August 2014) at paragraph 24.7.3
[123] Regulation 13(3) and 13(3A) to 13(3F) VAT Regulations

makes out VAT invoices on behalf of its registered subcontractor) and sends a copy of the invoice to the supplier with the payment. The suppliers must agree to self-billing. Details of the self-billing procedure are covered in VAT Notice 700/62 (September 2014), some parts of which have the force of law.

Authenticated receipts[124]

The authenticated receipt procedure (not to be confused with self-billing) allows a supplier to issue an authenticated receipt for payment instead of a normal VAT invoice. The time limit for the issue of an authenticated receipt is the same as for a VAT invoice.

The procedure can only be used when all of the following conditions are satisfied:

(1) Services, or services together with goods, are supplied in the course of the construction, alteration, demolition, repair or maintenance of a building or of any civil engineering work.

(2) The contract provides for payments for such services to be made periodically, or from time to time.

(3) The receipt contains all the particulars required of a VAT invoice.

(4) No VAT invoice or similar document which was intended to be or could be construed as being a VAT invoice for the supply to which the receipt relates is issued.

An authenticated receipt is not a VAT invoice and so its issue does not create a tax point for the supplier. The tax point for the supply is therefore solely determined by the receipt of payment by the supplier or, where the anti-avoidance rule described in **10.9.4** above applies, the date the work is completed.

An authenticated receipt is acceptable evidence for input tax purposes.

There is no definition of what is meant by 'authenticated' for this purpose but HMRC's view is that a receipt must be authenticated by the supplier and only after payment has been received.[125]

---

[124] Regulation 13(4) VAT Regulations
[125] HMRC VAT Manual at VATREC14020

10.11 Summary of VAT liability of supplies of building services

New building	Designed as dwelling	ZR
	To be used solely for a relevant residential purpose	ZR
	To be used solely for a relevant charitable purpose	ZR
	Other building	SR
Adaptations of buildings for use by the disabled	The provision, extension or adaptation of a bathroom, washroom or lavatory The provision of ramps or widened doorways or passages to allow access	ZR
	Other	SR
Conversion of existing building	1. Which is a non-residential building into a dwelling or dwellings or a into a building intended for use solely for a relevant residential purpose where the supply is to a housing association	ZR
	2. Which results in a changed number of dwellings	RR
	3. Which does not contain any multiple occupancy dwellings into a multiple occupancy dwelling or dwellings	RR
	4. Which is not being used for a relevant residential purpose into premises intended to be used solely for that purpose	RR
	5. Not falling within 1-4 above	SR
Renovation/alteration	Of qualifying residential premises (which have to have been empty for a two year period)	RR
	Approved alteration to a protected building under the transitional rules applying until 30 September 2015	ZR
	Other	SR
Reconstruction	Of any building	SR
Repair/maintenance	Of any building	SR
Civil engineering	Developing a permanent park for residential caravans	ZR
	Other	SR

11 Partial Exemption and the Capital Goods Scheme

Where a taxable person makes both taxable and exempt supplies (as they often will do if they are making supplies of property), input tax recovery is usually restricted as only input tax that relates to taxable supplies can be recovered. This is referred to as partial exemption.

This chapter only outlines the partial exemption rules, and anyone who is or may be partially exempt should seek specific advice as to their effect on his particular situation. The partial exemption rules are set out in Part XIV of the VAT Regulations.

The capital goods scheme covers input tax incurred in respect of land and property (and computers) above certain values. Under the scheme, the owner of the capital item must review the extent to which the item is used to make taxable supplies over a period of time (five or ten years) and make an adjustment where appropriate.

11.1 Effect of being partially exempt

A business which is partially exempt must restrict the amount of input tax it claims. Input VAT that is attributable directly to exempt supplies cannot be recovered. Also, a proportion of the VAT on the businesses overheads (the residual VAT after apportionment) cannot be reclaimed as this will relate to both taxable and exempt income. A suitable method of apportionment needs to be used and unless the standard method is used, it must be agreed with HMRC. Special rules apply to input VAT on capital items (see **11.4** below).

Where a partly exempt business prepares VAT returns and deducts input tax on a quarterly or monthly basis, the input tax deduction is provisional. The business also has a longer period at the end of which it is required to review the extent of its allowable input tax and revise its deduction accordingly. In general, the longer period ends on the last day of the quarter ending March, April or May and the adjustment is known as the annual adjustment. Newly registered traders have a longer period known as a registration period.

Even if a partial exemption method has to be used, the de minimis limits referred to at **11.3** below may allow all the input tax to be recovered (subject to the normal rules).

11.2 Methods of apportionment

Any method that produces a 'fair and reasonable' result can be used. All methods should provide for direct attribution and apportionment of the input tax incurred. Direct attribution involves identifying VAT on goods and services which are used exclusively to make taxable supplies or exempt supplies: the former is deductible, the latter is not. Apportionment is required for the remaining input tax (e.g. on overheads) which cannot be directly attributed.

The standard method (use of which does not require HMRC's approval) apportions VAT on overheads by reference to use and is broadly a value-based calculation:

Standard method claimable percentage =

$$\frac{\text{Value of taxable supplies in the period (excluding VAT)}}{\text{Value of all supplies in the period (excluding VAT)}} \times 100$$

Alternatively, methods using the value of input tax incurred, cost centre accounting, transaction counts, staff numbers or any other mutually agreed method. Taking time to choose the correct method can be cost-effective, and a method that is easy to operate has considerable merit.

11.2.1　Special method override

Any method that is not the standard method must be agreed with HMRC as a special method. Any agreement will require the person seeking to apply it to state that the proposed method will produce a fair and reasonable result. Where the special method is not producing a fair and reasonable result the 'special method override' will come into effect. This override requires the VAT incurred to be apportioned according to use until a new special method can be agreed. The special method override only applies where HMRC serve a notice that the override is to apply. Before the issue of the notice, the person affected will have the opportunity to amend their special method to one that is acceptable to HMRC.

11.2.2　Standard method override

Where the standard method is used it may be necessary to consider the standard method override. This override prevents VAT being reclaimed under the standard method if the 'use of the VAT' relates to exempt activities, but the standard method allows for VAT recovery. This override only has to be applied where the amount of VAT that has to be apportioned (the residual VAT) exceeds £50,000 (or £25,000 for a group undertaking). Unless the amount of VAT that is being reclaimed is unfair and unreasonable it is unlikely that either override will be applied. The introduction of the overrides increases uncertainty and it is necessary to continually review the VAT position and recovery of input tax.

11.3 De minimis limits

A business is treated as fully taxable if the amount of input tax that relates to exempt income (both directly and apportioned from overheads) is less than £625 per month on average and less than 50 per cent of the total amount of input tax incurred.

The calculation must be undertaken on a quarterly basis (or monthly or annually if monthly or annual VAT returns are used). An annual adjustment must then be carried out. This annual adjustment recalculates the VAT recovery for the whole year. Any over claim or under claim of VAT actually made during the year when compared to the annual calculation is then adjusted in the VAT period following the VAT year-end. The VAT year-end is 31 March, 30 April or 31 May depending on the VAT quarter.

When applying the de minimis provisions to a longer period, any treatment of relevant input tax as attributable to taxable supplies in any VAT period is disregarded, and no account is to be taken of any amount or amounts which may be deductible or payable under the capital goods scheme.

Example: Standard method of apportionment and de minimis

Sales for Year		Input Tax for Year	
Exempt	£100,000	Attributed to exempt income	£ 3,000
Taxable	£100,000	Attributed to taxable income	£10,000
		Residual input tax	£8,000
Total	£200,000	Total	£21,000

Apportionment of Residual VAT

Irrecoverable Residual   = $\frac{£100,000 \times £8,000}{£200,000}$ = £4,000

Exempt input tax =   £4,000 + £3,000   = £7,000

As the exempt input tax is £7,000, it is below the de minimis limit and all the input VAT (£21,000) can be reclaimed.

11.4 Capital goods scheme
Part XV VAT Regulations

The capital goods scheme was introduced on 1 April 1990. The scheme applies to VAT which businesses incur after that date on capital items which fall within the scheme.

The general aim of the scheme is to displace the rule that the recovery of input tax should depend on the initial use to which those capital items are put. Instead, input tax recovery will be dependent upon the use to which these capital items are put over a longer period of, normally, ten years for land. The way the scheme does this is by initially allowing input tax to be recovered in the normal way with later adjustments, dependent on the use to which the capital item is put, which can result in an additional recovery of input tax by the business or a claw-back of input tax by HMRC. The adjustments are intended to reflect any change in use of the capital item (between taxable and exempt use) since the initial attribution of input tax was made. Provided that there is no change in use there is no adjustment.

When a 'capital item[1]' falling within the scheme is acquired, the normal rules for claiming input tax apply:

(1) if it is used wholly in making taxable supplies, input tax is recoverable in full;

(2) if it is used wholly in making exempt supplies, none of the input tax is recoverable; and

(3) if it is used for making taxable and exempt supplies, a proportion of the input tax may be claimed under the partial exemption rules.

Where, subsequently, in the adjustment period for that item there is a change in the extent of taxable use, an input tax adjustment has to be made to take account of this. If taxable use increases, a further amount of input tax can be claimed and, if it decreases, some of the input tax already claimed must be repaid.

With effect from 1 January 2011, the capital goods scheme also takes into account fluctuations in the extent to which a capital item falling within the scheme is used for business/non-business purposes.

The capital goods scheme has little impact on businesses making only taxable supplies, but they should keep the appropriate records in case later exempt supplies are made. Businesses that are partly exempt will have to make adjustments to reflect the changing use of capital items over the capital goods scheme adjustment period.

The capital goods scheme: a word of warning
The rules are complex and have changed may times since they were first introduced. This chapter only outlines the capital goods scheme, and is no substitute for specific advice where the rules may apply.

11.4.1 Capital items falling within the capital goods scheme
Regulations 112 and 113 VAT Regulations

---

[1] For capital items falling within the scheme see **11.4.1** below

Capital items to which the capital goods scheme applies are any items within (1) to (6) below which the owner (or person who holds an interest) uses in the course or furtherance of a business carried on by him, and for the purpose of that business. Only items (1) to (3) are property-related. Items (4) to (6) are included in the list for the sake of completeness and are not dealt with further.

The scheme does not apply to assets acquired or expenditure on assets held solely for resale (stock-in-trade).[2] If an asset is used in the business before it is sold, it is no longer treated as an asset held solely for resale and the capital goods scheme will apply; conversely if a capital item is acquired for use in the business but is sold before being used, it is no longer treated as a capital item.

All values are VAT-exclusive. In respect of capital items acquired on or after 1 January 2011, non-business use is accounted for under the capital goods scheme and hence the value in question is the full tax-exclusive value.

Capital items from 1 January 2011:

(1) Land, a building or part of a building or civil engineering work or part of a civil engineering work where the value of the interest supplied to the owner is £250,000 or more (excluding any zero-rated or exempt elements).

(2) A building which the owner alters, or an extension to an annexe which he constructs, where additional floor area is created in the altered building of 10 per cent or more of the original floor area before the work was carried out. The value of the work must be £250,000 or more (excluding any zero-rated or exempt elements).

(3) A building or civil engineering work which the owner refurbishes or fits out where the value of the expenditure on the taxable supplies of services is £250,000 or more (excluding any zero-rated elements). However, only capitalised expenditure is included – not repairs and maintenance costs charged to the profit and loss account.

(4) A computer or item of computer equipment, where the owner incurs VAT-bearing capital expenditure on its acquisition, the value of which is at least £50,000.

---

[2] Regulation 112(2) VAT Regulations

(5) An aircraft, where the owner incurs VAT-bearing capital expenditure on its acquisition, construction, refurbishment, fitting out, alteration or extension, the value of which is at least £50,000.

(6) A ship, boat or other vessel, where the owner incurs VAT-bearing capital expenditure on its acquisition, construction, refurbishment, fitting out, alteration or extension, the value of which is at least £50,000.

Self-storage
Regulation 113A VAT Regulations

From 1 October 2012 where the owner of land, a building (or part), or a civil engineering work (or part) (or a person to whom he has granted an interest in that item) uses that item to make a grant that falls within Item 1(ka), Group 1, Schedule 9 (self-storage facilities excluded from exemption[3]) and the owner has, no later than 31 March 2013, decided to treat the item (which would not otherwise be a capital item) as a capital item; and has made a written record of that decision specifying the date it was made, then £250,000 is substituted by £1. No adjustment of deductions of input tax should be made for any intervals ending before 1 October 2012 that fall within the period of adjustment for the capital item.

This is to enable businesses affected by the change in the liability of the grant of self-storage facilities with effect from 1 October 2012 to recover the input tax on buildings that are not otherwise capital items, and which are used to provide self-storage facilities. Without this provision, input tax on such buildings incurred before the change in liability would be irrecoverable as exempt input tax.

Capital expenditure[4]
This is not defined in the legislation. 'Capital expenditure' is normally expenditure capitalised for accounting purposes. HMRC will not normally challenge a business's capitalisation policy for the purposes of the capital goods scheme, except in cases of avoidance or abuse.

In some cases charities may incur expenditure of a capital nature on land and property which is not capitalised in their accounts (for example, certain heritage buildings, churches etc.). This is generally because the charity does not have unfettered freedom to exploit or dispose of the land or property concerned. This will not prevent expenditure that is essentially capital in nature from being adjusted under the capital goods scheme.

---

[3] See **3.2.14** above
[4] See VAT Notice 706/2 'Capital goods scheme' (October 2011) at paragraph 4.1

11.4.2 The value of a capital item

The value of a capital item is the VAT-exclusive value of the item. Only the value of standard or reduced-rated taxable supplies of capital items is included. Before 1 January 2011, the value of a capital item was determined by reference only to the business-related expenditure. With effect from 1 January 2011, the value is determined by reference to total expenditure on an asset. This includes both business and non-business expenditure on the asset.

Where expenditure is incurred on a capital item before and after 1 January 2011, it is necessary to determine the amount of business-related expenditure incurred on the asset up to 31 December 2010 and the total amount of expenditure (business and non-business) incurred on or after 1 January 2011. If the sum of these amounts exceeds the relevant capital goods scheme threshold, the asset falls within the capital goods scheme.

Estimated values[5]

If a business does not know whether a project exceeds the value threshold for the capital goods scheme until all invoices have been received it will need to estimate the value of the supplies it has received.

If a business estimates that the value of relevant supplies will exceed the value threshold for the scheme, the item will become a capital item. Even if it finds later on that the value does not reach the threshold, the item remains in the scheme and it should continue to make adjustments as necessary. If a business does estimate the value of a capital item it will need to keep all the documents it based its estimation on, such as a contract, as HMRC may ask to see it.

11.4.3 The adjustment periods

Regulation 114 VAT Regulations

Adjustments are made over ten successive intervals. Intervals are normally but not necessarily annual. If, at the time of the owner's first use, the number of intervals exceeds the number of complete years that the owner's interest in the capital item has to run by more than one, the number of intervals should be reduced to one more than the number of complete years that the owner's interest has to run, calculated from the date of the owner's first use (but not to less than three intervals). In such a case, the denominator in the fraction for the method of adjustment (see **11.4.5** below) should be adjusted accordingly.

---

[5] See VAT Notice 706/2 'Capital goods scheme' (October 2011) at paragraph 4.5

Where a business (or part of a business) which includes capital items falling within the scheme is transferred as a going concern,[6] so that no VAT is charged on the transfer, the buyer has to continue to operate the scheme in respect of those capital items.[7] The effect of this is that the purchaser may become subject to a claw-back of input tax which the vendor has previously claimed. Equally, the purchaser may be entitled to recover input tax incurred by the vendor. In these circumstances a buyer will require details of the capital items that are being transferred, the date of acquisition, the initial input tax, the amount recovered and any adjustments made and provision to this effect should be included in the contract.

Where capital item is sold before the end of the adjustment period, the adjustment for the interval in which it is sold is the final adjustment for that item, and must include all adjustment amounts for any remaining intervals.

11.4.4 Amount subject to adjustment

Before 1 January 2011, only VAT on the business-related expenditure on an asset (i.e. input tax) fell within the capital goods scheme. With effect from 1 January 2011, all of the VAT on an asset (in this instance input tax and non-business VAT) falls within the capital goods scheme. Where expenditure is incurred both before and after 1 January 2011, the VAT on the business-related expenditure incurred up to 31 December 2010 and the total VAT incurred on the asset on or after 1 January 2011 fall within the capital goods scheme.

11.4.5 How the adjustments are made

Regulations 115-116 VAT Regulations

The adjustment is calculated by dividing the total input tax on the capital item by the number of intervals in the adjustment period and multiplying the result by the 'adjustment percentage'.

The 'adjustment percentage' is the difference (if any), expressed as a percentage, between the extent to which the whole or part of the capital item was used or to be used for making taxable supplies at the time the

---

[6] See **12.11.2** below

[7] By reason of regulation 112(4)(a) VAT Regulations which may, however, be called into question by the decision of the European Court in *Staatssecretaris van Financiën v Pactor Vastgoed BV* (Case C-622/11) (10 October 2013 unreported) that 'the Sixth Directive must be interpreted as precluding the recovery of amounts due following the adjustment of a VAT deduction from a taxable person other than the person who applied that deduction'

original entitlement to deduction of the input tax was determined under the partial exemption rules; and the extent to which it is so used, or treated as used as the result of a disposal under **11.4.6** below, in the subsequent interval in question.

Where the owner of a building within these provisions grants or assigns a tenancy or lease in the whole or part of the building and the premium (or if no premium is payable the first payment of rent) is zero-rated, any subsequent exempt supply arising from the grant (e.g. rent) is disregarded in determining the extent to which the building is used in making taxable supplies.

This is best explained using a simple example.

Example: capital goods scheme adjustments
If a partially exempt business purchases a building which it will occupy for business purposes at a cost of £400,000 and the vendor charged VAT of £80,000 the building cost is clearly in excess of the capital goods scheme limits. VAT will need to be adjusted to reflect any change in use over the next ten years.

If in the VAT accounting period when the building was purchased, the company made half exempt, and half taxable supplies (and the building was used to make this these supplies), half of the VAT incurred on the capital item can be claimed as recoverable input tax under the normal partial exemption rules. At the end of its partial exemption year, the company looks back over the whole year and adjusts the VAT reclaim to reflect the whole year's activity. An adjustment would be made to the original £80,000 attribution to account for any differences. If during the year the building was used to make supplies which were 40% taxable and 60% exempt, there would be a repayment due to HMRC of £8,000 (10% of £80,000).

At the end of the second year, the trading pattern may have changed so that the business has made 65% taxable sales. Accordingly, the business is able to make an adjustment to recover additional VAT to reflect the increased taxable use of the building made in that year. The additional amount recoverable is 25% (65% less the original 40%) of one tenth (as it is a ten year adjustment period) of the original VAT amount. That is, 25% of $\frac{1}{10}^{th}$ x £80,000 = £2,000.

Adjustments over the remaining intervals will follow a similar pattern.

11.4.6   Disposals of capital items during the adjustment period
Regulation 115(3)-(38) VAT Regulations

Where capital item is sold before the end of the adjustment period, the adjustment for the interval in which it is sold is the final adjustment for that item, and must include all adjustment amounts for any remaining intervals.

The provisions outlined below also apply to the part disposal of a capital item. Therefore, references in this paragraph to the supply of a capital item cover the supply of whole or part of a capital item.

If a capital item is sold without ever having been used, HMRC do not regard it as a capital item for the purposes of the scheme. Otherwise, where, during an interval other than the last interval, the owner of a capital item:

(1) supplies it; or

(2) is deemed to supply it on ceasing to be a taxable person; or

(3) would have been deemed to supply it on ceasing to be a taxable person but for the fact that VAT on the deemed supply would not have been more than £1,000 (whether by virtue of its value or because it is zero-rated or exempt),

then:

(a) if that supply is a taxable supply, the owner is treated as having used the capital item for each of the remaining complete intervals wholly in the making of taxable supplies; and

(b) if that supply is an exempt supply, he is treated as not using the capital item for each of the remaining complete intervals in making any taxable supplies.

The effect of these rules is as follows:

(1) For the interval in which the capital item is sold, the adjustment is calculated (or, if it is the first interval, input tax is reclaimed) in the normal way as if the capital item had been in use for the whole of that interval.

(2) For any remaining complete intervals in the adjustment period, the recovery percentage will be 100% where (a) above applies or 0% where (b) above applies, but subject to the 'disposal test'.

'Disposal test'

Where the total amount of input tax deducted or deductible by the owner of a capital item as a result of the input tax initially recovered on the capital item, any adjustments already made under the scheme (and any final adjustment that is required as a result of the sale of the item) would exceed the output tax chargeable on the supply of the capital item, then the owner must pay to HMRC, or (as the case may) be may deduct, such an amount as results in the total input tax deducted or deductible being equal to the output tax chargeable on the supply of the whole or part of the capital item.

The disposal test is an anti-avoidance measure to ensure that partly exempt businesses do not obtain an unjustified tax advantage, for example, by making a substantial exempt supply of a long lease of a property followed immediately by the taxable disposal of the freehold for low consideration. HMRC do not intend that the disposal test should be applied to bona fide commercial transactions. Given the policy objective, the disposal test will not be applied:[8]

(1) where the owner disposes of an item at a loss due to the market conditions (such as a general downturn in property prices);
(2) where the value of the capital item has depreciated;
(3) where the value of the capital item is reduced for other legitimate reasons (such as accepting a low price for a quick sale);
(4) where the amount of output tax on disposal is less than the total input tax only because of a reduction in the VAT rate;
(5) where the item is used only for taxable (including zero-rated) purposes throughout the adjustment period (which includes the final disposal).

Where there is no 'unjustified tax advantage', a business need not apply these provisions and it is not necessary to apply to HMRC for a specific ruling. An 'unjustified tax advantage' is normally one arising from an avoidance scheme where the owner seeks to secure an amount of input tax that would still be subject to adjustment under the scheme, were it not for the sale of the item, less any output tax due on the sale.[9]

Where there is an unjustified tax advantage, a business must calculate the net tax advantage (i.e. the overall benefit derived from the avoidance device, normally the amount of input tax that would still be subject to adjustment under the scheme were it not for the sale of the capital item less any output tax due on the sale) and then work out how much of the net tax advantage is unjustified. Normally this could be achieved by using the ratio that the value of the final taxable sale bears to the value of both the exempt supply and the final taxable sale.

[8] See VAT Notice 706/2 'Capital goods scheme' (October 2011) at paragraph 11.2 and Business Brief 30/97 'Statement of Practice on a Budget change to the capital goods scheme' (19 December 1997)
[9] See VAT Notice 706/2 'Capital goods scheme' (October 2011) at paragraph 11.2

12 Transfer of a Business as a Going Concern ('TOGC')

Section 49 and Article 5 Value Added Tax (Special Provisions) Order 1995[1]

The transfer of a business (or part of a business) as a going concern is potentially a non-supply and, therefore, disregarded for VAT purposes. In a property context this can be relevant to both occupiers and investors.

The purpose of the TOGC provisions is twofold:

(1) to help businesses by improving their cash flow and avoiding the need to separately value assets which may be liable at different rates, or are exempt and have been sold as a whole, and

(2) to protect the revenue by removing a charge to tax and entitlement to input tax where the output tax may not be paid to HMRC

Where TOGC treatment applies no VAT needs to be charged on the value of the assets. This can be important to the parties as it prevent the transferee suffering a cash flow disadvantage on the payment of the VAT which would otherwise be chargeable. TOGC treatment can also provide a real saving in a property transaction because the consideration is VAT-free, so reducing the SDLT charge (if it is not a TOGC and VAT is due, then SDLT will be due on the VAT element).

The VAT-free treatment as a TOGC is mandatory where it applies. If VAT is charged in error, the purchaser has no legal right to recover it from HMRC, and should look to the vendor to reimburse it. HMRC's attitude will, however, largely depend on whether or not the vendor has accounted to them for the VAT.

12.1 The legal framework for TOGC treatment

Article 19 of the VAT Directive provides that:

'In the event of a transfer, whether for consideration or not or as a contribution to a company, of a totality of assets or part thereof, Member States may consider that no supply of goods has taken place and that the person to whom the goods are transferred is to be treated as the successor to the transferor.

Member States may, in cases where the recipient is not wholly liable to tax, take the measures necessary to prevent distortion of competition.

---

[1] SI 1995/1268

They may also adopt any measures needed to prevent tax evasion or avoidance through the use of this Article.'

Article 29 of the directive gives effect to article 19 in relation to services.

The UK rules in this respect are in article 5 of the VAT (Special Provisions) Order 1995 which is made under section 5(3)(c). Article 5(1) provides that, subject to the special rules in article 5(2) which apply where certain property assets form part of a TOGC[2]:

'there shall be treated as neither a supply of goods nor a supply of services the following supplies by a person of assets of his business -

(a) their supply to a person to whom he transfers his business as a going concern where -

   (i) the assets are to be used by the transferee in carrying on the same kind of business, whether or not as part of any existing business, as that carried on by the transferor, and

   (ii) in a case where the transferor is a taxable person, the transferee is already, or immediately becomes as a result of the transfer, a taxable person or a person defined as such in section 3(1) of the Manx Act;

(b) their supply to a person to whom he transfers part of his business as a going concern where -

   (i) that part is capable of separate operation,

   (ii) the assets are to be used by the transferee in carrying on the same kind of business, whether or not as part of any existing business, as that carried on by the transferor in relation to that part, and

   (iii) in a case where the transferor is a taxable person, the transferee is already, or immediately becomes as a result of the transfer, a taxable person or a person defined as such in section 3(1) of the Manx [VAT] Act.'

12.2 The general conditions for TOGC treatment
Article 5(1) Value Added Tax (Special Provisions) Order 1995[3]

(1) The transferred assets must be business assets transferred as part of a going concern.

(2) The transferee must use the assets acquired in carrying on the same kind of business as that carried on by the transferor.

---

[2] See **12.8** below

[3] SI 1995/1268

(3) The transferee must be a taxable person or as a result of the TOGC become a taxable person.

(4) Where only part of a business is transferred, that part must be capable of separate operation.

These general conditions are considered in detail at **12.4** to **12.7** below. The three additional conditions which apply to certain property assets are considered at **12.8**.

12.3 TOGCs: Some drafting points

Even where a transfer appears to fall within article 5, the best course of action is to have a clause dealing with VAT in the agreement, because there is always a risk that a sale will in fact fall outside the TOGC treatment provided for in article 5.

Accounting for any VAT on the sale is the liability of the vendor and it is for him to decide whether TOGC treatment applies. When acting for the vendor it should be ensured that the vendor reserves the right to recover VAT from the purchaser in addition to the price in the event that the sale falls outside article 5.

The dangers of not dealing with VAT clearly in the sale documentation are illustrated in *CLP Holding Company Limited v Singh and Kaur*[4] where the Court of Appeal considered whether a purchaser was liable to pay VAT on the purchase price of a freehold commercial property. The contract, which incorporated the Standard Conditions of Sale (Fourth Edition), stated that sums payable were VAT exclusive and any obligation to pay included an obligation to pay VAT in respect of that payment. However, the Special Conditions, which took priority over any conflicting Standard Conditions, defined the 'Purchase Price' as £130,000. The Court held that the sale contract, properly construed, did not oblige the purchaser to pay VAT in addition to the Purchase Price. The vendor, therefore, had to account to HMRC for VAT out of the £130,000 it received.

The Court's reasoning was that it is necessary to consider what a reasonable person, with 'all the background knowledge' at their disposal, would have understood the contracting parties to have meant. Of critical importance seems to have been that the purchase price was agreed and paid a considerable time before completion. The vendor, through its lawyers, confirmed that it had received 'all of the sale monies of £130,000 on this matter', with no mention of VAT. In response to the standard requisition

---

[4] [2014] EWCA Civ 1103

seeking confirmation of the exact amount payable on completion there was again no mention of VAT.

The vendor should, initially, also look for an indemnity against interest and penalties. If there is a real doubt about whether the provisions of article 5 will apply, the vendor should consider requiring the purchaser to deposit an amount equivalent to the VAT that may become due pending application to HMRC for unofficial clearance although this can only be sought where 'an unusual aspect has been identified in a potential TOGC.'[5]

The vendor's right to recover VAT from the purchaser can, with one exception, be made conditional on him providing the purchaser with a valid tax invoice. However, when in the exceptional case the vendor is deregistering for VAT purposes after the sale his right to recover any VAT which is due should not be fettered in this way, since once he has deregistered he cannot issue a valid tax invoice.

VAT on the sale may be recoverable by the purchaser as input tax but not in all cases – for example, it will not be recoverable as of right where it should not have been charged because the provisions of article 5 apply to the transfer – so it is also in the purchaser's interest to get it right. VAT is likely to be a cash-flow cost to the purchaser even where it is recoverable.

When acting for the purchaser, the stance should be that the vendor must take a view as to whether or not article 5 applies and once he has decided, he should either charge VAT or not, as the case may be. However, in many circumstances the vendor will insist on being able to recover any VAT that is payable from the purchaser in addition to the price. If this is the case then the purchaser should always require that any payment of VAT is conditional on receiving a valid tax invoice. In most cases, this should not present the vendor with any difficulties. As mentioned above, it is only when the vendor is proposing to de-register for VAT purposes that difficulties will arise because then the vendor will not be able to issue a tax invoice.

12.4 General condition (1): business assets transferred as part of a going concern

The TOGC rules do not apply to the transfer of non-business assets of a taxable person.

---

[5] See paragraph 9.1 of VAT Notice 700/9/12 'Transfer of a business as a going concern' (December 2012)

The business whose assets are being transferred probably needs to be trading, or only closed temporarily, although it does not need to be profitable and could be in receivership. In VAT Notice 700/9/12,[6] HMRC say that:

> 'There must be no significant break in the normal trading pattern before or immediately after the transfer. The "break in trade" needs to be considered in the context of the type of business concerned, this might vary between different types of trade or activity. For example, HMRC do not consider that where a "seasonal" business has closed for the "off-season" as normal at the time of sale, that there has necessarily been a break in trade. In addition, a short period of closure that does not significantly disrupt the existing trading pattern, for example, for redecoration, will not prevent the business from being transferred as a TOGC.'

HMRC see a VAT group as a single entity for these purposes, so that, for example, the letting of a property to another member of a VAT group is not a business capable of TOGC treatment and the tribunal in *Intelligent Managed Services Ltd*[7] (where the transferee was making supplies only to a group member), in effect, agreed with this view.

Until the decision of the First-Tier Tribunal in *Robinson Family Limited*[8] HMRC considered that there must be a 'transfer' of the assets in the sense of a 'handing over' of something owned by the transferor to the transferee, so that the grant of a lease which is the creation of a new asset out of an existing asset could not form part of a TOGC. HMRC also used to be of the view that the asset transferred must continue to exist after the transfer, so that the surrender of a lease which then merges with the superior interest could not be the transfer of an asset to which TOGC treatment applied. This was sometimes dealt with by means of a 'declaration of non-merger'.

The facts in *Robinson Family Ltd* were that in 2004 a property development company purchased a 125 year lease of a site in Belfast, and redeveloped it, constructing six commercial units. The company's lease prohibited assignments of part so when the company subsequently sold one of the new units, it granted a sub-lease of it. The company did not account for VAT on the sale, treating it as a TOGC on the basis that it was the transfer of a property letting business. HMRC had accepted that sufficient preparatory acts had been undertaken by the company to constitute a letting business.

---

[6] 'Transfer of a business as going concern' (December 2012) at paragraph 2.3.6
[7] [2013] UKFTT 741 (TC)
[8] [2012] UKFTT 360 (TC)

HMRC issued an assessment charging tax on the sale on the basis that the creation of the sub-lease was not the transfer of an asset. The tribunal allowed the company's appeal holding that the unit was an asset of the company's letting business, which it had transferred as a going concern:

'79. While not technically binding on this Tribunal, the Tribunal's decisions in the case of *Fox*[9] and *Morton Hotels*[10] were very helpful. In the former case, the Tribunal upheld the transfer of a business notwithstanding that the transferee carried on business in terms of occupation on a different legal basis from that of the original deemed transferor.

80. In the *Morton* case the Tribunal again relied on the substance as against the form and, in that particular case, held that there was a TOGC even though the transferor had owned the freehold of the business premises and the transferee had entered into a sale and leaseback of the premises so that, at the end of the transaction, it occupied as a tenant rather than as a owner of the freehold.

81. The principle of substance over form is clearly well established and is one which the Tribunal finds amply applies in the current factual situation. It seems wrong to this Tribunal that a transferor should be denied the ability to treat the transfer of a business as a "non supply" simply because it is (as in this case) required to document it in a particular way.

82. In such situations, one must look to the substance of the transaction and, where the transferee is, in effect, carrying on exactly the same business as the transferor, then prima facie the TOGC Provisions should apply.'

Following the decision in *Robinson Family Ltd*, HMRC announced three shifts in policy[11]:

(1) accepting in principle that the surrender of a lease can be a TOGC for VAT purposes;

(2) confirming that the change announced in Revenue & Customs Brief 30/12[12] on whether the grant of a lease can be a TOGC applies generally and is not confined to property letting businesses; and

---

[9] (VTD 18441)

[10] (VTD 20039)

[11] Revenue & Customs Brief 27/14 'VAT: changes in policy on TOGCs' (9 July 2014)

[12] 'HMRC's position following the decision of the tax tribunal in the case of *Robinson Family Ltd*' (16 November 2012)

(3) accepting that a person acquiring a completed dwelling or relevant residential or charitable business as part of a TOGC inherits 'person constructing' status and is capable of making a zero-rated first grant of an interest[13].

Section **12.9** below says more about TOGC treatment for a property letting business.

Morland & Co plc[14] concerned the sale of 98 tenanted pubs. The seller was an investor which had been letting the properties to a brewer which had then sub-let them as tied houses, whereas the buyer was a brewer who let the pubs itself. The sale was not subject to the leases to the investor. The operation of the public houses had not formed a part of the seller's business, since it had leased them to a single customer. Accordingly, the seller had not transferred part of its business as a going concern.

Availability of TOGC treatment before trading commences – selected case law

A sale of development land to another developer was seen as a TOGC in *The Golden Oak Partnership*[15] where the vendor had undertaken preliminary work including the construction of driveways and provision for electricity, gas and sewerage. *The Golden Oak Partnership* was distinguished in *Gulf Trading and Management Ltd*,[16] where the tribunal held that a sale of development land was not a TOGC. In this case the vendor had merely erected fencing and engaged surveyors and architects.

In *Dartford Borough Council*[17], the Council sold land to an investor, with the benefit of an agreement for lease to a supermarket chain of part of the proposed development. It had spent over £7 million on preparatory work, including work to roads, power lines and a watercourse. The Tribunal rejected HMRC's contention that the sale was not a TOGC and allowed the appeal, finding that 'at the time of sale the appellant was carrying on an economic activity' in relation to the site. The investor was continuing the economic activity of obtaining rental income from the site, which had previously been carried on by the council. Accordingly the sale of the freehold constituted the transfer of a going concern.

---

[13] See **4.3.1** above for more detail
[14] (VTD 8869)
[15] (VTD 7212)
[16] (VTD 16847)
[17] (VTD 20423)

In *Royal College of Paediatricians and Child Health*[18] terms for the purchase of a property for occupation by the College were agreed with a seller, and the College instructed its tax advisers to achieve the most VAT efficient structure for the purpose. The advice provided indicated that VAT could be saved if the purchase were to be structured as a TOGC (as the College was partly exempt). To achieve this result, existing tenants of the College (who occupied part of its existing building and who intended to move with it) entered into an agreement for lease of part of the property with the seller before the College entered into an agreement to purchase the property. The advice was that since the seller was carrying on a property business, this would be sufficient to make the sale to the college a TOGC. The tribunal agreed that the sale of the building subject to that agreement for lease was the transfer of a property leasing business, and its transfer to the appellant was a TOGC. In coming to this conclusion the tribunal followed *Dartford* as:

> There it was held that the disposal of a development site by its owner with the benefit of the agreement for lease fell within TOGC relief. In observing that the Commissioners' decision that it did not so fall had been based on a misunderstanding of the legal nature of an agreement for lease, the Tribunal [in *Dartford*] said:
>
> "15. It is clear that [the Commissioners] had no idea what an agreement for lease was and thought it no more than 'a statement of intent to lease'"

It is a well established principle of English law that equity looks on that as done which ought to be done so where, for example, possession is held under an agreement for a lease, of which specific performance would be ordered, the parties are treated in equity as being in the same position with regard to their respective rights as if a lease had been granted.[19]

---

[18] [2013] UKFTT 202 (TC)

[19] *Walsh v Lonsdale* (1882) 21 ChD 9, (CA); *Zimbler v Abrahams* [1903] 1 KB 577 (CA); *Gray v Spyer* [1922] 2 Ch 22 (CA);*Tinsley v Milligan* [1994] 1 AC 340 at 370, (HL), per Lord Browne-Wilkinson; *Jerome v Kelly (Inspector of Taxes)* [2003] STC 206. The maxim may be applied twice, e.g. where V agrees to sell to P, who agrees to grant a lease to T: *Industrial Properties (Barton Hill) Ltd v Associated Electrical Industries Ltd* [1977] QB 580 (CA)

12.5 General condition (2): assets to be used by the transferee in carrying on the same kind of business

In *Zita Modes Sàrl v Administration de l'Enregistrement et des Domaines*[20] the European Court was asked whether the transferee had to carry on the same type of economic activity as the transferor and held that it did not. However, the transferee had to carry on the business and not shut it down. The tribunal in *Intelligent Managed Services Ltd*[21] agreed with HMRC that this latter statement justified the UK's restriction that the same business must be carried on by the transferee even though this wording does not appear in the VAT Directive.

The Tribunal said:

> 'Although the phrase the 'same kind of business' does not appear within Article 19, it is clear from the decision of the ECJ in Zita Modes... that, for there to be a ... TOGC the transferee must intend to operate the business transferred, i.e. the business of the transferor. It must therefore follow that this will inevitably be the same kind of business as that previously carried on.

> As such, in our judgment, the 'same kind of business' requirement in Article 5(1)(a)(i) of the VAT (Special Provisions) Order 1995, is, clearly compatible with EU law as stated in Zita Modes ...'

Zita Modes Sarl concerned the sale of a Luxembourg clothing business to a perfumery business. The European Court held that, where a Member State had introduced non-supply treatment for TOGCs, this must apply:

> 'to any transfer of a business or independent part of an undertaking. ... The transferee must however intend to operate the business or the part of the undertaking transferred and not simply immediately to liquidate the activity concerned and sell the stock, if any.'

This second condition is about the transferee's intentions at the time of the transfer – it is not about what actually happens although this might be the best evidence of the intentions), nor about what the transferee could have done.[22] The transferee does not need to intend to carry on the same kind of business for very long. An intention immediately to sell the business, or to close it down, will prevent TOGC treatment.

---

[20] (Case C-497/01) [2005] STC 1059

[21] [2013] UKFTT 741

[22] *Hartley Engineering Ltd* [1994] VATTR 453 distinguishing the earlier decision of the High Court (QB) in *CCE v Dearwood Ltd* [1986] STC 327

In the light of the decision of the tribunal in *Kwik Save Group plc*,[23] HMRC do not generally see a TOGC arising in the context of a sub-sale. If A agrees to sell to B, and B agrees to sell to C, there are successive supplies A-B and B-C, rather than a potential TOGC A-C, even if completion is direct from A to C and B never carries on business using the transferred assets.

There are further issues with property transactions where the purchaser is a nominee. These are looked at in **12.10** below.

Selected case law - same kind of business
In *ICB Ltd*[24] the purchase of two quarries was not a TOGC, since the intention of the transferee was not to carry on a quarrying business but to acquire a convenient source of raw materials for use in an existing business. The transferee had not purchased any goodwill, debtors or work in progress.

In *Bo Jones*[25] the tribunal found that the sale of nightclub premises which the purchaser was intending to convert to a restaurant was a TOGC because the nightclub remained open for a week after the purchase. The tribunal found that the purchaser had, in fact, purchased the night club as a going concern.

In *Hallborough Properties Ltd*[26] a company which carried on a property investment business purchased a head lease. The seller who was a developer had granted a 25-year underlease a year before the sale, and had opted to tax. The buyer also opted to tax, and reclaimed input tax on the purchase of the head lease. HMRC rejected the buyer's claim on the basis that the sale constituted a TOGC. The tribunal dismissed the buyer's appeal, holding that the letting and management of the property was a part of the seller's business, consisting of the receipt of rental income, notwithstanding that it was a developer not a property investor, and this was the same kind of business as that for which the buyer was intending to use the head lease.

12.6 General condition (3): transferee must be a 'taxable person' or, as a result of the TOGC, become a taxable person

A 'taxable person' is defined in section 3(1) as a person who 'is, or is required to be registered under this Act'. If the transferor is a 'taxable person' the transferee must already be a taxable person, or must immediately become a taxable person as a result of the transfer. The latter is

---

[23] [1994] VATTR 457
[24] (VTD 1796)
[25] (VTD 6141)
[26] (VTD 10849)

often the case, since the transferee must take account of the turnover from the transferring business, or from the part being transferred, in determining when and whether it must register.[27]

The rules do not allow for the transferee to be VAT-registered in another jurisdiction, other than the Isle of Man.

If the transferor is not a taxable person, the status of the purchaser is irrelevant.

12.7 General condition (4) Transfer of part of a business capable of separate operation

If part of a business is being transferred, it must be 'capable of' separate operation. This is normally taken to mean that the part being sold must not depend on other business activities of the vendor which are being retained by him. It is not necessary for that part to be operated separately. The sale of one let property out of a portfolio, or of one shop out of a chain, could qualify as a transfer of part capable of separate operation.

12.8 Additional conditions for certain property assets to be included in a TOGC

Article 5(2), 5(2A) and 5(2B) Value Added Tax (Special Provisions) Order 1995

Three further conditions have to be complied with where the assets of the business include land or properties which would be subject to VAT if they were sold otherwise than as a TOGC. The following property assets fall into this category:

(1) property over which the transferor (or a relevant associate' of his within the meaning of paragraph 3, Schedule 10) has exercised the option to tax and the supply of which to the transferee would 'but for' that option be exempt as falling within Item 1, Group 1, Schedule 9;

(2) the freehold in a partly constructed building (other than a building designed as dwellings or for relevant residential or charitable use) or civil engineering work;

(3) the freehold in a building (other than a building designed as dwellings or for relevant residential or charitable use) or civil engineering work which was completed in the previous three years.

If the business to be transferred includes the above kinds of property assets TOGC treatment will only be available where:

---

[27] Section 49(1)

(1) the purchaser opts to tax the property and that option to tax has effect from the earliest tax point[28] in respect of the property asset (the 'relevant date'); and

(2) written notification of that option to tax is given[29] to HMRC on or before the relevant date; and

(3) the purchaser notifies the vendor by the relevant date that the anti-avoidance provisions in article 5(2B) Value Added Tax (Special Provisions) Order 1995 do not apply to it (see below).

These additional conditions apply if the transaction would, without TOGC treatment, be standard rated, either because the transferor has opted (and the option would have effect in relation to it) or because the sale is of a freehold new building or civil engineering work.

If these conditions apply and the purchaser fails to meet them, the transfer of the property asset will not be (or form part of) a TOGC and will be taxable at the standard rate.

'Relevant date' - Higher Education Statistics Agency Ltd v CCE[30]

A company ('HESA') purchased a rented property at auction. The vendor had opted to tax the property, and it was accepted that the letting of the property constituted a business. Following the exchange of contracts (and payment of a deposit), HESA opted to tax the property. Customs issued a ruling that tax was chargeable on the transfer.

HESA appealed, contending that the effect of article 5 of the Value Added Tax (Special Provisions) Order 1995 was that the transfer should not be treated as a supply. The tribunal[31] rejected this contention and dismissed the appeal. The transfer was to be treated as a supply, unless the transferee had opted to tax 'no later than the relevant date'. The effect of article 5(3) was that the relevant date was the date of the contract, rather than the date of completion. The tribunal observed that conveyancing solicitors were generally aware of HMRC's view that 'where it is intended that the transfer of otherwise taxable property is to be regarded as the transfer of a going concern, then the purchaser must elect prior to the tax point relating to the transfer'.

---

[28] For tax points see **2.2** above

[29] In VAT Notice 742A 'Opting to tax land and buildings' (April 2014) HMRC say that 'By 'notified to HMRC' we mean that the purchaser has properly addressed, pre-paid and posted the appropriate form or letter to us (or faxed it to us)'

[30] [2000] STC 332 (QB)

[31] (VTD 15917)

HESA appealed to the High Court, which upheld the tribunal decision. Moses J held that 'the relevant date is the date when the deposit was paid'. Since HESA had not opted on or before that date, it was liable to pay output tax on the purchase. (The requirement to notify the exercise of the option by the relevant date was not introduced into article 5 until 18 March 2004.)[32]

As well as notifying HMRC of the option, the purchaser must notify the vendor that the provisions of article 5(2B) of the Value Added Tax (Special Provisions) Order 1995, do not apply to him. This is normally included as a standard clause in the sale agreement and sometimes takes the form of a warranty.

The transferee (which for this purpose includes a 'relevant associate' within the meaning of paragraph 3, Schedule 10) cannot give this notification if either of two conditions is met:

(1) The asset that is to be transferred to him is a 'capital item' in his hands, whether or not the transfer is regarded as a non-supply under the TOGC rules.

(2) His supplies of the property asset 'will, or would fall, to be exempt supplies' because of the application of the anti-avoidance rules in paragraph 12 of Schedule 10.[33]

TOGC treatment depends on the notification being given, so there can still be a TOGC if the notification is incorrect.

Although article 5(2B) is intended as an anti-avoidance measure,[34] it can be a problem in normal commercial transactions. An example would be where the purchaser is obtaining finance for its acquisition of a property from a bank that is coincidentally a major tenant, or a member of whose corporate group is a major tenant. This will normally mean that the purchaser's option will be disapplied under the anti-avoidance rules in paragraph 12 of Schedule 10, (although only in relation to supplies under the lease to the bank) so that it cannot give the necessary notification to the vendor that article 5(2B) will not apply. The purchaser will incur VAT, not all of which (because of the exempt letting to the bank) will be recoverable.

---

[32] By the Value Added Tax (Special Provisions) (Amendment) Order SI 2004/779

[33] Described in **9.14** above

[34] See Budget Notice 30/04 'VAT: Commercial buildings – anti-avoidance' (17 March 2004) for a description of the scheme the provision (along with the anti-avoidance rules introduced at the same time into paragraph 12, Schedule 10) was intended to counter

12.9 Property letting and TOGCs

The sale of let property may qualify for TOGC treatment if it the sale of a property letting business or part of such a business. As noted in **12.4** above, HMRC do not see the letting of a property between members of a VAT group as a business capable of TOGC treatment. So there is no TOGC if the only tenant is VAT grouped with either the vendor or the purchaser.

Where a number of properties are sold together, only some of which are tenanted, the question can arise whether there is a single TOGC or whether each property must be considered separately. For example, a developer may build various commercial units and wish to sell them. The units may be untenanted, but tenants may be being actively sought, and some units may be tenanted, or they may all be let.

In Notice 700/9/12[36], HMRC say (at paragraph 6.4.1) that:

> 'The transfer of a number of sites or buildings where some of the sites or buildings are let, or partially let and some are unlet, needs to be considered on a case by case basis. The nature of the sites or building and their use are all factors for consideration. It is important to look at whether the assets can be identified as a single business or an identifiable part of a business. In addition all the [other conditions for a TOGC] would need to be met. For example the sale of a chain of shops or pubs could be a TOGC whereas the sale of a grouping of disparate properties might not.'

12.9.1   TOGCs of properties let or held to let - HMRC's views

VAT Notice 700/9/12 gives some examples of HMRC's views on TOGCs and non-TOGCs in the context of investors and others disposing of property that is held to let.[38] HMRC's examples are reproduced below in the form of a table.

---

[36] 'Transfer of a business as a going concern' (December 2012)
[38] Ibid – see sections 6.2 and 6.3

Capable of being a TOGC	Not capable of being a TOGC
Sale with the benefit of an existing lease or sub-lease	Sale subject to temporary occupation only without the right to occupy after sale)
Sale when let but subject to initial rent-free period and sold during that period	Sale of empty property which is being marketed
Sale when let but not yet occupied by tenants	Sale of lease granted out of freehold[39]
Sale of freehold[40] when tenant has been found and agreement for lease in place but before lease signed so purchaser takes subject to agreement for lease	Grant of sublease[41]
Sale of a site by a developer which consists of a mixture of let and unlet, finished or unfinished properties to a single purchaser	Sale where existing lease from vendor is surrendered before completion even if tenants under a sublease remain in occupation[42]
Sale of freehold[43] of one of a number of let properties owned by seller	Sale of freehold to an existing tenant of the whole premises as the transferee would not be carrying on the same kind of business as the transferor
Sale of partially-let building provided that 'the letting constitutes economic activity'	The grant of a lease to the new owner of a business carried on from the building which the previous tenant has sold as a going concern after surrendering his existing lease
The purchase of the freehold and leasehold of a property from separate sellers without the interests merging, provided that the purchaser continue 'to exploit the asset by receiving rent from the tenant'	

---

[39] Query the tenability of this position now given the decision of the First-tier Tribunal in *Robinson Family Limited* – see discussion in **12.4** above

[40] Logically the same should hold good for the assignment of a head lease

[41] See **footnote 39** above

[42] This appears to be based on the decision in *Morland & Co plc* (see **12.4** above)

[43] Logically the same should hold good for the assignment of a head lease

12.10 TOGCs and transfers to nominees

Where property is held on trust, it is usually the beneficiary, rather than the nominee or legal owner, who is seen as making the supplies to tenants.[44] The TOGC rules do not deal with this adequately where the transferee is a nominee, since those rules require it to be the transferee who carries on the business.

To deal with this, HMRC accept that the vendor, nominee purchaser and beneficiary can agree that the beneficiary will be treated as the transferee for the purposes of the TOGC rules. This only applies where the business being transferred is a property letting business, and where the identity of the beneficial owner is known to the transferor.

HMRC suggest the following form of wording:

> 'X, Y and Z confirm that they have agreed to adopt the optional practice set out in Customs' Business Brief 10/96 in relation to the purchase of the property pursuant to an agreement dated () between X and Y.
>
> Following the transfer of the property Y will hold the legal title as nominee for Z, the beneficial owner.'

Alternatively the point can simply be written into the sale agreement, provided the beneficiary is a party to this.

The arrangement is optional. If it is not used, the sale will be treated as a supply to the nominee, and not as a TOGC.

Further details are in VAT Notice 700/9/12.[45]

12.11 TOGCs: summary of main VAT consequences

Where the transfer of assets is a TOGC it is not a supply and no VAT is chargeable. There is a saving if the sale would otherwise be subject to both VAT and stamp duty land tax. There are no VAT cash-flow considerations for the parties.

12.11.1 Input tax

HMRC have confirmed[46] that input tax related to a TOGC, for example, on professional fees, is recoverable according to whether the activity transferred is taxable or exempt. For the transferor, input tax on expenses

---

[44] 'Transfer of a business as a going concern' (December 2012)

[45] In VAT Notice 700/9/12 'Transfer of a business as a going concern' (December 2012) at 2.6

[46] Originally in Business Brief 08/01 (2 July 2001) now in VAT Notice 708 'Partial exemption' (June 2011) at paragraphs 15.5 to 15.7

that relate wholly to the transfer (for example, legal fees) should be treated as an overhead of that part of the business being transferred. For the transferee, the input tax on costs that relate wholly to the acquisition of assets acquired as a result of a transfer of a going concern, will be recoverable to the extent that they will be used in making taxable supplies. This is based on the judgment of the European Court in *Abbey National plc v CCE*[47].

The facts of *Abbey National* were that a company, which was a member of a banking group, carried on a life assurance business and held a number of properties as investments. It sold a property which it had let out, and in respect of which it had opted to tax. The sale of the property was treated as the transfer of part of a business as a going concern. The representative member of the group reclaimed input tax on the solicitors' fees in relation to the transfer.

HMRC issued an assessment on the basis that, since a TOGC was not a supply for VAT purposes, the input tax on the legal fees could not be directly attributed to taxable supplies and had to be treated as residual input tax within regulation 101(2)(d) VAT Regulations. The representative member appealed and the High Court referred the case to the European Court for a preliminary ruling on the question of whether, in circumstances where a member state had exercised the option in article 5(8) of the Sixth Directive,[48] the transferor might deduct the VAT on the costs of the services acquired in order to effect the transfer.

The European Court ruled that where, in accordance with article 5(8) of the Sixth Directive:

'the transfer of a totality of assets or part thereof is regarded as not being a supply of goods, the costs incurred by the transferor for services acquired in order to effect that transfer form part of that taxable person's overheads and thus in principle have a direct and immediate link with the whole of his economic activity. If, therefore, the transferor effects both transactions in respect of which value added tax is deductible and transactions in respect of which it is not', it followed from article 17(5) Sixth Directive[49] that he may deduct only that proportion of the value added tax which is attributable to the former transactions. However, if

---

[47] (Case C-408/98) [2001] STC 297
[48] Now article 19 of the VAT Directive which is the vires for the UK TOGC rules
[49] Now article 173.1 of the VAT Directive

the various services acquired by the transferor in order to effect the transfer have a direct and immediate link with a clearly defined part of his economic activities, so that the costs of those services form part of the overheads of that part of the business, and all the transactions relating to that part of the business are subject to value added tax, he may deduct all the value added tax charged on his costs of acquiring those services'.

12.11.2 Capital goods scheme

Where a business (or part of a business) which includes capital items falling within the capital goods scheme[50] is transferred as a going concern, the transferee has to continue to operate the scheme in respect of those capital items for the remainder of the adjustment period on the basis of the transferor's original input tax attribution but by reference to the transferee's use of the item[51]. This can result in additional recovery of input tax by the transferee or a claw-back of input tax previously reclaimed by the transferor from the transferee by HMRC.

The transferee will need access to the transferor's capital goods scheme records to be able to comply with this obligation and this should, where possible, be provided for in the contractual documentation otherwise the transferee will have to rely on the provisions of *VATA* referred to in **12.11.3** below to get the necessary information.

12.11.3 Business records

The preservation of the records of the transferor's transactions remains, with effect from 1 September 2007, the responsibility of the transferor, unless HMRC, at the request of the transferor, direct otherwise.[52] The transferor must make documents, information and records available to the transferee to the extent necessary for him to meet his VAT obligations.[53] In addition, HMRC may disclose to the transferee any information relating to

---

[50] For the capital goods scheme see **11.4** above

[51] By reason of regulation 112(4)(a) VAT Regulations which may, however, be called into question by the decision of the European Court in *Staatssecretaris van Financiën v Pactor Vastgoed BV* (Case C-622/11) (10 October 2013 unreported) that 'the Sixth Directive must be interpreted as precluding the recovery of amounts due following the adjustment of a VAT deduction from a taxable person other than the person who applied that deduction'

[52] Regulation 6(3)(f) VAT Regulations

[53] Section 49(4) and 49(5)

the business whilst it was operated by the transferor to enable the transferee to meet his VAT obligations.[54]

12.11.4 Registration/deregistration

The transferee will generally need to register for VAT, if it is not already registered. This will necessarily apply if the transferor was registered or should have been registered, and the transferred businesses turnover counts as the transferee's in determining whether and when the transferee should register.[55] Provided the transferee is not already VAT registered he may take over the transferor's VAT registration number following a TOGC by using Form VAT 68.[56] Any VAT liabilities would be transferred with the VAT registration number.[57] If the whole business is transferred, the transferor will generally need to deregister.

12.11.5 Transfers into VAT groups

If the transferee is a member of a partly exempt VAT group, it may have to account for VAT on a 'self-supply' of any assets included in the TOGC, the supply of which would otherwise be subject to VAT.[58]

---

[54] Section 49(6)
[55] Section 49(1)(a)
[56] Regulation 6 VAT Regulations
[57] Ibid
[58] Section 44

13 Property Supplies relating to Caravans and Caravan Parks

Caravans are often used as dwellings. Consequently some 'caravan-related' building work and property supplies are afforded zero-rate relief.

13.1 Caravan park works

Services supplied 'in the course of construction' of any civil engineering work necessary for the development of a permanent park for 'residential caravans', and which relate to the construction, are zero-rated.[1] Specifically excluded (and therefore standard-rated) are:

(1) the separate supply of architectural, surveying, consultancy or supervisory services;

(2) the hire of goods on their own (e.g. plant and machinery without an operator, scaffolding without erection/dismantling, security fencing and mobile office); and

(3) the private use of goods.

'Building materials', supplied by the person providing the above services and incorporated into the site in question, are also zero-rated.[2]

The construction of a civil engineering work does not include the conversion, reconstruction, alteration or enlargement of a work.[3]

A caravan is not a 'residential caravan' if residence in it throughout the year is prevented by the terms of a covenant, statutory planning consent or similar permission[4]. The development of a holiday park of fixed caravans, or parks for touring caravans, is, therefore, normally standard-rated.

The VAT incurred on other works, such as the construction of pitches, roads, and toilet blocks such works can only be reclaimed if taxable supplies are made. If the site is for permanent pitches and exempt fees only are charged, the VAT incurred cannot be reclaimed and becomes a cost.

13.2 Caravan pitches

Items 1 and 1(f), Group1, Schedule 9

The provision of 'seasonal pitches' for caravans, and the grant or assignment of 'facilities' at caravan parks to persons for whom such pitches

---

[1] Item 2, Group 5. Schedule 8

[2] Item 4, Group 5, Schedule 8 - for 'building materials' see **10.7.1** above

[3] Note (15), Group 5, Schedule 8

[4] Note (19), Group 5, Schedule 8

are provided, are taxable at the standard rate. Other supplies are exempt. The option to tax has no effect in relation to a pitch for a residential caravan.[5]

From 1 March 2012 a 'seasonal pitch' is a pitch, other than an 'employee pitch,' on a 'holiday site', or a 'non-residential' pitch on any other site.[6]

'Employee pitch' means a pitch occupied by an employee of the site operator as that person's principal place of residence during the period of occupancy.[7]

'Holiday site' means a site or part of a site which is operated as a holiday or leisure site.[8]

'Non-residential pitch' means[9] a pitch which is provided:
(1) for less than a year; or
(2) for a year or more and is subject to an 'occupation restriction',
and which is not intended to be used as the occupant's principal place of residence during the period of occupation.

'Occupation restriction' means any covenant, statutory planning consent or similar permission, the terms of which prevent the person to whom the pitch is provided from occupying it by living in a caravan at all times throughout the period for which the pitch is provided.[10]

In *HMRC v Tallington Lakes Ltd*[11], licence agreements for caravans provided that, in accordance with relevant planning permission, they could not be occupied during February of each year. However, the licensor was not enforcing this restriction. The High Court held that the effect of the section 171B(3) *Town and Country Planning Act 1990*, was that the local authority had retained the right to enforce the original planning permission which prevented occupation during February. The fact that Tallington had allowed some owners to breach that condition did not prevent the definition of 'seasonal pitch' from applying. Accordingly, the supplies did not qualify for exemption.

---

[5] See **9.12** above

[6] Note (14), Group 1, Schedule 9

[7] Note (14A), Group 1, Schedule 9

[8] Note (14A), Group 1, Schedule 9

[9] Note (14A), Group 1, Schedule 9

[10] Note (14A), Group 1, Schedule 9

[11] [2008] STC 2734 (Ch D)

Following the tribunal decision in *Ashworth*[12], HMRC accept that a pitch is only to be regarded as 'seasonal' if it is on a site, or part of a site, which is advertised or held out for holiday use.[13]

The effect of the above is that exemption applies to the provision of pitches:

(1) on permanent residential sites where caravans can be lived in at all times throughout the year;

(2) on sites for travellers where the caravans are used as principal private residences;

(3) for restricted occupancy periods provided that the site is not advertised or held out for holiday/leisure use, and the pitch is intended to be used as the occupant's principal private residence; and

(4) on any type of site (including holiday/leisure sites) if the pitch is occupied by a warden or other employee of the site operator as his principal private residence.

13.3 Caravan rental

The supply of rented accommodation in any caravan or mobile home is exempt unless the accommodation is 'holiday accommodation'[14] which is standard-rated under Item 1(d), Group 1, Schedule 9.

---

[12] [1994] VATTR 275

[13] See VAT Notice 701/20/12 'Caravans and houseboats' (January 2014) at para. 4.1

[14] See **3.2.14** above

HMRC Forms and Guidance

R &C Briefs8

VAT Forms

VAT Notices10

INDEX